THE GOVERNANCE OF INDIA

AS IT IS AND AS IT MAY BE

THE GOVERNANCE OF INDIA

AS IT IS AND AS IT MAY BE

GOVINDA DAS

GYAN

Published by

Gyan Publishing House
5, Ansari Road
Daryaganj, New Delhi-110002
Phone: 011-47034999, 9811692060
E-mail: books@gyanbooks.com

Distribution Network
gyanbooks.com
India, USA, Canada, UK, Australia

ISBN: 978-93-7225-344-3 (PB)

2nd Impression 2025

Printed at: Gyan Press, Delhi.

THE GOVERNANCE OF INDIA:
AS IT IS AND AS IT MAY BE
Author: GOVINDA DAS

THE GOVERNANCE OF INDIA

AS IT IS AND AS IT MAY BE

A Hand-Book of Progressive Politics

BY

GOVINDA DAS.

PREFACE.

This short book has a long history behind it. In the very earliest years of the Indian National Congress, I spoke to Mr. A. O. Hume about the desirability of preparing a series of handbooks, something like Sir Henry Craik's series on "The English Citizen—His Rights and Responsibilities," which, while describing the actual administration of the country in its different departments, would also enlighten the Indian citizen as to its dark spots and suggest ways for their removal—in short, a series which would help to qualify the public to become rationally articulate and to avoid mere declamation and vague generalities. The suggestion could not be taken up at the time, and for many years afterwards, my own very limited energies were taken up by educational and social activities. But though put aside for the time being, the idea was not given up by me.

Nearly twenty years ago, in my leisure moments, I sketched out a rough syllabus for a work on the Indian Government, and circulated it among a few friends, in the hope that some would be willing to take up at least some parts of it. But my hopes were not fulfilled. As a last resource, I began to fill up the syllabus myself. But my chronic ill-health would not allow of my devoting the time necessary to compile it while also engaged in the work of the Central Hindu College which was founded in Benares, about the same time, by a dozen 'idealists,' with Mrs. Besant as the leading exponent and worker, and which absorbed all my little energies.

In connection with that movement, I wrote a book on *Hinduism*, which had a fairly large circulation. In that book I tried to bring together as much information as possible about the countless forms of the current (and also the less-known) beliefs and practices of Hinduism, and also to point out as impartially—indeed, perhaps over-strongly, as some of my friends think—the degenerations, superstitions and mal-practices of current Hinduism, as in this book I endeavour to mark the defects of the current methods of the Government, while describing them. In both books, the underlying idea has been the one I had in mind when placing the suggestion mentioned above before the late Mr. Hume; but of course, my realisation of it has been most lamentably defective.

When after nearly two decades of strenuous work by friends and helpers of that unique educational experiment in this country, the Central Hindu College—unique because of the constant and fraternal co-operation of Indian and European workers, with a total absence of race and color prejudice between them and with the presence of the good old Hindu joint-family feeling between the managers, the staff and the students—it developed into the Benares Hindu University with a new management and new methods, the older workers have felt free to take to other work, in keeping with their humble capacities for the service and towards the uplift of the country.

My friend Mr. G. A. Natesan, the enterprising and patriotic editor of *The Indian Review*, insisted on my doing at least some part of the old scheme myself. The five chapters printed here are the result of his energetic persuasions. Of the remainder I give the syllabus as an appendix to this work, in the hope that some one with greater knowledge and opportunities may complete them.

I may point out that though there is a good deal in common between the suggestions put forward in this book and in the scheme of the late Mr. Gokhale sketched by him on his deathbed in 1916, and the famous memorandum of the Nineteen Indian Members of the Imperial Legislative Council and the still later scheme put forward by the Indian National Congress of 1916 in consultation with the All-India Muslim League, there are some serious differences also. I feel that some of these differences are of vital importance and that it will be to the good of the country to express them clearly and unhesitatingly. The present 'demands' are but the logical outcome of the Minto-Morley reforms, and when these demands are not identical, they are necessarily the outcome of the different experiences and thoughts of the people advocating them. One point however must be singled out and emphasised to our utmost power namely, the admission of Indians to the inmost sanctuary of the administration. For this tremendous innovation we Indians can never be too thankful to Lord Morley but for whom this significant change may have been deferred to the Greek Kalends. In its way this breaking down of the exclusiveness of the political caste system is as fraught with the future good of India as was the mightier innovation of Buddha in the sphere of the life of the spirit, when he broke down the exclusiveness of the Brahman and put the non-Brahman on a footing of spiritual equality with him.

I would like to call the special attention of every one concerned with the good government and prosperity of 'The Indian States' to chapter III. In treating of this subject, covering such a vast extent and with next to no full and reliable guidance, avoidance of pit-falls becomes almost impossible. There is every likelihood, therefore, of my not having escaped these wholly. My justification for having attempted the treatment is that I have written with a single eye to the welfare of a third of the land of

India with seventy millions of peoples and seven hundred Princes and Chiefs, whose interests are so inextricably mixed up with those of British India, that the progressiveness or the backwardness of the one inevitably reacts for weal or woe on the other. Even my mistakes of omission and commission will have been of service if they stimulate thinking and dissipate inertia ; bring light, however feeble or coloured, into dark places and rouse the people responsible for their prosperity into wholesome activity.

My very bad health and consequent incapacity for unbroken application to work, combined with the publisher's very natural and proper impatience and reminders against delays over 'copy' and 'proofs' is responsible for rather serious defects of matter and of manner, for which I can only crave the indulgence of the reader. I am indebted to my brother, Babu Bhagavan Das, M.A., better known for his labours in the field of Ancient Philosophy than of modern politics, for having carefully revised the book in proof, and reduced at least to some extent the defects above referred to.

It may be mentioned here that after this work was put into the press another with the same title has been published in Bombay. But the printing of this work had advanced so far that its title which had been already mentioned also in advance references in the press could not be changed. That work, though its title is the same, is very different in conception and execution from this, being an exposition of and commentary on the Government of India Act.

Durgakund, BENARES.
Vijaya-dashami, 1974. GOVINDA DAS.
OCTOBER 25, 1917.

CONTENTS.

THE GOVERNANCE OF INDIA

PART I

Problems of Administration

CHAPTER I

THE INDIA OFFICE

It was a serious omission not to have so enlarged the sphere of the enquiry of the Decentralisation Commission as to bring within its purview the methods and machinery of the India Office. For, in spite of recent great constitutional changes and much devolution of power, the real power behind the throne is the India Office, and it is essential that the powers and functions of the Secretary of State for India be brought into greater harmony with the present state of affairs in the country by a very much greater devolution of his powers to the Governor-General in *Legislative* Council. It becomes, therefore, incumbent upon every Indian publicist to devote a great deal of thought to the ways and means by which to secure that the Secretary of State in Council, and, still more, individually, cease to be the predominant partner in the dual Government of India, make over much more fully than at present the power of initiative to the Imperial and Provincial Governments in India itself, and retain only enough power to veto actions which may be positively mischievous or to stimulate initiative when mere lethargy or powerful vested interests hamper progress. In short, the powers exercised by the Secretary of State for India should not be dissimilar to the powers exercised by the Secretary of State for the Colonies over the four self-governing Dominions.

Unfortunately there are few publications dealing with the subject and none from the inside, so to say. Consequently, it becomes a very difficult task to avoid falling into pitfalls unawares. Chesney, in Chapter XXI of his *Indian Polity*, acutely points out again and again, that "our administrative system" is full of "legal fictions" and exclaims, "Great is the force of official shams" when animadverting on "the illusive effect of form in constitutional affairs." On page 367, he emphatically remarks:

> But, as has been pointed out more than once in this work, in order to appreciate the full effect of the administrative changes effected by a change in the law, we must go behind the verbal provisions, and examine its effect on the actual course of procedure.

He points out how even the advisory function of the Council is not properly utilised by its not being utilised *in time*. Effective consultation "depends on the point at which, in the course of deliberation, its advice is recorded." If it is not sought from the very beginning right through every stage, it may fulfil statutory obligations, but it will be of no real help. Ilbert's *Government of India* deals naturally only with the statutory provisions establishing the official machinery and is of little help in throwing light on the *actual* working of the department.

The statutory provisions, which have been consolidated in the *Government of India Act*, 1915, cover a period of one hundred and forty-five years beginning with 1770, when the first Act was passed in the reign of George III. In this long period vast political changes have occurred, and scientific discoveries with their practical applications to every-day life have completely altered the conditions of existence which had existed for untold millennia. Is it any wonder then that the methods and machinery of the India Office require considerable re-modelling before they can become helpful instead of being harmful ?

The Colonial Office has "learnt some wisdom" after losing America in 1776, as was pointed out by Lord Crewe, who had long been the Secretary of State for the Colonies before becoming the Secretary of State for India, in one of his speeches in the House of Lords, and since then, we have seen, how discontented and rebellious Canada has been transformed into a perfectly loyal and helpful part of the Empire, the penal settlement of Australia into the powerful Australian Commonwealth, and the mutually hating—with the bitterest hatred possible—Boer and Briton of South Africa have become so utterly loyal after the grant of self-government, that the Boer Generals, who were so foremost in fighting the English, are the Ministers in the South Africa of to-day and have swept their old allies the Germans out of that vast continent.

The way to India in those days was round the Cape of Good Hope, in sailing ships at the mercy of the winds. There was no Suez Canal, no railways, no telegraphs, no marconigraphs, no turbine and motor-driven steamers. So, with the utmost possible powers of statutory control, the actual stringency cannot but have been much less than is possible now with all these scientific appliances to hand, keeping the India Office into continuous touch with India, and giving a possibility of stringency and force to the old rules which were beyond the ken of their promulgators.

In view of a great deal of nonsense that has been talked by some of the more rabid Anglo-Indian dailies in this country about the autocratic way in which Lord Morley has dealt with the Government of India, his treating the Governor-General and his Council as mere delegates, as hands and mouths for the Secretary of State to make audible in this country his voice and carry out his instructions, it becomes necessary to say a few words about what should be the proper relations between these two august authorities which would work for the benefit of the Indians. The howl raised by the Anglo-Indian Press will deceive nobody who knows the real reasons at the bottom for this outcry against a liberal and not indolent Secretary of State. If Lord Morley had chosen to mark time and say ditto to the views of the Anglo-Indian community at large and give no political privileges to the "natives," nothing would have been heard against him. Fortunately for us, though coming to a new office at an age when most people would have been glad to be able to rest, his liberalism has been an active faith, and has been worked out in practice causing a natural discontent amongst those possessors of vested interests who are unwilling to lay aside even a tithe of the power and prestige so long enjoyed unhampered and unquestioned by any outside authority.

As far as Parliamentary Statutes are concerned, it needs no pointing out that the Secretary of State for India is absolutely master of the situation. He is a greater autocrat than the Tsar of all the Russias,* or the German Emperor, or even the President of the U. S. A., strange and incredible as it may sound to those who do not realise that a Republic is not always a really democratic form of government, where the considered *will of the people* is supreme.

But the exigencies of the situation, common-sense, and the necessity of having to deal with men who are not 'Orientals' but of the same blood and breeding as themselves, and who can and do make their voices heard amongst that British public which is the ultimate master of both, exercise a great deal of check on any tyrannical handling by the Secretary of State of European officials. So, as long as responsible Govern-

* The Tsar was forced to abdicate on March 13, 1917, and the new Russian Cabinet is now exercising supreme powers hitherto vested in the Monarch.

ment is not established in India, as it is in Canada, in New Zealand, in Australia, in South Africa,—which question is not so wholly beyond the pale of "practical politics" as interested persons would have us believe —it is absurd to kick against the exercise of the authority by a Secretary of State, which exists in him through the power of statutes.

But there is another set of circumstances, which not only Anglo-India but India feels to be a case of injustice and against which there is no remedy, and mere protests seldom avail. It generally happens in financial cases only, when a money burden has to be put on this Dependency in the interests of the dominant partner. Then no Cabinet seems to be strong enough to mete out even-handed justice and the Constitution provides no remedy. Lower down I suggest a plan to allow equitable adjustments in all such cases, where the Government of India is opposed to the policy of the Home Government and dislikes to have to carry it out, and is further backed up by a strong feeling in the country against the measure sought to be imposed upon it and against its interests. For cases like these where a strong-handed, unsympathetic Secretary of State, mostly ignorant of India and its various and rapidly changing conditions, and unmindful of its interests, appointed more for his political views on Home questions and his services to the party in power than for his personal knowledge and fitness for the post, pulls the wires from London and keeps the puppets dancing in India, some ways and means have to be found to bring regulating pressure on him. We have also had cases where perfectly incompetent persons, but whom the party in power dare not disoblige, were put in as Secretaries of State for India as if the misgovernment of this "brightest jewel in the British Crown" were of little moment—as truly it is from the standpoint of mere party Government.

If the Government of India is to be merely the delegate of the British Government and meant merely to see that the orders of the India Office are literally carried out—as they were in the days of Lords Lytton and Elgin, the latter going to the extent of deliberately enunciating and defending the theory of mandate from Home in the Imperial Legislative Council—then it would be far better to abolish all this complicated and costly machinery of the Government of India and replace it by one High Commissioner at the Indian end of the cable. This will secure both economy and despatch. This idea, when put forward so nakedly, would, of course, be scouted by everybody; though unfortunately for us Indians, wherever the interests of India and England conflict, the former have to go to the wall. No Secretary of State is strong enough to withstand the tremendous social and political pressure of parties, corporations and even individuals.

It may be incidentally noticed here that so far not a single *ex*-Viceroy, or *ex*-Governor has been made a Secretary of State for India. Is it that a first-hand knowledge is considered to be a drawback for the efficient discharge of the duties connected with the office?

One can quite realise that while the permeation with only that sort of knowledge that comes of intimate association, in one's youthful and impressionable days, with the scum of India—the low paid, venal and cringing subordinate revenue, police and jail staff of a District, and its criminal population—should rightly be a bar even to the headship of a Province ; but one wholly fails to see why a five years' intimate acquaintance and at a mature age, with all that is best in the land and its people, should not be utilised in this high office. It is unfortunate that mere party convenience should be the sole consideration in the appointment of the Secretary of State for India.

It may be all right where the subordination to the India Office is in matters of such principles and actions as are far-reaching in their consequences, affecting the well-being of the British Empire as a whole; but in matters of every-day administration, in matters that concern the economic, social, and political well-being of the teeming millions of this country, the position should be one of freedom : the Secretary of State's authority held in abeyance and coming into activity only as an Appellate Court.

The reasons for such an extraordinary concentration of powers in the hands of a single individual, practically irresponsible as long as he has the Cabinet with him, and not even bound to consult it, is due to historical causes, into which we need not enter here. It is a relic of the days of the East India Company and its conflicts with the Ministers of the Crown till the

Crown obtained the necessary powers of over-riding the authority of the Company, by its own uncontrolled and autocratic authority.

The conditions of the British Government of India, namely, through an alien executive, owning neither allegiance nor responsibility to the ruled, are such that neither the Viceroy nor the Secretary of State can, profitably to the Indians, be permitted to go his way unchecked by the other. The people of the country have no real and effective voice in dealing with the policy and principles actuating the springs of administration, which are wholly in the hands of a close Bureaucracy and which all unconsciously has come to regard itself as not merely the ruler of the land, but in conjunction with the British merchants in the country, as its owner, its proprietor, as a landlord is of his estate. It is to *them* that loyalty is owed by the people, and not so much to the Constitution or even to the Crown. All criticism of *their* actions is *lese majeste*, sedition ! The "man on the spot" quite naturally is unwilling to part with any of the powers that he has been exercising in his 'paternal' way for so many generations. He does not feel that he exists *for the people*, and not *they* for him. He does not feel that loyalty has to be *mutual*. Oligarchies are proverbially tenacious of *their* powers and privileges ; and so whenever any question of devolution of powers to the *people* comes up, they oppose it strenuously. It should be clearly realised in this connection that the great devolution of powers advocated by almost all of the official witnesses before the Royal Decentralisation Commission was to *themselves.* They, one and all, resented interference and meddling, with what they regarded as their own proper work. They would not be hampered either by the authority of an official hierarchy above them, or by a non-official *popular* authority below them. Witness the strenuous resistance to the Indian proposal of District Councils, or even for such an elementary but basic demand for bare justice and freedom from oppression and terrorism as lies at the root of the universal cry for the separation of Executive and Judicial powers.

For all such cases it is absolutely essential that there should be plenary authority in England till the Indian Legislatures have come into their own, to override the selfish views of the local administrations. But for all those cases where principles and policies do not come into conflict with the long enjoyed powers and privileges of the Bureaucracy but instead concern themselves with the improvement of the administration at large, "the man on the spot," *aided and advised* by elective councils, might be trusted almost wholly. In all such cases he will be far more alive to the needs of the moment than any distant authority could possibly be, and besides there is no personal bias in such cases distorting judgments from, though unacknowledged but ever-present, personal motives.

High authorities like Sir George Chesney, Sir John Strachey, Sir Charles Dilke—to give only three names out of many—are all for giving a complete measure of power to India to administer itself. A couple of quotations from Sir Charles Dilke's *Problems of Greater Britain* and Sir John Strachey's *India* will bring out the meaning of the above statements more clearly. Speaking of the Secretary of State for India, and the Government of India, the former says :—

Even their [the Government of India's] official representative [the Secretary of State] himself is subject to pressure from his constituency, which may render him upon some questions but a half-hearted friend. (P. 408.)

To exemplify this statement of his and thus to bring it home to his readers, he cites the notorious case of the abolition of Import Duties. This abolition, he says, has been a triumphant success but unfortunately it was carried, as has been shown, by interested pressure from Lancashire and against a considerable amount of Indian feeling.

Unfortunately for this optimism born of Free-trade bias, this "triumphant success" has turned out to be an unmitigated failure, and the Duties had to be re-imposed. Showing yet again and unmistakably the black hand of "interested pressure" in the imposition of Excise Duties on cotton goods, Sir John Strachey, the official apologist, says :

Pressure, however, not easy to resist, is sometimes brought to bear upon him.—[The Secretary of State.] (P. 53, 2nd Edition.)

If he had dared to be fully truthful, he might have added that this pressure is invariably transmitted to India. For, did not Sir John himself succumb to it in the Viceroyalty of Lord Lytton over the Customs question and defend his action vigorously in *The Finances and Public Works of India*, a book published by the Strachey brothers? What shall we say to the honesty and truth of official versions *versus* non-official?

One has only to compare the admissions of Sir Charles Dilke and the indignant denials of Sir John Strachey. Finally, Sir Charles Dilke most truly remarks that questions of this class will increase day by day

> in which the Government of India would have a general local opinion upon its side, and as we should not dream of imposing our ideas in such matters by force upon Self-Governing Colonies, and as we do not, in fact, impose upon many of the Crown Colonies, there is a great deal to be said for allowing Home Rule to India with regard to them.

The late Mr. R. C. Dutt, in his *India in the Victorian Age*, in approvingly commenting on J. S. Mill's evidence, makes the following remarks :—

> It is next to impossible to form in one country an organ of government for another which shall have a strong interest in good government. "There can be little doubt that the irresponsible Government of the Secretary of State has also been attended with many hurtful results." There is no real control over the Secretary of State's action, similar to that which was exercised on the Court of Directors by the Board of Control; no periodical enquiries were made into the present administration, as inquiries were made into the Company's administration at every renewal of their Charter; and no jealous and salutary criticism, like that to which the Company was subject, restrains and corrects the action of the present Indian Government. And the results of this irresponsible administration have not been altogether happy. To confine ourselves to financial matters only, the annual revenues of India averaged thirty millions sterling in the last five years of the Company's administration; and out of this sum, only three and a half millions were remitted to England for Home Charges. By the last year of Queen Victoria's reign, 1900-1901, the revenues had been nearly doubled, amounting to fifty-five millions, excluding Railway and Irrigation receipts, although the extent of the Empire remained much the same and the wealth and income of the people had certainly not increased. And a sum exceeding seventeen millions were remitted to England as Charges. This enormous economic drain (increased fivefold in less than fifty years) would have been impossible under the rule of the East India Company. (P. 184.)

Similar is the import of the statements made by Lord Lawrence in his answers to Henry Fawcett, namely, that, the Secretary of State cannot stand the pressure of people who have votes and whose interest is not the Government of India for the good of the Indians but for their exploitation in the interests of the commercial classes of England. (P. 340 *ibid.*)

Sir Charles Trevelyan also (p. 378 *ibid*) made similar remarks :—

The Queen's Government has shown itself profuse and squeezable . . . . . The influences which press upon the Government outside, through the Press and through their influential supporters, have altogether been too strong, and every safeguard has been overborne.

Lord Salisbury also repeats the same old tale in his evidence. (P. 386.) Lord Curzon, also with his blunt outspokenness in his speech before the Indian Mining Association, unhesitatingly blurted out that British officials and British merchants were alike here for purposes of exploitation.

Now, let us see if there are any means for counteracting the pressure of English interests on the Secretary of State, and so of allowing a freer hand to the Government in India. How this latter is to be widened and prevented from falling completely a prey to Bureaucratic influences and Anglo-Indian prejudices, whether mercantile or official, has been suggested in the succeeding chapters.

To begin with, the 'Home' Government of India, in England

does not correspond in character to the Government of the British Dominions beyond the Seas. From the executive point of view, and apart from the legislative supremacy of Parliament, the Colonies are governed by the King-in-Council, acting on the advice of the Secretary of State for the Colonies. But India is governed by the King-Emperor on the advice of the Secretary of State for India. (Anson: Law and Custom of the Constitution, Vol. II, Part II, p. 83.)

Then we come to the India Council. The recent

changes introduced in the Constitution of the Council may and probably will improve its present working. But the criticism that will rightly have to be levelled against its present Constitution is, that all these recent changes but touch the fringe of the evil; they are superficial, they merely tinker with the old machinery and do not go down to the very root of the mischief; they but provide palliatives instead of a radical cure for the deep-seated trouble. But most likely these recent tinkerings are but preliminaries to changes of a far-reaching character. It would be useful to offer, therefore, a few suggestions as to what would constitute a good and profitable adaptation in the interests of India.

(1) The salary of the Secretary of State for India, and the Parliamentary Under-Secretary, should be a charge on the British Budget. This is a demand of the most elementary justice. We do not ask that the expenses of the establishment of the Secretary of State and other India Office expenses should be a charge on the British revenue. This is *less* than what the British Government is doing for the Colonial Office. History justifies our demand completely. For the first time and most arbitrarily was India saddled with the salaries of the Indian Secretary of State and his Parliamentary Under-Secretary in 1858. Up till then from 1784, for a period of 75 years, it was a charge on the British Budget. The Board of Control, which was established in 1784, was to consist of six Commissioners, namely, the Chancellor of the Exchequer,

the Secretaries of State—there were only two in those days—and not more than three other members, who too must be Privy Councillors. *The salaries of the three ex-officio Commissioners were paid out of the revenues of England*, while those of the nominated Commissioners were a charge on the revenues of India. It will thus be seen that we are doubly justified in our demands, that (*a*) there should be no invidious distinction on this question between the treatment meted out to the Colonies and to India, and further (*b*) we are historically justified in our demand, which asks only for a reversion to the old system.

If this were granted, then the unpleasant insinuation made in certain quarters that this great constitutional change was quietly made for the deliberate purpose of keeping Indian questions out of Parliament would be given its quietus. That the interference of Parliament is bitterly resented by the Indian Bureaucracy is too well known to need enlarging upon. Paget, M.P., is a standing caricature in all Anglo-Indian papers and clubs, so much so that even Lord Morley was forced to criticise their attitude and defend Parliamentary interference. In *The Nineteenth Century and After*, for February 1911, he wrote:—

> That, however decorously veiled, pretension to oust the House of Commons from part and lot in Indian affairs—and this is what the tone now in fashion on one side of the controversy really comes to—must lead in logic, as, in fact, to the surprising result of placing what is technically called the Government of India, in a position of absolute irresponsibiliiy to the governed. Now, this, whatever else it may be, is at daggers drawn with the barest rudiments of democratic principle. So, for that matter, is it incompatible with Divine right or the autocracy of the sword? Even the fiercest Oriental tyrant always ran some risk of having his throat

cut or his coffee poisoned, if he pushed things too far . . . . No Government can be trusted if it is not liable to be called before some Jury or another, compose that Jury how you will, and even if it should unluckily happen to be of dunces.—(Quoted from A. Rangaswami Ayengar's *The Indian Constitution*.)

What the effect of placing the salary of the Secretary of State, and the Parliamentary Under-Secretary, on the British Exchequer will be, is put tersely by Lord Courtney in his *Working Constitution of the United Kingdom*. He says :—

No part of the expense involved in the Government of India comes before the House of Commons in Committee of Supply. The salary of the Colonial Secretary is voted by Parliament, and there is thus a possibility of annually reviewing his policy in the full activity of the Parliamentary Session. The salary of the Indian Secretary of State is paid by India and never comes before the House of Commons. At the end of the session, generally after the Appropriation Bill has been read a second time, the Indian Budget is submitted; and this consists of the review of the financial situation in India followed after a desultory discussion by a resolution simply affirming that the Indian accounts show certain totals of income and expenditure. It may be doubted whether this does not betray too great a jealousy of the House of Commons. If the salary of the Indian Secretary of State were submitted like the Colonial Secretary's to a vote, the opportunity for a real debate would be given which, experience suggests, would be used rather than abused.

No Indian could profitably add to these weighty pronouncements of Lord Morley and Lord Courtney.

(2) The Government of India Act, 1915, Section 27, Clause (7) reads :

The auditor shall lay all his reports before both Houses of Parliament with the accounts of the year to which the reports relate.

This submission leads to no action, nor under the circumstances can it be of any earthly use; unless and until the scope of the above clause is enlarged by the addition of some such words as—"*and such reports with the account shall forthwith be referred to the Public*

Accounts Committee of the House of Commons;" then and then only will the scrutiny of the Indian Budget become a reality instead of the annual farce that it is at present.

(3) The members of the Secretary of State's Council should be fourteen, of whom not more than four should be taken from among the eminent British public workers and appointed by the *King in Council*, as was the good old practice in the days of the Board of Control, and not by the Secretary of State for India; and not more than two should be appointed by the Government of India, while not less than eight should be elected from among the eminent Indian public workers by the non-official members of the Provincial and Imperial Legislative Councils of India, so that every Major Province might be represented. The *personnel* of the India Office is made up almost entirely of retired Anglo-Indians, so the views of the Government of India, i.e., of the I.C.S., are not merely fully well known but are as a matter of fact fully carried out; so it can do very well even without these two representatives. *Under the Act, as it stands, every one of the fourteen members may be Indians and none need be a European, if the Secretary of State so chose.* Their tenure of office should be only for five years.

The statutary provision (Section 3, Clause 1 and 3), that out of a minimum of *ten* members, *nine* must have served or resided in British India is again a relic of the compromise of 1858, by which the Court of Directors appointed by the Court of Proprietors, and the Board of

Control appointed by the British Government, were fused into the present-day Secretary of State and his Council, and there is no good reason for its continuance to-day.

The East India Company, naturally anxious about its dividends, stipulated, as the price of compromise, that the major part of the members should be men who, either through service or trade relations with India, were pledged to its *commercial* interests. These interests were further to be safeguarded by making the appointments independent of the Secretary of State by making them *elective* and their tenure for life. The Government of the day astutely made no serious objections—if they made any—to this triple line of defence. Any such resistance might have alarmed the Court of Directors and wrecked the whole measure. The Cabinet knew that all these safeguards were mere cobwebs which could not restrain for a moment the actions of the Secretary of State, whom other sections of the Act had made all powerful.

That this question of the *elective representation of the British commercial interests* was ever present in the mind of the British Cabinet, is made very clear in the Earl of Derby's speech when introducing the Third Government of India Bill after the First Bill, that of Viscount Palmerston, and the Second Bill, that of the Earl of Ellenborough, had come to grief. He said on this point:—

There was another proposition of the Government which did not meet with seeming great favour; I mean the proposition by which they endeavoured to obtain, what it was very difficult to

secure, a representation of the commercial interests connected with India in the Council. We proposed in that Bill to supply that deficiency by giving the appointment of four of the Councillors to the Constituencies of the largest towns connected with the trade to India. That proposal was, I believe, a good one in itself, but it did not meet with such an amount of support in Parliament, or in the country, as would justify us in insisting on its adoption. The conclusion at which we then arrived was, that with a view to secure the three great requisites of intelligence, experience. and independence in the Councillors, it is necessary that a portion of their body should be elected; that another portion should be nominated, and that all the parties elected should have served, or should at least have resided, for a considerable period in India, and should, consequently, have possessed opportunities of obtaining a knowledge of the feelings and of the wants of the people of that country.—(*Indian Constitutional Documents*, Edited by P. Mukerji. P. 125-126.)

On the suggestion of Earl Grey, the Court of Directors, which consisted of eighteen members, was given the power to elect seven members from among themselves, *vide* Government of India Act 1858, Section 8.

The Indian demand that not less than half the Councillors shall be elective has no novelty about it. The principle of elective members, who should be conversant with the feelings and wants of the people of India and whose number was not to be less than half of the total number of members, was whole-heartedly agreed to by both the Liberal and Conservative Ministries of the day and embodied in the Act of 1858. But sixty years, which have produced political self-consciousness amongst us, have most unfortunately stimulated a reactionary policy—not in the British Parliament, and the British People—but among the retired pro-Consuls, like Lords Curzon, Sydenham, MacDonnel, and others, and in the India Office itself manned, as it has been for years now, by obsolete Anglo-Indians. Even such a sympathetic and liberal Secretary of State as Lord Crewe could not advance beyond a "panel of forty Indians" to be nominated by the non-official members of the various Legislative Councils, and from which he was to select two! The Earl of Derby, when introducing the Third Government of India Bill of 1858, *defended* the two absolute limitations imposed on the Secretary of State in the ever to be remembered words:—

> **The first of those limitations will arise in the case of the election of members of the Council. It is obvious that that election would be a farce if the authority of the Secretary of State were to be paramount in the matter.—(P. 128, *Indian Constitutional Documents.*)**

India, with one voice, rejected this travesty of the elective principle, and further pointed out how utterly impracticable was the idea of getting forty good men and true who would be prepared to expatriate themselves to a very inhospitable climate for seven long years.

We owe it to Lord Morley's prestige, and courage that a slight progress in the right direction has been made and that two *bona fide* Indians have been members of the India Council since the days of his Secretaryship. His successor Lord Crewe attempted to give these appointments a statutary basis, but his Bill was unfortunately still-born.

That no person, however sympathetic, alert and intelligent he may be, can adequately represent people who are of a different nation than himself, is a well-worn truism, and it would be impertinent to enlarge upon this fundamental principle of all sound Government. One quotation from the speech of Sir Charles Wood in the House of Commons, when introducing the *Indian Councils Bill* of 1861, will show the utter futility of the assertions of those persons who not only insist in season and out of season that a foreigner can represent the wants and aspirations of 'natives,' but who go to the ludicrous length of asserting, with all the fervour of fanatics, that he can do so *far better* than a 'native' can! Sir Charles said :—

> It is notoriously difficult for any European to make himself intimately acquainted with either the feelings or opinions of the Native population, and I was struck the other day by a passage in a letter from one of the oldest Indian servants, Sir Mark Cubbon, whose death we have had recently to regret. He had been in the service for sixty years; he had administered the affairs of Mysore for nearly thirty years, he had been living in the most intimate intercourse with the natives, possessing their love and confidence to an extent seldom obtained by an English officer, and yet he said, 'that he was astonished that he had never been able to acquire sufficient acquaintance with the opinions and feelings of the natives with whom he was in daily communication.—(Page 168, *Indian Constitutional Documents.*)

Can there be a more emphatic contradiction than the above of the Bureaucratic assertion that it is the Anglo-Indians who are the real voice of the people, and not men of our own flesh and blood! If this was so in those old days when Indians were less self-conscious, and the colour prejudice almost non-existent, what shall we say about the immensely greater difficulties of a sympathetic understanding of the Indian position when he has become so much more self-conscious, and the British, not only in India, but all the world over, have developed *colour sight* most markedly.

The India Council is almost purely an advisory body and not an administrative machine like a

Cabinet with individual Ministers in Executive charge of the different departments of a Government, hence the absolute necessity of a majority of Indians in it, otherwise the first requisite "Experience" will be at a discount; of these being Elective, otherwise the second requisite "Independence" would be at a discount; and, finally, of the Electorate consisting of the non-official members of the Legislative Councils, otherwise the third requisite "Intelligence" will be at a discount in the Council of the Secretary of State. Thus and thus only can the three "requisites" of the Earl of Derby be properly satisfied.

It is wholly proper that it should be nothing but a purely advisory body, with no administrative functions, but one before which *every matter* should come up. The Secretary of State should be bound to consult it collectively, and hold weekly meetings for the purpose. He should be bound to take it into his fullest confidence. The eight elected Indian members should occupy a position somewhat similar to that occupied by the High Commissioners accredited to the Colonial Office by the Dominions possessing responsible Government.

With regard to the emoluments of the Indian members of the India Council, the proposal of Lord Crewe that they be given an expatriation allowance of £600, in addition to their salary as Councillors, was an eminently just one; though unfortunately a certain section of the press of Bengal misled by mere *doctrinaire* considerations strenuously objected to this perfectly sound principle. I would even go further and say that these should be paid £2,000 as consolidated salary, and the non-Indians the present £1,000.

It is curious that of all persons it should be Sir George Chesney who advocates the portfolio system with its individual responsibility for the India Council. That one with such an antecedent as his, of long and intimate connection with the Government of India, could advocate a system which would place that Government at the whims of individual retired Anglo-Indians full of old prejudices is passing strange. Such a system stands self-condemned.

The anomalous position of the Council is itself due to historical causes. It is the legal successor of the Court of Proprietors, of the Court of Directors, and the Board of Control, none of which, of course, could control the actions of a Minister. As long as his appointment is the offspring of Parliamentary Government and Ministerial responsibility, he is bound to be the predominant partner in the concern. His decision will continue to be the final one till such time as India also gains Home Rule.

Such a change by removing the invidiousness inseparable from the status of the Councillors and preventing their being wrongly regarded as active participants in the day-to-day business of administration, and so jointly responsible with the Secretary of State will also help to remove the complaint of Sir George Chesney (*Indian Polity*, p. 375) and of others that the Secretaries of the various departments of the

India Office who, as far as their legal status is concerned, are mere clerks—have far more power than any of these Councillors. This is due to their having direct access to the Minister and receiving *their* orders straight from him, without reference to the Councillors. It is an absurd complaint arising out of mere hurt vanity. They forget that the responsibility is that of the Secretary of State, and he shares it with nobody else.

This Secretariat Government is a serious drawback in the Government of India also, diminishing as it does the Minister's control over the Secretariat, and consequently his responsibility very largely. But unlike that at the India Office, the evil is remediable here. The British Prime Minister would not communicate with the staff of any office *unless he was acting in conjunction with the political head of the office*, but the Secretaries in the Indian Government stand in immediate relation to the Viceroy, and he may confer with or instruct any of them *without reference* to the member of his Council in charge of the department concerned. (Anson, Vol. II., Part II., p. 88.) So also is the case in the Provincial Governments. It has got to be brought into line with the British practice.

The necessity of changing the Constitution of the India Council cannot be better put than was done by J. S. Mill in the report he drew up for his employers —the Court of Directors. The Report says :—

The means which the Bills provide for overcoming these difficulties [of the Government of one nation by another] consist of the unchecked power of a Minister . . . . The Minister, it is true is to have a Council. But the most despotic rulers have Councils

The difference between the Council of a despot, and a Council which prevents the ruler from being a despot is, that the one is dependent on him, the other independent; that the one has some power of its own, the other has not . . . . The functions to be entrusted to it are left in both [Bills] with some slight exceptions to the Minister's own discretion. That your petitioners cannot well conceive a worse form of government for India than a Minister with a Council whom he should be at liberty to consult or not at his pleasure . . . . That any body of persons, associated with the Minister, which is not a check, will be a screen.—(R. C. Dutt's *India in the Victorian Age*, pp. 226, 228.)

The argument is unanswerable so far as it goes. As it is impossible to make the Council into a "check," so neither should it be permitted to be a "screen," which is best done by turning it into a purely advisory board but which must be consulted at every step.

(4) The *Secret* Department should be abolished at once. It has been the cause of so many Frontier Wars, of internal and external annexations, and generally of financial trouble to India. This parent of so much mischief in the past, and pregnant with many more in the future, is an inheritance from the dead old days of the dual government of India, when the Minister appointed by the Crown was often at loggerheads with the various Boards and Courts of the East India Company, and used this method for imposing his will and setting theirs aside. For when once any definite line of action had been started, there could be no withdrawal, it had to be persisted in to the bitter end.

The Earl of Derby's statement in the House of Lords about the second limitation on the very full powers of the Indian Secretary of State, *viz.*, that,

the only other limitation will be with regard to the expenditure of the revenues of India. With regard to this expenditure we must bear in mind the effective and *bona fide* control over the

Secretary of State by an independent body, such as I hope this Council will be.—*Indian Constitutional Documents*, p. 128.)

Alas for official optimism, *the effective and bonâ fide control* has proved to be a complete fraud. The Earl of Derby himself could scarcely have been genuinely persuaded of the effectiveness of the control provided by the statutory provision, as will be seen below from a further quotation from the same speech. A matter has only to be put in this Secret Department by the Secretary of State, and any number of millions of Indian Revenue may get dissipated, and the India Council and the Government of India may sit in despair helplessly wringing their hands. If the archives were to be thrown open to an independent investigation of the doings of this department, one is afraid the record would be found to be black indeed.

Richard Brinsley Sheridan, known to our graduates as a clever dramatist only, was in his days a sturdy politician, a friend of Charles James Fox and a member of the House of Commons. He published in 1788 a pamphlet called *A complete statement of the two Bills for the better government of the British possessions in India brought into Parliament by Mr. Fox and Mr. Pitt with explanatory observations.* In this comparative study of the two Bills, which he had originally delivered as a speech in the House of Commons, among other matters, he with keen insight fixed on this glaring departure from the Bill of Fox and, in fact, from all known principles of Constitutional Government, as one which would lead to endless mischief. He says :—

"The Secret Committee, created by Mr. Pitt's Bill in the Court of Directors, is an instrument of Government unlike anything existing in any other country, or anything to be found in the history of all past governments. A body of men in authority (the Court of Directors) acting under a delegated trust from their constituents, (the East India Company) take an oath on their election to support the interests and rights of the Company. These Directors are then bound by law to choose a Secret Committee from among themselves, which Secret Committee are to take an oath to be "true to the trust reposed in them by the Directors"; but to obey only such orders and directions as they shall receive from the Board of Control, which orders and directions they swear also never to communicate to the Directors, who appoint them, without the consent of the said Board of Control. This Secret Committee have no power of originating or directing anything to be done of their own authority, still less, by suggestion or instruction from the Directors. All the Governments and Presidencies, however, in India, are bound to pay a faithful obedience to their orders and dispatches, and to answer the same upon the same terms of secrecy, "as if such orders and directions had been issued and transmitted by the Court of Directors of the said United Company."

If it were worth reasoning or arguing upon, it would be no difficult matter to prove that this crooked system of involved mystery and contradictory duties could never have been meant for any fair purpose of good government. Facts, however, make reasoning on the subject unnecessary. The institution had scarcely taken place, with the addition of the *oath*, added in the Explanatory Act passed in 1786, before this committee, appointed for the purpose of issuing the secret instructions of the Board of Control, relating to matters of *war* and *peace*, are directed to manage, as a *matter of secrecy*, the *settlement of an old debt* due from the Nabob of Arcot to the Company.

Nothing could be more clearly out of the spirit and meaning of the Act of 1784, than this measure. The Board of Control had already assumed an arbitrary power of settling the debts due from the Nabob to *individuals*, as *matter connected with revenue*. The Directors conceived they might at least have been permitted to settle *their own* debt, which was their property and stated as part of their effects to Parliament; but this was discovered to be—*matter connected with negotiation.* The Board of Control had no power to issue their orders, through the *Secret Committee*, with respect to matters of *revenue*; but with respect to *treaties*, with *Native Princes*, they had: accordingly the settling a sufficient security for an old and public debt to the Company, due from a dependent on their Government, was converted into *a negotiation of State*, deemed a matter of secrecy, and withdrawn even from the knowledge of those who alone had any title to the debt. The Directors apply to their Counsel; and they are truly informed by

Mr. Rous, that "the whole effect of the last Regulation Bill, in constituting the two Boards of Directors and of Commissioners, the one proposing measures, and the other, after representation, finally deciding, will be lost, as far as concerns the Government of Madras, *if the intercourse with the Nabob shall be confined to the Secret Department*, because this intercourse involves directly, the arrangements respecting the military force, and indirectly *every interest of that settlement*."

The dispute comes before the Court of Proprietors, who resolved, on the 30th of June 1786, "that the construction of the Act of the 24th of his present Majesty, under which the right Honourable Board of Commissioners for the affairs of India have claimed to exercise the powers in instances before the Courts, is *subversive of the authority of the Court of Directors* and the *chartered rights* of the Company, recognized and confirmed by the said Act; and tends to establish a *secret system of Government, highly dangerous to the interests of the Public and the Company*."

It was further *resolved unanimously*, "that this General Court do return thanks to the Court of Directors for the *firmness* with which they have *maintained the rights of the Company* against the *claims of the Right Honourable Board of Commissioners for the Affairs of India;* and that the spirited protest of Mr. Samuel Smith merits the approbation of his constituents.

Upon this the Court of Directors resolve, that "it is expedient to apply to the Legislature for a further explanation, and more correct limitation of the powers of the Board of Control. At the same time, however, with a very natural caution, they think it prudent to ask Mr. Pitt's *permission*, to do so first." Accordingly the Chairman, and Deputy Chairman, are directed to wait on the Chancellor of the Exchequer, and propose the following question: "If the Court of Directors, with the authority of the General Court of Proprietors, *shall think proper to apply to Parliament to* explain the powers of the Board of Control, with regard to the secret correspondence relative to the country powers of India, will *you* assist them in their application?

Here seems to have been a reasonable case made for a *Declaratory Law*, if (according to Mr. Scott) "a material difference of opinion between the Company and the Board of Control is a sufficient ground for one."

The Chancellor of the Exchequer, however, after due deliberation, answers, that "he cannot agree in the sentiments expressed in the Resolution concerning the conduct of the *Right Honourable Board of Commissioners for the Affairs of India, and does not see any ground for an application to Parliament on the subject*."

In a Court of Proprietors, these proceedings being reported, it was moved that a Committee be appointed to take into consideration the State of this Company, under the operation and effect of the last Act of the 24th and 26th of George III. Upon this a ballot was demanded, in which (the refractory conduct of the Court of Directors and Proprietors having created a considerable alarm) a proper *weight of influence* was exerted, and the question *passed in the negative.*

Mr. Samuel Smith's testimony on this occasion, as he has been a zealous friend to the *present* administration in Parliament, must be admitted to be at least free from party prejudice. He says, in the protest above alluded to, containing the reasons of his resignation:

"It will be in vain to contend that the *Patronage* is secured to the *Company* by the Act of Parliament; if *the Government is secret*, it will be absurd to suppose that the *Patronage will be open;* or that those *who have no voice in the measure* will have much concern, *if any, in the appointments;* if they have not, to what evils, so often foreboded as dangerous to this constitution, will not this *mysterious* Government of India expose us? And if this is to be contended as a *necessary mode of managing and controling the affairs of India*, it will, in my opinion, give rise to a question, whether, *under such circumstances of danger to the constitution, our Indian possessions are worth retaining?"*

A public situation, reduced to the mere *mechanism of official obedience*, can afford but little credit, even by the most rigid discharge of its functions. Circumscribed as the power of the Court now is, and by the interpretation given to the clause to which I allude, incapable of acting either with energy or effect, it *must ere long yield an easy surrender of its remaining rights to the encroachments, and vigilance of a more active control.* Thus circumstanced, the office of a Director may be the object of obloquy; and, though liable to a serious responsibility in the case of misconduct in others, is too subordinate to continue the post either of independence or honour.

It is, therefore, my intention to resign my trust to the Proprietors, conscious that while I held it, I endeavoured to discharge it to the best of my abilities, and with an integrity unimpeached.

India House,
June 13th, 1786. (Sd.) SAMUEL SMITH, *Jun.*

In fact, this transaction established the power of the Board of Control to act through the *Secret* Committee, UPON ALL MATTERS, and IN ANY MANNER they may think proper, without a possibility of check, and with scarce a probability of detection.

(Pages 32 to 35.)

We may, after this trenchant criticism, see what the Earl of Derby, who, by the very nature of his official position, could not but be an apologist, a whitewasher, in defending this weapon of autocratic, darkness-loving Government, had to say about this department. The admissions made by him are significant. In his speech in moving the second reading of the third Government of India Bill, he said :—

There is another provision, which, I think, your Lordships will believe to be absolutely necessary, for transferring to the Secretary of State that power which was exercised by what was called the Secret Committee of the Court of Directors, namely, the power of sending out orders and instructions to India on particular subjects, without previously communicating those orders and instructions to the Council. Now, I do not mean to say that that power has not in certain cases been abused ; I do not mean to say that it has not been too extensively employed ; but I am sure your Lordships will agree with me that, with regard to the two cases to which alone it is properly applicable, namely, the carrying on of war or of diplomatic arrangements with Native States, it is absolutely necessary the Secretary of State should possess the right of preserving entire secrecy even from the members of the Council.

The Earl of Derby naturally would not point out that this Secret Committee of the Court of Directors was but the 'hand' of the President of the Government Board of Control for pulling out his chestnuts from the fire, and that the poor Court of Directors were in no way responsible for its actions. From the date of Pitt's Act 1784, all real power and authority had been transferred from the Company to the Crown. (Chesney, p. 362). Sheridan in his pamphlet was acute enough to see through the veil that Pitt had drawn over the whole matter. He says :—

But, if anything further were wanting to show the fallacy of this pretended security to the rights of the Company, we find it amply made out in the notable devise of *compelling the Directors to establish a Secret Committee to be solely under the orders of the Board of Control.* This Secret Committee was accordingly soon employed *contrary* to the *professed purpose* of its institution, (p. 23).

Even if we accept the Earl of Derby's specious pleading, we may point out that conditions of affairs in 1917 are very different from those that existed in 1858. Now, there is no Native State problem. They have all been reduced to Feudal subordination and have loyally accepted British suzerainty.

The condemnation pronounced by General Sir George Chesney, M.P., who throughout his official career was intimately connected with the Government of India and was the military member—and so almost as important as the Viceroy or the Commander-in-Chief—in the closing years of his official life, is as below:

"One of the most important points to be provided for is the protection of the people of India, the taxpayers, from the infliction of improper and unfair charges. This was, no doubt, the object aimed at in the provision of the Act of 1858, that 'no charge should be placed upon the revenues of India without the sanction of the majority of the Council.' But this check is practically rendered nugatory by the power given to the Secretary of State to deal with business alone in the Secret Department. In the days of the East India Company, the Chairman and the Deputy Chairman of the Court of Directors were associated with the President of the Board of Control on this Committee; but now the Secret Department of the India Office is removed entirely from the view of the whole Council. And thus, while the sanction of the majority of that body is required to the granting of a gratuity or a pension of a few shillings a year recommended by the Government of India on behalf of some humble applicant, a Secretary of State may order, and has ordered, military operations to be undertaken by the Government of India, involving an expenditure of millions of money, not only without the sanction, but without even the cognisance of his Council. This is a flagrant defect of the system which was certainly not contemplated by the framers of it, and which calls urgently for remedy. The Secretary of State should undoubtedly have power to over-ride his Council. It could not be allowed that the policy of the British Government should be liable to obstruction by any other body than the Parliament which places it in power; but the interests of India demand that the Cabinet should at least be placed in possession of the opinions of those who are best qualified to judge of the effect of any measures proposed which will involve a financial burden on India; and while it should be recognised that in dealing with measures involving military operations, secrecy is a necessary condition, and that the maintenance of secrecy is not compatible with deliberation of a large body, yet, on the ground of justice to India, and to prevent rash and ill-considered action, the reconstitution of at least a part of the Council as a Secret Committee is undoubtedly required. At present such of the clerks as deal with the secret business of the India Office are placed in a more responsible and important position in the Council, they can at least make representations regarding the measures dealt with in these despatches, while the Council itself may be in absolute ignorance about them. (Page 371 to 373.)

(5) The statutory provision that members of the India Council must not be members of Parliament should be repealed. No convincing or for the matter of that any reasons have been given for such a drastic prohibition. On the contrary, the case for having some members of the Council in the House of Commons has been well made out by Sir Charles Dilke. He says :—

The Council is out of touch with the House of Commons, and adds no element of security to the side of the Indian Governments in contests with that House, which has little regard for its opinion. . . The Viceroy and his Council in Calcutta are face to face with the House of Commons with little to protect them, except the single voice of the Under-Secretary of State or of the Secretary of State.—(*Problems of Greater Britain*, p. 407.)

It might be helpful to recall that no such unmeaning and curious limitation was imposed upon the members of the Board of Control, *all* the six Commissioners of which might sit in either House of Parliament. The retrograde measure was sought to be imposed for the first time in the first India Bill of 1858, and from which it was bodily taken over in the third India Bill of 1858, without a word of explanation or justification. Viscount Palmerston in his speech introducing the first India Bill of 1858, in calling attention to this innovation, said :—

> We do not propose that the Councillors shall be capable of sitting in Parliament. We think there would be great inconvenience in such an arrangement; that they would become party men; that they would necessarily associate with one side or the other in this House, and that with changes of administration, the relations between the President and the Councillors might then become exceedingly embarrassing.—(*Indian Constitutional Documents*, p. 112.)

Now all this is very feeble and unconvincing. The relation of the Secretary of State to his Council is not that of the political head of a department and its permanent officials, but is analogous to that of a Minister and the Legislature. There can be no question of official discipline here, these councillors having no routine duties, or any office work to perform; the Council and the Secretary of State are not required to present a united front.

(6) In all cases of serious difference of opinion between the Secretary of State and his Council, the Secretary, before taking any action, should be bound to lay the whole case before three other Members of the Cabinet, who should be jointly responsible for the action proposed to be taken, and a State paper embodying the reasons for the proposed course of action should be issued to the India Council and to the Government of India.—(Sir George Campbell, *India As It May Be*, Chapter I.)

(7) In cases of difference of opinion between the Government of India and the India Office, or between the latter and the War Office or the Treasury, which

would saddle India with some financial burden, the Secretary of State when he is inclined to resist, which is all too rare a phenomenon, can be, and is always, overborne by his colleagues in the Cabinet. Having no Indian electors to conciliate, no Indian votes in the Parliament to reckon with, he as well as the Cabinet naturally take the line of least resistance and never hesitate to transfer the obligation incurred for British benefits to Indian shoulders. The only method which would be a safeguard against such unblushing transactions would be a tribunal removed from the din of political strife. *The Judicial Committee of the Privy Council would be an ideal body for adjudicating upon all such questions.*

It follows from all this that there should be no such entity as *Secretary of State in Council*, nor *Committees of the Council of India*, to whom administrative charge of departments of the India Office may be made over.

The leaders of modern India, Hindu, Muslim, and Christian, have been steadily awakening to the fact that the existence of the India Council is an insuperable bar to the full development of representative institutions in this country and to our obtaining the status of an autonomous Dominion of the British Empire. The National Congress has attacked it, (*vide* the brilliant speech of Mr. Eardley Norton made in the Congress of 1894). The Muslim League has attacked it. So far back as 1853, when it was being created, its creation was denounced in an able pamphlet, *Plan for the future Government of India,* by James Silk Buckingham (2nd Edition) with all the fullness of his knowledge gathered in the course of forty years, experience of things Indian. He, in 1818, became the editor of the first daily journal published in India as he himself tells us. He goes to the root of the matter by bluntly asking, "Is such a consultative Council indispensable, or even necessary at all?" He answers straight, "I am clearly of opinion that it is not." The pamphlet deserves a careful study even after the lapse of so many years.

It is a body, as has been fully shown above, wholly helpless to either resist the actions of the Secretary of State, or to spur him into action when he is inclined to be lethargic; while it serves as a most effective screen for the auotocrat. Its sinister influence, however, comes into play where the interests of the people of India clash with those of the dominant hierarchy of European officials and European merchants. Its vast patronage in the matter of those appointments which are not through the door of competitive examinations, all exerted against the interests of the sons of the soil, is an ever standing grievance.

All the suggestions put forward above for mending this machinery are meant only for such time as the machinery does not get scrapped. These, if adopted, it is hoped, may turn a baleful agency into a beneficial one. The suggestions about the eight elected Indian High Commissioners are irrespective of the factor of the India Council. These we must have.

(8) All revenues or moneys raised or received by the Government of India should vest in the Governor-General in Council, and not as at present in the Secretary of State acting for His Majesty the King Emperor. They shall form one consolidated Revenue Fund to be appropriated by the Legislative Council for the purposes of the Government of India.

This is the most important item in the devolution of the powers of the Secretary of State to the Governor-General in Council.

(9) The continued existence of the Stores Department is the cause of much justifiable complaint on the part of traders and merchants in India. It should forthwith be abolished, for, as long as it exists, the Government will be bound to provide gist for its mill and the many 'philanthropic' resolutions about buying stores in this country will remain largely a dead letter. Its abolition will force the Government to look nearer home for the supply of the goods wanted, and thus, instead of practically boycotting, encourage, commercial enterprise in India.

If the reforms suggested above are carried out, and the relations of the Secretary of State to the India Council adjusted to the newer conditions, and the Council itself modified in its *personnel* and constitution and brought up to date, then there would be removed the indictment of Sir John Strachey—himself for long a distinguished member of that body—that

> a body constituted like the Home Government of India is slow to move and sometimes obstructive, and its general policy has been conservative and cautious.—(*India*, 2nd Edition, p. 54.)

He might have pointed out, if he could have got over his Anglo-Indian prejudices and *esprit de corps*, that this was largely due to the very large employment of retired and effete Anglo-Indians as members and secretaries. It could not be otherwise, "regard being had to the innate indolence of most men, especially of old men," (Chesney's *Indian Polity*, 3rd Edition, p. 374) and to the force of lifelong prejudices contracted in the despotic atmosphere of their Indian surroundings.

(10) The real centre, round which revolves the whole question of the proper Government of India, is, however, neither the Secretary of State nor the Viceroy, but the Permanent Under-Secretary. The overwhelmingly important and, indeed, decisive part played by him in all questions of administration is fully brought out by Lowell in *The Government of England*, Vol. I, Part I., Chapter VIII—and the question is—how to bring this powerful official into direct touch with the rapidly changing conditions of things in India. The whole chapter deserves very careful study, especially the pages dealing with the colonial office; for, it is a very serious problem for all those interested in a *progressive* Government for India. The Secretaries of State come and the Secretaries of State go, but he sticks on for ever.

It is to be hoped that the change here suggested in the *personnel* of the India Council, and in the method of their appointment, would go a long way towards bringing the Permanent Under-Secretary of State into touch with the hopes and aspirations of progressive India. Lord Crewe's innovation in appointing to this post an Indian Civilian is fraught with mischief for the future of India. The Congress and Muslim League demand is that there shall be a native Indian Permanent Under-Secretary also.

(11) The British Prime Minister, Mr. David Lloyd George, has, in one of his speeches in the House of Commons, thrown out a suggestion that the English constitution might with profit adopt the French practice of having Parliamentary Commissions attached to each Ministry. This will enable the Parliament to be in far more direct relations with the government departments than is the case at present. If this suggestion materialises, it is bound to be an effective check on the vagaries of the India Office and its permanent staff and of great good to us. But there is the danger also of the present evils getting terribly intensified if, instead of honest and sympathetic members with no axes of their own to grind, members representative of vested interests inimical to Indian aspirations are permitted to be smuggled in. This will have to be guarded against most strenuously.

Before concluding the chapter, it would be well to discuss from the Indian point of view a question of very great importance, namely, whether India is to be kept clear of entanglement in English party politics or is to take its part in the fierce din and wrangle of party warfare.

The Anglo-Indian view is singularly unanimous, clear and emphatic on the point. On no account is the political neutrality of India is to be disturbed. In season and out of season, it is ever being dinned into British ears that if India is ever lost to the British Crown, it will be lost on the floor of the House of Commons. It was not the House of Commons, but a prestige-ridden, short-sighted, mean-minded, domineering Tory Colonial Office that lost America nearly a century and a half ago to the British Crown: and it was a liberty loving, high-minded, generous, prescient, democratic House of Commons that saved South Africa to the Empire. No better reply to these interested croakings can be given than in the wise and eloquent words of Viscount Palmerston when introducing the first India Bill of 1858. He said:—

However, we shall be told by some that the Government of India is a great mystery—that the unholy ought not to set foot in that temple—that the House of Commons should be kept aloof from any interference in Indian affairs—that if we transfer the Government to the Ministers responsible to Parliament, we shall have Indian affairs made the subject and plaything of party passions in this House, and that great mischief would arise therefrom. I think that argument is founded on an overlooking of the fundamental principles of the British Constitution. It is a reflection on the Parliamentary Government. Why, Sir, what is there in the management of India which is not mainly dependent on those general principles of statesmanship, which men in public life in this country acquire here, and make the guidance of their conduct. I do not think so ill of this House as to imagine that it would be disposed, for factious purposes, or for the momentary triumph of party, to trifle with the great interests of the country as connected with the administration of our Indian affairs. I am accustomed to think that the Parliament of this country does comprise in itself as much administrative ability, and as much statesmanlike knowledge and science as are possessed by any number of men in any other country whatever; and I own, with all respect for the Court of Directors, that I cannot bring myself to think that the Parliament of England is less capable of wisely administering the great affairs of State in connection with India than the Court of Directors in Leadenhall Street. I am not afraid to trust Parliament with an insight into Indian affairs. I believe,

on the contrary, that if things have not gone on so fast in India as they might have done — if the progress of improvement has been somewhat slower than might have been expected, that effect has arisen from the circumstance that the public of England at large were wholly ignorant of Indian affairs, and had turned away from them, being daunted by the complications they imagined them to be involved in, and because Parliament has never had face to face, in this and the other House, men personally and entirely responsible for the administration of Indian affairs. No doubt a good deal has been done in the way of substantial improvement of late years, but that which has been done I may venture to say has been entirely the result of debates in this and the other House of Parliament. And, so far from any discussion on India having worked evil in India, I believe that the greater part of those improvements which the East India Directors boast of in that publication, which has lately issued from Leadenhall Street, has been the result of pressure on the Indian administration by debates in Parliament and discussions in the Public Press. Therefore, so far from being alarmed at the consequences which may arise from bringing Indian affairs under the cognisance of Parliament, I believe that a great benefit to India, and through India to the British nation, will result therefrom. (Pages 116-117. *Indian Constitutional Documents.*)

May one be permitted to ask whether these reiterated loud proclamations are not due to a little fear of unpleasant investigations by Parliament. Similar outcries against Parliamentary interference were quite common in the days of the East India Company whenever the Charter was to be renewed and a Commission of Enquiry issued.

Unfortunately there is a grain of truth in the Anglo-Indian contention against Parliamentary interference which makes it so plausible. We see how the verdict goes against us wherever large questions of policy are concerned, and in the carrying out of which there may be some antagonism between the interests of the British taxpayer and merchant, and the Indian taxpayer and merchant. The opportunist Ministers cannot always afford to advocate justice. The Colonial

Conferences, the Imperial Federation Schemes, all ignore India—nay, gore her in her tenderest parts, Indian questions being always looked at with vulgar colour prejudice, and never on their merits. Unless and until India also becomes a factor to be reckoned with in the maelstrom of British politics, full justice will never be, cannot be, done to her.

This was not so even up to fifty years ago. It began to come into existence with the growth of Australia and of South Africa, and has become notoriously prominent latterly by the contagion of the Colonials, who are, through their politicians, their students, their merchants, influencing English life in so many directions, as also through the vested interests of retired Anglo-Indians. Lowell also gives some other reasons why the national temperament has changed. The proverbial old 'phlegm' has given place to almost 'French hysteria' as was markedly shown on the never-to-be-forgotten 'Mafeking' night in London. The whole town went almost mad when the long tension and agony of the strain of the Boer War was suddenly relieved by the news of victory. The *laissez faire* doctrine of the Manchester School of Economics has disappeared and been replaced by socialistic and 'paternal' doctrines. The new Imperialism is inimical to the aspirations of non-White and non-Christian nationalities, its humanitarianism confines itself largely to men of its own blood. English Ministers are after all human beings, and they have to tack their sails to the breeze of the moment, if they are to avoid foundering. So the habit of treating the urgent symptoms, and not going behind them in search of ultimate causes, is very strong. Even Mr. Gladstone had to confess that he had never been "able sufficiently to adjust the proper conditions of handling any difficult question, until the question itself was at the door." Such an attitude makes far-sighted policies looking for results in the distant future impossible. Parliamentary legislation has become a scramble where the most persistent and influential get what they want. "The motives for winning over the various classes in the community by yielding to their wishes" are very strong. "Under the late conservative administrations, complaints were made of doles to the landowners, the Church of England and the publicans; now, under the Liberals, of concessions to Non-conformists and to the Trades-Unions." (*The Government of England*, Vol. II. Chapters LXV-LXVI.) Every interest that can bring to its help the pressure of votes in the Parliament, and can make any question 'acute,' is certain of a favourable hearing.

It is impossible to prevent the discussion of Indian questions in the Houses of Parliament, and equally impossible that the discussions should not take a party turn. Lord Morley's India Councils Acts, notwithstanding his strenuous efforts to keep out discussion on party lines, were discussed largely on party lines, and Lord Morley had to conciliate the Opposition by throwing overboard many a provision for which India had been pressing.

Why is it that India, "this brightest jewel in the English Crown," is not even thought of in connection with Imperial Federation Schemes? Why was it that it had no voice in the Colonial Conferences? What is the *real* objection to a policy of Protection? It is India that stands in the way. It is felt that the demand for Fiscal Autonomy on her part could not well be refused with any show of even political, to say nothing of ethical, decency, nor could be light-heartedly met for fear of selfish commercial votes.

If India is to be governed in the interests of its people, it must enter the arena of party politics. Everybody is much too busy with affairs nearer home to spare time and energy for seeing full justice done to a people who are dumb. Even the Secretary of State for India is a party politician owing his Cabinet rank to his English work and not Indian. It is not on questions of Indian policy that a Cabinet is ever wrecked. All this talk about keeping Indian questions out of party polemics looks very much like a convenient cloak for covering them up and thus preventing their becoming urgent symptoms to add further perplexities to an already overburdened and harassed Cabinet.

(12) Finally, India should be allowed direct representation in Parliament for the purpose of making its voice heard in the home of its rulers. Till the time that the question of giving India an autonomous government on the lines of Australia, of New Zealand, of South Africa, of Canada, is solved, how are we

to voice our demands in the Houses of Parliament, if not through Indian representatives? The plea put forward against direct Colonial representation, "that the Colonies would interfere with England, or England would rule the Colonies far too much" (Lowell, Vol. II, p. 436) cannot hold good of India. Her Parliamentary representatives would be too weak—we do not ask for more than twenty members in the House of Commons and ten in the House of Lords (these to be appointed for a term of five years from among the Ruling Princes, the bigger Zamindars and the Cadets of their House)—to be able to interfere with English policy and, as India is not yet a Self-Governing Dominion, there could be no question of England ruling her far too much. It already rules fully.

French and Spanish, Dutch and Portuguese Colonies send representatives to their respective 'Parliaments.' If the representatives of Pondicherry can sit in Paris, cannot the representatives of its neighbour, Madras, sit in London with profit to their Constituencies and to England? The advantage of such a course would be immense. All questions would be threshed out in public, all chances of misunderstandings would be removed. The people, at large, would know the reasons for any line of action taken, and even if it is against their wishes, it would leave less of a soreness behind against the Government than is the case at present.

SUMMARY.

1. The position of the Secretary of State for India to be approximated as quickly as possible to that of the Secretary of State for the Colonies with regard to the Self-Governing Dominions.
2. The salary of the Secretary of State for India and of the Parliamentary Under-Secretary to be a charge on the British Budget.
3. If the Indian Budget continues to be submitted to Parliament, it should be referred to the Public Accounts Committee of the House of Commons, after presentation.
4. The Secret and the Stores departments of the India Office to be forthwith abolished.
5. The present India Council to be replaced by a Board of High Commissioners, eight in number, each one of whom is to represent a Major Province of India and to be elected by its Legislative Council and his salary of £2,000, to be on the Provincial Budget. The High Commissioners not to have any administrative functions, but only consultative and advisory.
6. The Secretary of State's control over Indian Finance completely, and over Administration very largely, to be made over to the Imperial and Provincial Legislative Councils.
7. All revenues and moneys raised or received by the

Imperial or Provincial Governments of India to be vested in the Governor-General-in-Council, or the Governor-in-Council, as the case may be, and not in the Secretary of State.

8. Till such time as India does not become autonomous, like Canada etc., all differences of opinion between the Government of India and the India Office, or between the latter and the British War Office or the British Treasury, to be referred to an independent tribunal like the Judicial Committee of the Privy Council foı adjudication.

9. The Permanent Under-Secretaryship of State for India should not be filled by retired Anglo-Indian Officials as has been done for the first time under the *regime* of Lord Crêwe. It is a perilous innovotion. The vested interests and class prejudices of a member of the I.C.S. are likely to prove prejudicial to the best interests of India.

10. India—whether directly under British rule, or only indirectly so, being those portions which are governed by its own native Princes—to be allowed to send representatives to both the Houses of Parliament.

CHAPTER II

THE IMPERIAL GOVERNMENT

The Royal Commission upon Decentralisation in India in their Report, issued in 1909, point out that under their terms of reference they could only enquire into the relations of the Government of India with the Provincial Governments, and into those of the latter with the authorities subordinate to them. They take care to state that they were precluded from dealing with the question of alterations in the control of the Secretary of State over the Indian Governments (Imperial and Provincial),

> except incidentally and so far as discussion of the relations between the Government of India and the Provincial Governments compels a reference thereto . . . . Similarly, we have not enquired into the relations between the Government of India and the heads of the Imperial Departments which they directly administer, such as Railways, the Post Office and Telegraph. We hold, too, that our terms of reference precluded us from enquiring into . . . . . the constitution and duties of the Civil and Criminal Courts.

It is perfectly true that most unfortunately for us the terms of reference were deliberately made narrow and were further circumscribed by the very rigid and technical interpretation put upon them by the Chairman of the Commission, who was the Political Under-Secretary of State for India, and was thus inevitably biassed *against* a liberal interpretation of the terms and *towards* an interpretation that would disturb the least the administrative system as it existed. This self-imposed limitation has been no less harmful than the other limitation, which prevented them from enquiring into the relations of the Secretary of State and the Government of India. The absence of the former would have helped to remove a very large number of the errors of the system of administration, which bear very harshly and injuriously on the people; while that of the latter would have paved the way to the granting of a large and liberal measure of Home Rule to the country.

We in India feel every moment of our lives how very necessary is an enquiry into the powers and duties of the Law Courts, the emoluments of the officers and their qualifications, the methods of appointment, and their relations to the Central and Local Governments, and to each other. Criminal, Civil, Revenue, all these Courts need a rehauling. But the enquiry that we demand is not of the type of the unfortunate Islington Public Services Commission, which has once again brought home to us the truth of the Biblical Parable of the Talents. If its recommendations are acted upon, then the Indian will be called upon to surrender even the little that he has got and the foreign element in the various services of the country which, considering the poverty of the country and the rate of payment for similar services in other civilized countries, is being already exorbitantly overpaid, will have further additions made to its emoluments and a larger monopoly of all the higher posts to the exclusion—

herein lies the pathos of the situation—of the sons of the soil.

No reason, even specious, has been made out for the avoidance of enquiry into the above-mentioned matter of the Law Courts, or of the relations of the Government of India and the Heads of the Departments directly administered by them. The Commission has coolly refrained from even the mention of such other Departments as the Law, the Military, the Foreign, each under the control of a Member of the Executive Council of the Governor-General. All these should have been enquired into. Nor have the relations of the Local Governments and the Heads of the various Departments subordinate to them, like the Public Instruction, the Police, the Foreign, (each Local Government has also such a Department) the Judicial, and others been enquired into.

The Foreign Department does not deal only with the affairs of such States as are really situate *without* the boundaries of India, but it deals also with the 700 odd Native States and only the most determined optimist or the rosiest-hued official apologist can assert that it is perfection. Further the Chief Commissionerships are annexes of this Department and are directly controlled by the Governor-General. Surely an enquiry here would have been fruitful of results. The Military Department, the cause of so much bitter feeling and public quarrel between the late Lord Kitchener, Lord Curzon, and Lord Middleton (then Mr. Brodrick, Secretary of

State) ending in the resignation of his high office by Lord Curzon, should not have been left severely alone. It is true that, later, another Commission, under the Presidency of Lord Nicholson, sat at Simla in the Viceroyalty of Lord Hardinge, but its findings have been treated as a dead secret and nobody outside the charmed circle knows anything about it. The repeated attempts to drag its findings into light, both in the Governor-General's Legislative Council and in the Parliament have proved wholly abortive.

An enquiry into the Law Department would have shown that it has continued to be the Cinderella of the family since the days of Macaulay, its first head, and has not yet come into her own, other Departments continuing to usurp her heritage.

All this is very far from being satisfactory or hope-inspiring. No real progress towards honest Decentralisation by a genuine association of the people with the government of the country, with ever accelerated pace, is possible, unless and until the limitless Statutory powers of the Secretary of State over the Central and Local Governments in India are very considerably abrogated. My purpose in pointing out all these shortcomings is that some future Commission of Enquiry should not be permitted to have its scope so narrowed, but should make a *full* and *genuine* enquiry into the *entire machinery* of administration, as was done in the olden days when the East India Company's Charter had to be renewed periodically. It is for such a wide Commission that the National Congress has been pressing for years.

Still more necessary and very urgently needed is a Retrenchment Commission. Expenditure has been going up by leaps and bounds. Salaries are being increased, special allowances are being granted, highly-paid posts are being multiplied, and taxation is becoming ever more burdensome, while the economic condition continues to be deplorable.

THE VICEROY.

Coming now to the main thesis of this chapter, we find that in dealing with the powers of the Supreme Government, its constitution and its machinery, the very first factor that attracts attention is the Viceroy, his qualifications, his status and his powers.

There does not seem to be much danger of this, the finest post in the British Empire, becoming a preserve of the Indian Civil Service. So far there has been only one departure from the invariable practice, and the chances are few indeed of that departure becoming a precedent. The magnificent political patronage involved is not likely to be surrendered by either of the powerful parties ruling England. The Viceroy will continue to be a nominee of the party in power for the time being. Both parties have, however, recognised that the post is not to be made a party-question in the American sense of 'spoil to the victors,' which would spell ruin to any serious and proper administration of this country. It goes without saying that the post is a reward for recognised party help, and it will continue to be bestowed only on those who have rendered conspicuous service to the party that happens to be in power when the post falls vacant, and are also otherwise fully qualified by administrative and political experience. But some queer notions of dignity prevent a commoner being appointed. Lord Curzon's case seems to be decisive on the point. If the choice of the Prime Minister falls on a commoner, he will be ennobled before being sent out. Another point is that no Viceroy-designate is likely to repeat the mistake of Lord Curzon, who, while accepting ennoblement, did not wish to be exiled from the House of Commons. He found that after years of almost kingly dignity, he was no longer fit to stand the rough and tumble of the House of Commons. Such superior positions cannot but tell on the moral fibre of a man, and the shadow of "the divinity that doth hedge a king" comes, in however modified a form, to unfit him for the ordinary heckling of the House of Commons politics, quite as effectually as if he had been born an aristocrat.

Coming back to the question of the class from which such exalted personages are to be chosen, there is little danger of their ever being chosen from the Royal family. The political and other reasons against such a step would overwhelmingly be against any English Cabinet making such a choice. But it is necessary to say something about this subject from the Indian point of view, as suggestions to that effect have been made, from time to time, by persons in this country, of diametrically opposed political views. Neither radical, nor conservative, neither plebian nor aristocrat, neither Hindu nor Mussalman has realised what the establishment of such a miniature Royal Court would mean to India as a whole. They have been simply led away by the glamour of the idea, added to, perhaps, a semiconscious feeling that the 'pseudo-aristocrats' of the Indian Civil Service would not then be able to hold their heads so very high as they do now in the absence of genuine aristocracy from their own land, and who give themselves such annoyingly superior airs not only where the "native" is concerned, but also in their dealings with men from their own land whether official or merchant, journalist or traveller, if they have the misfortune to be out of the charmed circle of the I. C. S. Its snobbery is limitless. These bad manners are not of recent growth; but are of fairly old standing. J. S. Buckingham, in his *Plan for the Future Government of India*, to give only one instance and that too from a rather later day pamphlet, published in 1853 (2nd edition), animadverts strongly on the wide-spread evil. For Europeans to come suddenly, he says:—

> From a society composed wholly of Europeans, to one in which they are surrounded chiefly by dark-skinned Asiatics—greatly their inferiors in rank, emolument, and position is to beget in them a supercilious contempt for a race so different from their own, and whom they seem to think they are specially appointed to overrule and command; and this haughtiness of disposition towards the Natives is daily fostered by the examples and customs by which they are surrounded. (P. 26.)

Every psychologist knows that this sort of bumptiousness is not the outcome of any inherent evil special to the English character, but merely the vulgar manifestation of the exuberant feelings of the successful man; of the top-dog in the battle of life.

Because we dare not retaliate as we do when we meet with such behaviour in persons of our own hue and political standing, therefore the continuing sore.

From the point of view of the good of the sweating and teeming millions of India, nothing could be more retrograde than such an appointment, if English party politics could ever compose their differences to the extent of sinking their beneficial rivalry and agreeing to set up a simulacrum of a Royal Court with a Prince of the blood Royal to preside over its destinies. Apart from the inevitable fact that in Oriental surroundings, it is sure to attempt to eclipse the rather thin splendour of the English Court itself, which could not be tolerated, it would be financially ruinous to poverty-stricken India. If this is not enough argument to check the ardour of the champions of Royalty, we might remind them here that the Viceroy is a hard-worked official with a splendid training behind him and not a merely superfluous ornament, whose functions are purely social. Now, how many Royal Princes are there, who could be trusted to have even average abilities or average application to business? Bagehot, an undisputed authority, says on this point of Royal ability :-

> He can be but an average man to begin with; sometimes he will be clever, but sometimes he will be stupid; in the long run he will be neither clever nor stupid; he will be the simple, common man who plods the plain routine of life from the cradle to the grave. His education will be that of one who has never had to struggle; who has always felt that he has nothing to gain; who has had the first dignity given him; who has never seen common life as in truth it is. It is idle to expect an ordinary man born in the purple to have greater genius than an extraordinary man born out of the purple; to expect a man whose place has always been

fixed to have a better judgment than one who has lived by his judgment; to expect a man whose career will be the same whether he is discreet or whether he is indiscreet to have the nice discretion of one who has risen by his wisdom, who will fall if he ceases to be wise.

Theory and experience both teach that the education of a Prince can be but a poor education, and that a Royal family will generally have less ability than other families. What right have we then to expect the perpetual entail on any family of an exquisite discretion, which, if it be not a sort of genius, is at least as rare as genius? (*The English Constitution*, Ch. iii.)

It is nearly half-a-century since Bagehot wrote, and his delineation of Royalty is as true to-day as it was when he wrote. The English Royalty alone has improved since his day, largely because, as has been most happily described, the British Empire has become a crowned Republic.

A Royal Court will be a hindrance rather than a help to the good government of the country. Court influence, as we see in highly-civilised and largely-democratic Europe, even in the 20th century, is not always an unmixed blessing :—

What these influences are everyone knows; though no one, hardly the best and closest observer, can say with confidence and precision how great their influence is.—(Bagehot.)

These sinister influences, as Bagehot calls them, come to the surface off and on when one *camarilla* is exposed by another *camarilla*, causing horrible scandal and intense bewilderment as they did in Germany some years ago, and very recently in Russia and have done in every European Court from time to time.

The time of the Court, unfitted for business will, then, be naturally taken up wholly with the frivolous ceremonials and the fripperies of Government to the detriment of incessant, unpleasant, hard, vast, complicated and miscellaneous daily work which must be done if chaos is not to be produced. In fact, as it is, the present social functions of even a non-Royal Viceroy take up too much of his time and are unfortunately tending day by day to become quite as important factors as his administrative functions. It is necessary to raise this warning voice in time before it also becomes a 'burning' question. The question is already beginning, to be asked by the taxpayer, whether all this lavish display is right and proper, while famine after famine is laying the land desolate and killing off peasants and cattle by the million, to say nothing of the vast havoc caused by such ever-present diseases, as cholera, plague and malaria. He naturally asks: Who are the people that benefit by all this extravagance and display? The social amenities of gubernatorial life are for a handful, who are not of the land. These entertainments are the preserves of the European official and non-official populations of the hill and plain capitals, and sometimes a stray Native Chief. How does it benefit the teeming millions of India who have to provide the wherewithal for these grand shows? India is only the poorer for these costly social displays. Sir Frederick Lely has some acute remarks in his *Suggestions for the Better Government of India* on this point. He says (p. 15):

> I may note in passing that the Governor should never visit a town without making a not excessive but tangible gift to the public. A Budget Grant of, say, Rs. 25,000 in all every year for this purpose would be of *infinitely more political use than the sumptuary allowance for diners and dances to Europeans.* (The italics are mine.)

The author has touched here a very sore point of the Anglo-Indian administration of India, and while not meaning it, has shown how very English and insular are the surroundings of the Governors and how the Indians are wholly excluded from them. Incidentally this also raises the whole question of the extravagant sumptuary allowances to these highly-paid Heads of the Administrations. It is an ever-increasing burden, and there seems to be no check upon it. Why should it not be abolished altogether, or at least reduced to reasonable dimensions? Do the Governors-General, the Governors, the Lieutenant-Governors in Canada, Australia, South Africa, New Zealand, etc., get any, and if so, what allowances over and above their salaries, and for what purposes?

The question of salary naturally comes in here. The Governors-General of Canada, Australia, South Africa, each receive only £10,000 a year. Even the Emperor's own uncle received that much only as the Governor-General of Canada. Surely this is ample emolument; and there is not a shadow of reason or justice for burdening poverty-stricken India with fully double that rate. The household arrangements of the Indian Viceroy, and the Governors, which are probably on a more magnificent scale than in any other possession of the Crown, also badly call for the pruner's hands. For all this lavishness and display is due to a fancied necessity of vying with the fabled gorgeousness of the 'barbarous' Orient, and certainly not to any inherent necessity of the case.

Before going on to deal with the qualifications, powers and functions of a Viceroy, some remarks might be made about the tenure of his office. No legal limit is fixed to the term of office, but a custom has grown up which fixes it at five years; and this is the case not only for the Viceregal term of office but also of many others, for instance, the Subordinate Heads of Administrations, the Executive Councillors, and so on. It was not so in the earlier days. Five years is too short a period for any new man, however clever and hardworking he may be, to get at the heart of his new duties sufficiently to leave his impress on them when the time for his relinquishing of them comes. The statutory life of the House of Commons till very recently was 7 years, which means that the life of the Executive was also 7 years. If this was found advantageous up to only a few years back in England, where the incomers do not come into wholly new surroundings nor are they wholly new men—the case frequently being that they had previously filled that very office or had been in any case in the Cabinet and knew something of the inner working and the policy governing their particular departments, though might not have had anything to do with it actually, much more should it be advantageous in India. For both these conditions are absent in the Indian employment. The person appointed knows nothing of the work he is going to do. He only brings a trained intelligence and a wide experience to bear upon the work. He has to learn painfully, laboriously, all the minutiæ not only of his own department but also of every other. He has to gather special experience before he becomes fit to deal with the complex work of the departments to fit himself for his duties as the Prime Minister, correlating and controlling the whole vast machinery of the Government. Then, again, none of these appointments go again a second time to the same person, much less a third time, as they often do in England. Taking all these factors into consideration, it would seem to be the wisest course to copy the practice of the United States of America which fixes the time-limit at four years for the Presidentship, and if the President has proved himself to be a wise and capable head, he is elected for a second term of four years. A further equally wise, constitutional practice has grown up of not permitting a third term. Why should not such a good practice be adopted in India also? For all those offices in which, according to present practice, the tenure is limited to 5 years, it should get restricted to 4 years, with the distinct understanding that if the holder of it has proved himself to be a wise, progressive and sympathetic Governor or Minister he should be re-appointed for a further 4 years' term, by the Crown, *on a petition by the Legislative Council concerned.* Such a change will not only reduce the admitted evil of too rapid changes of portfolios but will have for us also the inestimable advantage of a quicker removal of unsympathetic or incapable holders of these exalted offices and of permitting of the lengthening of the tenures of such as have proved, in their first term, that the good of India and of Indians is their first consideration. It cannot be said that this lengthening of the term of office would destroy the freshness of view of the holder of the office. There can be such a thing as too much freshness of outlook! Let us be given the very best man possible for the work and then let him be allowed time to deliberately work out his ideas and not forced either to be in a hurry, or kept merely marking time as one is sure to do who feels that there is not time enough for him to carry through any work which he may set his hand to and which may be unpleasant or distasteful to a successor, who, unable to shove it aside and forced to go on, is almost sure to bungle it.

We may now take up the important questions of the qualifications, powers and functions of a Viceroy. We may take it that the jobbery that used to be perpetrated in the earlier days in the appointment of Governors and Governors-General is a thing of the past; but India feels and resents, that even now the British Cabinet does not fully realise its tremendous responsibility in the matter and does send out men who do not bring credit to their patrons and their country. A few concrete examples taken from the days when the sovereignty of India had not been assumed by the British Crown—for it may be unwise to name later instances—would bring home to those who have not made any particular study of Indian History in the British period, of the sinister influences deflecting the choice of Ministers from men fit for such exalted positions, to men who are a scandal. Very unpleasant tales are told not only about the lesser lights, like Chief-Commissioners, Lieutenant-Governors, and Governors, but even about such exalted persons as Viceroys!

Buckingham says:—

Lord Moira, it is now well-known, was sent out at the request of the Prince Regent, to enable him to repair a shattered fortune, ruined chiefly by advances to that profligate prince for the most unworthy purposes; though the embarrassments of the noble lord were so great, that all his allowances as Governor-General and Commander-in-Chief were insufficient to pay even the interest of his debts; and, on his return from India, his carriage and horses, the only visible property he had, were seized by his creditors, and he died at last in debt and exile, as Governor of Malta. His successor, Lord Amherst, was selected by Mr. Canning from personal, rather than public, motives; and when he plunged the country into the first Burmese War, and exhausted the Indian Treasury, Mr. Canning admitted in the House of Commons that, though he was deemed sufficient for the task of ruling such an empire in a state of peace, the contingency of war had not been calculated on. Sir William A'Court, afterwards Lord Heytesbury, was chosen by Sir Robert Peel, as being one of his political party; but though approved by the Court of Directors, he was recalled by the Whigs just on the point of his embarkation, and Lord Auckland, one of their family compact, though highly objectionable to the India Directors, as being thought deficient in ability, was sent out instead—chiefly, it is believed, because he was poor as a nobleman, and India was a fine field for repairing or making a fortune. The Marquis of Tweeddale at Madras, Lord Falkland at Bombay, and other Governors that might be named, owed their appointments entirely to their political connections with the Government of the day, the question of their fitness weighing only as a feather in the balance, compared with political and family considerations. (*Plan for the Future Government of Indies* pps. 18-19.)

This same pamphlet (pps. 49-50) has the following quotation taken from William Howitt's work, *Colonisation and Christianity*, about the peccadilloes of Lord Amherst:—

Yet, amidst all the poverty and wretchedness, behold such contrasts as the following: Even so recently as 1827, we find some tolerably regal instances of regal gifts to our Indian representatives. Lord and Lady Amherst, on a tour through these provinces, arrived at Agra. Lady Amherst received a visit from the wife of Hindoo Rao, and her ladies. They proceeded to invest Lady Amherst with a present sent for her by the Baiyza Bai. They put on her a turban, richly adorned with the most costly diamonds, a superb diamond necklace, ear-rings, anklets, bracelets, and amulets of the same, valued at £30,000 sterling! A complete set of gold ornaments, and another of silver, was then presented. Miss Amherst was then presented with a pearl necklace valued at £500, and other ornaments of equal beauty and costliness. Other ladies had splendid presents the whole value of the gifts amounting to £50,000 sterling! In the evening came Lord Amherst's turn. On visiting the Rao, his hat was carried out and brought back on a tray covered. The Rao uncovered it and placed it on his Lordship's head, overlaid with the most splendid diamonds. His Lordship was then invested with other jewels to the reputed amount of £20,000 sterling! Presents followed to the members of his suite. Lady Amherst took this opportunity of retiring to the tents of the Hindu ladies, where presents were again given: and a bag of Rs. 1,000 to her ladyship's female servants and Rs. 500 to her interpreters.

Out of the loot of Sindh General Napier received £70,000 as his share and the well paid post of the Governor of that Province which he had conquered against the wishes of his superiors. Every raid and annexation provides rich loot and decorations both to the civil as well as the Military powers.

These are the "gold and diamond diggings" which the appointment of a Governor-General opens to the successful occupant of this lucrative post: and thus it is that political and family interests and intrigues are so rife on every vacancy to obtain this rich prize, whether the individual be fit or unfit for the duties of his high and important station. It goes without saying that the theory is that England will send out the very best man it can. But even if the theory is not vitiated in practice, as shown in the quotations, above, it must be pointed out at once that this Superman will not be the man for work if he is wanting in humanity, in genuine sympathy. Hard-grainedness, mere intellectual brilliance, efficiency—fetish-worship is not wanted. What is wanted is transparent sincerity, whole-hearted sympathy. On the intellectual side, over and above his other current equipments, he must be a sound financier and businessman. He must be an economically-minded man, and up-to-date in the real (as apart from the book-taught theorists') workings of the Political Economy that is being actually practiced by the various Nations of the West. He must possess enough strength of character and honesty of purpose to keep steadily before himself the good of India and not allow himself to be made a party to its hurt. Of few Indian Viceroys can it be said that they have not succumbed to the interested pressure of either the Imperial Services here or the European tradesman, whether here or in England. Is he to be largely only a costly and decorative representative of the Majesty of Britain, with no real powers; or is he to be something more than a mere mouthpiece of the Secretary of State for India, for the time being? Is he to exercise his own personal judgment or to be a mere delegate for the carrying out of the policy of the English Cabinet? These questions have become necessary, for it seems that the increasing trend of opinion is to regard a Viceroy as a person without much voice. It is not meant that there should be no control; but the incessant, harassing control, against which every Viceroy who was strong has complained and to which every Viceroy who was weak has succumbed, should be put a stop to. What is contended is, that the subordination should not be *undue* and that the man on the spot advised and aided by Native Indian opinion through enlarged Executive and Legislative Councils, should be trusted more, and that if he is overruled, as sometimes he may have to be, the world should be given an opportunity of judging for itself. A Lord Elgin weakly announces in Council that he is but a mandatory of the Secretary of State as also his Executive Councillors, and that they must carry out at all hazards the policy enunciated at Home irrespective of its suitability to Indian conditions; or a Lord Lytton upsets Indian Financial stability with a grim famine stalking in the land, or a Lord Minto has to face a huge deficit, under similar famine conditions, because under the fiat of a Secretary of State for India—though he be the honest and conscientious Lord Morley—the revenues of India have to be surrendered to the all-devouring maw of the Army to the tune of 45 lakhs; and when papers are asked for, they are refused under the too common plea of State necessity!

The evil has been of long-standing. So far back as the reign of the Duke of Argyle at the India Office, this doctrine of the *complete* subordination in *all* matters of the Government of India to the Home Government, was laid down unequivocally by that statesman in a despatch to the Indian Government. It was re-affirmed later by the Marquis of Salisbury during his reign at the same office. Now, such a doctrine even when not rigidly adhered to—as it is not, one must recognise, in India—is fatal to all efficient and progressive administration. The reduction of the Viceroy and his Ministers to the status of merely intelligent telegraph operators at the other end of the wire would be supremely ludicrous were not the action pregnant with terrible consequences for the future of the British Rule in India. Which Colonial Secretary would dare to lay down these principles and apply them to any British Colony? The Colonial Office dare not open its lips even in cases of such flagrant injustice as is meted out to the Asiatic subjects of the King by such recently conquered and annexed Colonies as those of South Africa, even when one of the ostensible reasons, by an irony of fate, given by Mr. J. Chamberlain for going to war with the Transvaal, was the savage and oppressive way in which they treated the Indian emigrants! Under the present regime their condition is very much worse than it was before the terrible war, which was undertaken to right their wrongs! It was fondly hoped in India that the Royal Decentralisation Commission will point out some effective way out of this scandalous state of affairs but, as has been pointed out above, we were once more doomed to disappointment and the fond hope was shattered.

The only means of bringing about this eminently just Indian demand is to abolish the India Council and to put the India Office on a footing similar to that of the Colonial Office and allow India to be governed *in* India. A comparative study of (1) the Letters Patents creating the various Governors-Generalship, (2) of the

Commissions appointing the Governor-General and, finally, (3) the Instructions issued to each, will show us our manifold disabilities.

One more suggestion, before dealing with the Indian 'Cabinet.' Why should not the Viceroy and the Heads of the Provincial Governments have Indians as Joint or Assistant Private Secretaries ?

THE EXECUTIVE COUNCIL.

We may turn our attention now to the Executive Council of the Viceroy. I have already said above that the term of office of the Members of this Council should be limited to four years but open to one more re-appointment if the Legislative Council petitions for such. While on the subject I may point out the extreme inadvisability of the present practice of not making the term of office of the Imperial and Provincial Ministers co-extensive with that of the Imperial or Provincial Head. His political demise should invariably be followed by that of his Councillors. No Viceroy or Governor should have the power to appoint Ministers for his successor, as they invariably do now. All Ministers should be bound to put their resignations in the hands of the succeeding Viceroy or Governor within a month of his taking office. This will give the necessary free hand for the appointment of a cabinet homogeneous in its political connection, and not one whose integral parts are ever warring against each other. The importance and in fact the necessity of such a constitutional practice will be fully admitted when it is remembered that unlike the Colonial Governors, the

Indian Governors hold the position occupied by the British and Colonial Prime Ministers and are not merely ornamental Heads.

Another and no less important point is, that they should have no prospects of further preferment under the patronage of the Viceroy. Indeed, it is scarcely appropriate that gentlemen appointed to these high offices by the King should look to any lower anthority for further preferment. At present the inducement that a Viceroy can offer to *every* Member of his Executive Council to be subservient to him is by titles and decorations, but these are not sufficiently solid—though attractive enough—to appeal overmuch to these high and responsible officers; but the case of *some* of the Members who belong to the Indian Civil Service, for instance, is very different. The five Lieutenant-Governorships, under the patronage of the Viceroy, are sufficiently dazzling bribes for any but those who have the most robust conscience and the most exquisite sense of duty. It is an open secret that under the guidance of masterful Viceroys, very divergent despatches are sent 'home' to the Secretary of State. With but a trifling change in the *personnel* of his 'Cabinet,' a succeeding Viceroy, if differently minded from his predecessor, can always get a 'hundred' reasons recorded for a change of policy. This temptation would be removed from the path of both by the raising of the status of the Provincial Administrations to that of Governorships, and by sending young men of outstanding merits from the public life of England as Governors.

5

Sir George Chesney is perfectly justified in his contention about the probable misuse of this great power, seeing what human nature is as a rule. He quotes Mill approvingly:—

> The advisers attached to a powerful and perhaps self-willed man ought to be placed under conditions which make it impossible for them, without discredit, not to express an opinion, and impossible for him not to listen to and consider their recommendations.

That this fear is not wholly hypothetical is borne out by what little is known to the outside world of at least two of the Viceroyalties, namely, those of Lords Lytton and Curzon. Such an uncompromising and cautious bureaucrat as the late General Sir George Chesney would not have voiced it if there had been wanting solid reasons for such a damaging statement. Mr. S. S. Thorburn, who rose to the highest rungs of the official ladder short of the Lieutenant-Governorship of the Punjab, has also some very strong comments on this state of affairs in his work, *The Punjab: In Peace and in War*.

It is, of course, not proposed to touch in any way the final power of veto with which the Viceroy is invested; but it is necessary that his powers of initiating a new line of action should be limited by some well-devised constitutional checks for those cases where he wishes to act in *opposition* to the advice of his responsible Ministers and his Legislative Council, and the question is not one of merely suspending by the power of veto some course of action. Some very well-known and most flagrant abuses of this power might be cited as instances here. The repeal of the cotton duties by Lord Lytton in the teeth of the almost unanimous opposition of his Executive Council, under the disingenuous plea of Free Trade, by which nobody was deceived except perhaps the late Sir John Strachey, but really to catch Lancashire votes for his party, as was openly alleged in that very Council meeting itself, was one. Later, again, India has been made to smart under another grievous fiscal injustice, that of the Cotton Excise Duties under Lord Elgin; yet again another burden was cast on poor India by Lord Lansdowne anxious to carry favour with the Services in the shape of the ruinous Exchange Compensation Allowance, and the juggling with the Currency of the country, causing an artificial Government-created depreciation of the silver held in the country which some day is sure to result in a terrible crash.

As the shears have to be applied to the lavish expenditure of the Anglo-Indian Government all round, it is necessary that the emoluments of these Ministers should also be somewhat reduced. A reduction of Rs. 1,000 per month is not too much to ask for. The pay could well stand at Rs. 5,000 a month instead of Rs. 6,000 as at present. It might well be allowed to be a little lower than that of the British Ministers, which is only £5,000 a year. It will still be equal to that of the Chief Justices of the Indian High Courts, except that of Bengal, and whose pay too might now be very well put on the same level.

Sir George Chesney, in his *Indian Polity* (p. 139), has pleaded hard for the appointment of a Private Secretary to each one of the Executive Councillors and one of the reasons advanced is that he has so many social duties to fulfil that he ought to be relieved of the drudgery of writing letters himself, accepting the engagements or refusing them, so as to be able to devote more attention to his official duties! It would be more to the point that the distracting social duties be lessened rather than helped to keep their hold on the Ministers! If a Private Secretary is a necessity under these circumstances, one can only say that the cogency of the arguments advanced does not appeal to one's reason. The depleted Finances of India can scarce bear to be saddled with this additional burden on such a frivolous plea; and if one might venture on a suggestion, it may be said that it would be to the benefit of the country—and in fact to their own health also—if such an absorbing round of social engagements were to be left to their womenfolk who are such martyrs to *ennui* in this country. His further contention that these Members exercise greater powers than the Provincial Governors and that therefore their emoluments and status should be higher than those of these Governors can only be ascribed to his bias due to his having been such a Member himself. The illogicality of the position would be easily brought home to readers if the counter suggestion were made to exalt the emoluments and status of the Secretary of State for Ireland or for India over that of the Irish or Indian Viceroy who, while exercising far less power, are certainly the most showy part of the machine.

We might, with advantage, go on now to offer some

criticisms on the functions of these Ministers and their numbers. At present there are only six. Originally there were only three. A Law Member was added later, then recently a Commercial Member, and only the other day an Education Member, while the post of the Member for Public Works has been abolished. Under the arrangement suggested here there would be eight, an addition of two to the present number or rather of only *one*, as the Commander-in-Chief has always been a Member, though an extraordinary one.

1. Minister of Finance and Revenue.
2. " " Justice.
3. " " War and Marine.
4. " " The Interior.
5. " " Commerce and Industry.
6. " " Foreign and Feudatory Affairs.
7. " " Education and Public Health.
8. " " Agriculture, Fisheries, Forests, and Irrigation.

It has been customary in India to attach Revenue to Agriculture, but, as I point out lower down (p. 78) this arrangement does not work for the benefit of the tillers of the soil. The attention of the Officer in charge being fixed more on the best means of raising an ever-increasing revenue than of improving agriculture and the lot of the cultivator. It is a better arrangement to combine income and expenditure under one head and thus enable the Minister of Agriculture to devote his attention solely to agricultural improvements and the condition of the peasantry.

THE WAR MINISTER.

With regard to the War Minister, affairs even now are in a very unsettled state. The unfortunate controversy between Lords Curzon and Kitchener was decided in favour of the Military power as against the supremacy of Civil control. It was a badly selected time for such a momentous controversy with such a strong-headed and popular hero of the time, fresh with the laurels won in the Boer War. It was but a repetition of, in its day the equally memorable and momentous controversy between two no less strong men—Governor-General Dalhousie and Commander-in-Chief Napier; but *then* the Civil power triumphed, and Napier had to go. The Conservative Ministry dared not risk their position in the country by accepting the Curzonian proposals which would have inevitably ended in the resignation of Lord Kitchener. So the interests of India were sacrificed to the exigencies of politics and Lord Curzon's resignation was light-heartedly accepted which, of course, left the position of that party in the country unaffected. It would have been very different if Lord Kitchener had resigned; all the Jingo element of the country would have been flying at the throats of the Cabinet Ministers of that day. Now that the Military Supply Membership too has been abolished, the Commander-in-Chief alone is left to represent, or rather to play the dictator, in all Military matters. Every right-thinking and constitutionally-minded person will see that this is a far from desirable arrangement and sure to break down under the stress of a great war.

The breakdown was staved off by the five peaceful years that followed since the previous sentences were written. But the terrible strain of the Great European War hopelessly broke down the Indian Army system. It was responsible for the horrible Mesopotamia scandals and though the Governments both of England and India tried to draw a veil over it all, they did not succeed, and, under the heckling of the House of Commons enough truth came out to make it necessary for the Indian Commander-in-Chief to resign, and for a Commission of enquiry to be appointed. Politically, this has saved the situation and the Report of the Commission has been treated as a secret document on the plea that it might help the Germans to know our weaknesses in that region!

Not one civilised modern State keeps up such an anomalous state of affairs. Even in India it is clear that the present arrangement is more or less tentative and not final, awaiting a definite solution. (See the *note* to Sir John Strachey's *India*, 4th Edition, p. 497, by Sir Thomas W. Holderness, Permanent under-Secretary of State for India, as also Chesney's *Indian Polity*, pps. 134-138, where there is a good deal of discussion over the old point of view.) It may sound absurd to suggest that the practice of England itself in the matter be followed and a Civilian Head of the Department installed; but what might reasonably be accepted is the suggestion of following the Continental system with regard to the post. Let the portfolio of War be held by a senior Army man, but—this is the crux—let him be dissociated from the *actual command* of the Army. That should be the business of officers on the active list. Abolish the post of the *Commander-in-Chief* with its dual duty, of actual command of the Army, and that of a Minister of War. Let the whole of the affairs of the Army be under a responsible Minister of War, and while the actual command of the Army will be centred in a General Staff and an Army Council as holds good in England, in France, in Germany—the direction of the policy will be the sole charge of the Minister advised by a mixed Council of Civil and Military experts as in England. It may look over-bold in an Indian—and withal, not an expert—to venture into such highly disputed regions, but, after all, it is the lay public that is most interested in seeing that peace and security are firmly established, and all disturbing inimical elements kept well cowed, but, at the same time, with the utmost economy possible.

It will be noticed that in the designation of the "Minister of the Interior" for the "Home Member," I propose to follow the sensible practice of the Continent and of the British Dominions—Canada, Australia, South Africa, New Zealand, etc.—rather than the English practice whose only recommendation seems to be long-standing usage ; in India, especially, the designation is a misleading one, suggesting duties connected with England, such as 'Home

Charges,' 'Home Government' and so on, aud which is obviated by the use of the word "Interior."

THE FOREIGN MINISTER.

With regard to the suggestion of appointing a separate Minister of Foreign and Feudatory affairs, it is necessary to say a few words. By present practice it is the Viceroy who is his own Minister in this Department and he is assisted by a Permanent Secretary, whose status is higher than that of the Permanent Secretaries of the other Departments. This is a very unsatisfactory state of affairs. If there is any department which requires a special and minute knowledge of affairs running back to hundreds of years, it is this. No Viceroy, however sympathetic and quick of understanding, can ever hope to deal adequately with the numerous and complicated cases always arising in this department, even if he had the requisite time to devote himself wholly to it which certainly he has not. What is the result? The proud and touchy Princes are left to the mercies of an irresponsible subordinate who, if things go amiss, naturally takes shelter behind the broad back of the Viceroy. This always keeps things in a ferment in scores of States at a time, among the 700 and odd feudatories. The Foreign Office also controls the administration of all those tracts of the country which are directly under the Government of India as, for instance, the Chief-Commissionerships. This is not as it should be. The Foreign Office should confine its attentions to those affairs only which are really "foreign and feudatory." The duties which are *foreign* to this department should be allocated to their own proper departments. Lord Hardinge, finding that the duties were too heavy for one Secretary, split up the Department into two, each under its own Secretary. The new Secretary is designated the Political Secretary and is charged with the affairs of the Native States. This is a step in the right direction and it is to be hoped that it will soon be completed by the appointment of a separate Minister.

I might just refer here to what I shall deal with, at greater length, in a later Chapter, *viz.*, the extreme advisability of suppressing the Political Departments under the various Provincial Governments and concentrating the whole work of dealing with the 700 and odd feudatories in one Imperial Department and of reorganising the Indian Political Service into one homogeneous body like the I. C. S. or, better still, the amalgamating of the two into one large body and the consequent complete eliminating of the superabundant military element from it, which has become wholly unnecessary under the present changed circumstances. This would be a very welcome innovation to all those Feudatories who are, at present, under Local control and subordination, and who will unquestionably feel that their status has been raised in some way which will be the first step in some future federation of all these states. This is one more reason why this department, like every other, should also be under its own separate Minister, for the work will have grown to be much heavier and more complicated: the relations of the Viceroy with it being similar to what they are with the other departments. The Viceroy, in fact, ought not to be in direct, personal charge of any portfolio, but simply the controlling, supervising, co-ordinating and unifying head of the whole machinery of administration. In short, he should be the Prime Minister of the Cabinet responsible for the *policy* of the administration and its larger details but not for the daily work of the Government; his interference being in no case carried to the extent of diminishing Ministerial responsibility for the efficient working of the Departments concerned.

It might be questioned why I propose the name Foreign and Feudatory. It is simply because I regard it as an anomaly that the Feudatories should be regarded as Foreign. I have not space here to dwell longer on this subject and, indeed, it is not necessary; for all that I have got to say about this, I shall say in my Chapter on *The Indian States*.

THE EDUCATION MINISTER.

To one unaccustomed to the Continental system, it might look odd to combine Education and Sanitation. But it is so in Germany, in France, and in many other States. And, indeed, on a closer inspection it does not look so very queer. 'A sound mind in a sound body' is a world-old truism, and it is only in the fitness of things that the improvement of the physical and mental health of the people should be under one direction. The Government of India has done wisely in combining them under one Minister. Some might urge that the combined duties would prove too heavy a burden for a single shoulder to carry. It will not be so. There will not be work enough for two such officers, for the real work of these Departments ought to be, and should be done, by the Provincial Governments, and the work of the Supreme Government should be more or less merely advisory and unifying and not of active interference. In connection with this, the suggestion that the I. M. S., with its Military organisation, should be replaced wholly as far as its Civil work is concerned, by a Provincial Civil Medical Service recruited largely in India is worthy of serious consideration. Its present monopoly of all the higher posts in the line, to the exclusion of the Medical Graduates of the Indian Universities and the consequent stunting of the growth of Medical knowledge in the country by the want of this spur to ambition, should not be permitted to remain unremedied any longer.

THE PUBLIC WORKS DEPARTMENT.

The suggestion to abolish the Public Works Department will probably come as a surprise to most persons, but it is a very old suggestion and was made by such an expert as the late Sir James Caird. It is to be found quoted in A. K. Connell's *The Economic Revolution of India and The Public Works Policy* (p. 190). I give it here in full as it exactly expresses what I wish to convey :—

The very costly Department of Public Works, as a General Office connected with the Viceregal Government, should be closed ; each Province should carry on its works as found most desirable., and as its finances admitted. Native Engineering talent should be cultivated and full scope given to it. Of the large body of officers employed in the Public Works Department in India, nearly four-fifths are English, and the native employees are generally kept in the most subordinate positions. Native Engineering talent has thus not only received little encouragement, but has been kept down by the present system. The existence of it is undoubted, but the men who would have been found to direct, in former times, are gradually disappearing. They were the hereditary leading masons who still in Native States keep their pre-eminence. Their merit and artistic taste have been always appreciated by the English Engineers and Contractors, and their special skill in Irrigation Works in a country, the chief art of which for ages has been the economical use of water, is fully recognised. This class of men, working in conjunction with the Native Banker, who manages the accounts, might become native contractors, either of whole or sections of work, and take the place of the more costly European. The elaborate account of English book-keeping and correspondence required by the Public Works Department, for which they were not fit, has excluded their practical and useful assistance from being taken full advantage of, and has necessitated the introduction of an entirely new class of Overseer, in the native of Bengal. If, instead of a Central Department attempting to deal with all India, each Province was left to its own guidance and responsibility, local wants would be listened to, local interests and sympathy would be aroused, Public Works would not be prematurely urged, and those most urgently needed would be first attended to. The local gentry and heads of villages would be called on to take a share in Local Administration, and Native Engineers and Contractors would be consulted and employed. This would raise their position and admit the development of the talent kept dormant under our present arrangements. Not only would the State be served by a much less costly instrumentality, but there would be gained also that continuity of design which is so liable to be broken by the change of European Engineers, obliged by the climate to seek health at Home. The costliness of the present system prevents many useful wants from being undertaken; the money goes so short a way. A change of this kind would tend to great economy, and would bring out as coadjutors with us in the administration of India the most ingenious class of native talent, better capable of aiding in the development of the country than even that large body of native officials now found so indispensable in the Judicial and Revenue Departments.

The wasteful nature of the Public Works Administration of the Government of India is very clearly brought out in the above extract, and the remedy suggested, namely, the total abolition of the Imperial Department, though a drastic one, is the only remedy for the prevention of extravagance and waste necessarily leading to the crippling of urgent works of a local nature. The abolition of the Department would naturally lead to the abolition of the costly and imported supervising Imperial Service. Some little beginning has been made towards this very desirable condition of affairs by the abolition of the office of the Member of Public Works. But the root of the evil remains untouched. The Imperial *Department* of Public Works has not been abolished but handed over to the Member for Revenue and Agriculture. This estimable gentleman will henceforth be an expert thrice-over! (1) As a revenue expert, his duties will be to see that the last pie possible is squeezed out from land; (2) as an agricultural expert, his duties will be to ensure that the peasant becomes as prosperous and wealthy as possible; and, finally, (3) as an engineering expert, his duties will be to spend as much money on Public Works as he can wheedle his colleague, the Finance Minister, to allocate to the Public Waste Department, as it is facetiously (and not altogether incorrectly) dubbed by irreverent wags.

The evidence of Mr. Jacob (pp. 98-120) and his note (pp. 192-194) in Vol. X. *Minutes of Evidence* of Hobhouse's Royal Decentralisation Commission, should be carefully studied by everyone interested in the mending or ending of this Department. The Report of the Commission (pp. 75-88, Vol. I), while pointing out the necessity for further Decentralisation, has not even touched this, the *crucial* point in the whole business. Now that the wise step of abolishing the Public Works Member has been taken, it only remains to complete it by abolishing the Imperial Public Works Department itself, and thus give us the full benefit of that step.

THE RAILWAY BOARD.

There might be a doubt as to how the Railways are to be managed by the Provincial Governments, seeing that their interests and workings are largely Imperial and only in a minor degree Provincial. This objection is easily met by pointing out that the Railways would continue to be very largely Imperial concerns and under the control of the Railway Board brought into existence by Lord Curzon, which, again, is attached to the Ministry of Commerce and is not under the Ministry of Public Works; so the abolition of this portfolio will in no way touch Railway interests to their harm. With regard to the composition of this Board, I would suggest that one with a first rate experience of Railway matters in the United States on it would be an invaluable acquisition; for, admittedly, the United States Railways, both as regards the comfort of the passengers and the interests of trade, are unsurpassed in their management. For this the Board should not be composed wholly of Europeans: there should be at least two Indians also on it.

THE CANAL BOARD.

A similar Board is even more necessary for canals. The pressure—political, strategic and commercial—is so overwhelming for new, and ever new, Railways and that too on costly broad-gauge principles, that unless there is a very strong and representative Canal Board to fight for the development of water-borne internal traffic by canals and rivers, for water storage and for irrigation canals, the interests of agriculture and of inter-provincial trade, are bound to continue to suffer. Irrigation Commissions and Inspectors-General of Irrigation without such a backing are only voices in the wilderness. Such a Board should be insistently demanded by our Legislative Councils, and should form a part of the proposed Ministry of Agriculture.

THE HOME DEPARTMENT
OR
THE DEPARTMENT OF THE INTERIOR.

To come to the 'Home' Department, it will be seen from the evidence of Sir H. H. Risley and the Memorandum on the Constitution and Duties of this Department in the tenth volume of the Decentralisation Report, that it is not only overwhelmed with an ever-increasing amount of work proper to the department, but also with a great deal of work which is certainly extraneous to it. Since the report of the Commission was issued, there has been some redistribution of work owing to the creation of the Ministry of Education and Sanitation, and the burden of matters outside the legitimate scope of its functions has been considerably diminished. But there still remains a very large amount of work, which comes within the sphere of a properly constituted Ministry of Justice, and there is no good and serious reason why this should be delayed much longer.

An outsider, with only a general knowledge of affairs pertaining to the department, can but suggest remedies of a general nature. The full working out of the scheme of redistribution of functions can only be undertaken by a departmental committee.

However, I attempt here a list of those main heads of business which are dealt with in the 'Home' Department now, but which properly belong to the Department of Justice.

(1) Escheats and intestate property.

(2) Jails, Reformatory Schools and Penal Settlements.

(3) Registration.

(4) Copyright.

(5) Law and Justice.

(6) Judicial Establishments.

Fancy the last two being under the 'Home' Department!

Now that Bengal has been raised to a Governorship, a proposal is made in some quarters that like the High Courts in every other Province, the Bengal High Court should also be brought under the executive control of its own Provincial Government and removed from that of the Government of India. This would be a most regrettable retrograde step. What is really wanted, in the interests of genuine British justice, is still further to enhance the prestige of the High Courts by not only handing over to them the full executive control of all Law Courts subordinate to them, and the abolition of the various Provincial Judicial Departments, or, to be quite accurate, of handing these over to the subordination of the High Courts, but —and here is the kernel of the situation—of attaching all the High Courts to the Government of India, under the Minister of Justice.

MINISTERS OR MEMBERS.

It should go without saying that every one of these Ministers should be appointed with a single eye to his fitness for the special work he has to do and that vested rights or personal predilections should not be allowed to sway the choice for these offices of prime importance. Yet it becomes necessary to say this, because it has not always been so in the past. To give an instance of such open jobbery, it is only necessary to mention the Public Works Department. Its Head was never an expert but a Civilian from either Bombay or Madras alternately. A fat berth had to be provided for one of these gentlemen irrespective of the efficiency of the Department!

It will also have been noticed that I propose the designation of 'Minister' for all these 'Members.' The former word is more dignified, is in universal use, and fits their present position — that of responsible administrative Heads of Departments — while the latter does not. The word 'Member' came into use in those early days when his was a merely consultative post and not an executive one as it has gradually grown to be. It is but right that this modern status of full responsibility should be publicly notified by the requisite change to the higher designation.

INDIAN MINISTERS AND SECRETARIES.

We come now to the very important question of the appointment of Indians to these high offices. This demand, though made by the Indians for a long time past, has only now become a question of practical politics through the transparent honesty and generosity of Lord Morley, backed up by a no less sympathetic and sagacious Viceroy like Lord Minto, both alike determined to do their best to see that the Queen's Gracious and Motherly Proclamation should be literally fulfilled and that the bar sinister of race be wiped off. But this concession, though a very great one, is very far from satisfying our legitimate demands in this matter. One membership is but the bitters before dinner serving only to whet the appetite and not to satisfy it. We want much more substantial fare of the purpose. We want that *not less than* one-half of the Ministers—Imperial and Provincial—shall be native Indians and, further, that *not less than* one-fourth of the higher grades of the Secretariats shall be manned by Indians. The present state of affairs by which while theoretically admissible to every one of these posts—they are, for all practical purposes, kept wholly out of them, is absolutely indefensible. We further want that *not more than one-half* of the Ministers shall be Englishmen chosen from among the ranks of men trained and educated in the public life of England, so that India may have the benefit of a wider outlook and larger experience of the outside world. More, the elected representatives of the people should have some voice in the selection of the Indian members of the Executive Councils and for that purpose a principle of election or of veto, or any other helpful devise should be adopted. Further, this eminently desirable charge should be brought about at once and not merely promised for some never-nearing future.

As is but natural, and, in fact, in the fitness of things, these various proposals for bringing the government of the country more into touch with the governed are being treated with a perpetual dustwind of flippant and shallow gibes and malicious contempt by the blindly self-interested Anglo-Indian Press. It remains to be seen whether they can throw sufficient dust in the eyes of the British electorate and intimidate the British Ministry from doing us this elementary justice.

Further, the people's representatives should be able to exercise some sort of veto on the appointment of the English Members of the Ministry. If the antecedents of the gentleman proposed to be appointed by the Viceroy as one of his Ministers, are such that the appointment would be obnoxious to the people, their representatives in the various Legislative Councils ought to have the power to prevent such an appointment.

ADVISORY BOARDS.

We may now take up the question of Advisory Boards to be attached to each of these Ministries and in making this suggestion we are not so very odd as some might think. There is precedence for such a step in the various Occidental States and even England itself. The British Prime Minister, Mr. Lloyd George, after an experience of their great utility in France is now advocating the creation of such Boards in England, in all those Departments where they do not exist now including even the Foreign, from which the Parliament even is most jealously excluded. That such Boards would immensely strengthen the hands of the various Ministers by bringing them into closer touch with the tendencies of the times than could otherwise be the case from their isolated position, there is no doubt. They would help them to see where action was imperative and where the ground was to be allowed to lie fallow. They would be feelers warning them of dangers ahead. The shortcomings of bureaucracies all over the world are well understood by all who have to live under them, but none, so far as I know, has voiced their limitations so clearly and so trenchantly as Bagehot, and I will take the liberty of quoting a few sentences from him on the subject of their deficiencies in support of the proposition I have advanced about providing some sort of help, in, as well as control over their actions. He says :—

It is an inevitable defect, that bureaucrats will care more for routine than for results ; or, as Burke put it, 'that they will think the substance of business not to be much more important than the forms of it.' Their whole education and all the habit of their lives make them do so. They are brought young into the particular part of the public service to which they are attached ; they are occupied for years in learning its forms ; afterwards, for years too, in applying these forms to trifling matters. They are, to use the phrase of an old writer, 'but the tailors of business; they cut the clothes, but they do not find the body.' 'Men so trained must come to think the routine of business not a means but an end—to imagine the elaborate machinery of which they form a part, and from which they derive their dignity, to be a grand and achieved result, not a working and changeable instrument. The very means which best helped you yesterday, may very likely be those which most impede you to-morrow—you may want to do a different thing to-morrow, and all your accumulation of means for yesterday's work is but an obstacle to the new work.' 'Not only does a bureaucracy thus tend to under-government in point of quality, it tends to over-government in point of quantity. The trained official hates the rude, untrained public. He thinks that they are stupid, ignorant, reckless—that they cannot tell their own interest—that they should have the leave of the office before they do anything.' 'A bureaucracy is sure to think that its duty is to augment official power, official business, or official members, rather than to leave free the energies of mankind; it overdoes the quantity of government, as well as impairs its quality. The truth is, that a skilled bureaucracy—a bureaucracy trained from early life to its especial vocation—is, though it boasts of an appearance of science, quite inconsistent with the true principles of the art of business. That art has not yet been condensed into precepts, but a great many experiments have been made, and a vast floating vapour of knowledge floats through society. One of the most sure principles is, that success depends on a due mixture of special and non-special minds—of minds which attend to the means, and minds which attend to the ends. The success of the great joint-stock banks of London—the most remarkable achievement of recent business—has been an example of the use of this mixture. These banks are managed by 'a board of persons mostly *not* trained to the business, supplemented by, and annexed to, a body of specially trained officers, who have been bred to banking all their lives.' 'If it is left to itself, the office will become technical, self-absorbed, self-multiplying. It will be likely to overlook the end in the means; it will fail from narrowness of mind; it will be eager in seeming to do; it will be idle in real doing.'

EXPERTISM.

Expertism and experts, that is to say, all the highest grades of all the Services in India manned exclusively as they are by imported agency, are the constant theme of praise in the Anglo-Indian Press, and, of course, in all the gubernatorial speeches and writings, but a couple of quotations from two such foremost men of England as Viscount Esher and Viscount Haldane, may bring some commonsense to our rulers in this land.

Speaking about Mr. Churchill, at that time Naval Minister, Viscount Esher says:—

> He is, however, by the exigencies of his position, largely at the mercy of experts. As a rule, experts are the most fatuous people in the world. An expert believes in his own specific. If he did not, he would not be an expert. These people are specially mischievous when they are engaged in crushing originality in a soaring mind. It was by the advice of experts that millions of money were spent by Lord Palmerston in fixed defences. It was by the advice of experts that Trincomalee was fortified and, before the fortifications were completed, was abandoned. It was by the advice of experts that the breakwater at Singapore was begun, and, again, by their advice, left unfinished. It is by the advice of experts that millions are being sunk at Rosyth, and before long it will be by the advice of experts that Rosyth is declared to be an unsafe anchorage for the British fleet. By the advice of experts fresh anchorage along the east coast will be erected, and more millions spent on fixed defences, which will, in their turn, prove to be useless. (*The Influence of King Edward and other Essays*, p. 164.)

If an equally well-informed and equally trenchant criticism could be made about the way things have been done in India, it would be an even more woeful tale of wastefulness, extravagance and incompetence.

Listen now to Viscount Haldane. He says :—

> Again, there is a large class of skilled work, some of it requiring long training, and even initiative, which is done better by competent permanent officials than by statesmen even of a high order. But when we come to the highest order of work, it is different. There is a common cry that this, too, should be left to the expert. There is no more complete misinterpretation of a situation. The mere expert, if he were charged with the devising and execution of high aims and policy, would be at sea among a multitude of apparently conflicting considerations. What is the relation of a particular plan to a great national policy and to far-reaching principles and ends? Questions like these must always be for the true leader and not for the specialist. (*The Conduct of Life*, p. 23.)

Finally one more quotation—this time from an Indian bureaucrat, Mr. Bernard Houghton, who served out his term of 30 years in the Indian Civil Service in Madras and Burma. He says:—

> Most bureaucrats seem to require from the people they govern a sort of reverent respect—reverence for their supreme wisdom, respect for the admirable manner in which they conduct the affairs of the nation. They are shocked at the display of any feelings incongruous with this attitude. A nation in their estimation, is best conceived of as a number of schoolboys working and playing happily under the supervision of benevolent and very wise schoolmasters. (*Bureaucratic Government*, p. 113.)

Can one hope that people, under the rule of a *system* which breeds such a mentality as that depicted by Mr. Houghton, ever arrive at the full stature of manhood?

Speaking of that breeding-ground of bureaucracy—the Secretariats—he observes:—

> The Secretariats are the very apotheosis of clerkdom, and they tend to infuse in those who labour in them a clerk's mean outlook on public policy. For this reason the fact naively admitted by Lord Curzon, that Lieutenant-Governors and other high officials are usually drawn from among the secretaries, and spend their early career in "devilling" in secretariats, has a certain sinister significance. Men so trained, and brought up in such surroundings, naturally tend to perpetuate the evils of a bureaucracy. So far from taking broad and generous views of the aspirations of the people, they are more likely to place in the forefront official views and official interests, and to regard official convenience as outweighing the public good. (pps. 81-82.)

If all this is true for Europe and England, it is true with a tenfold greater significance for India. For though the enormous *personnel* of the Indian bureaucracy is largely composed of native Indians, all its heads and the superior grades are filled with the foreign element; and hence most of our difficulties; for how can a person, short of an angel, enter into all the thoughts and feelings and aspirations of a people whom he dominates over for a few decades sighing all the time for the land of his birth? Ever talking of the "land of regrets" and "land of exile"—and never of the "land of promise," as it is to us—in every after-dinner speech, how can such a person command our whole-hearted affection and inspire real genuine trust? He may, and does, if at all liberal-minded and sympathetic, have our respect and our gratitude, but the fine flavour of sentiment will surely be wanting.

Width of outlook is not for the expert, nor the self-denial which will be only too glad to part with power and make over to the ward, who has gained his majority, his property that was in trust. In the fine peroration to his book, Bernard Houghton exclaims:—

> Though the Indian Civil Service were manned by angels from heaven, the incurable defects of a bureaucratic Government must pervert their best intentions and make them foes to political progress. It must now stand aside and, in the interest of that country it has served so long and so truly, make over the dominion to other hands. Not in dishonour, but in honour, proudly as ship-builders who deliver to seamen the completed ship, may they now yield up the direction of India.

Will his brethren in the service listen to these wise words of his—is the question of the moment. It is because of this that we demand men with House of Commons experience as heads of every one of our Provinces and as Executive Councillors.

REPORTERS-GENERAL.

There are a number of Imperial officers, known variously as Commissioners, Directors, Directors-General, and Inspectors-General. The report of the Decentralisation Commission has tried to steer a middle course with regard to these, for, while the Government of India was strongly in favour of retaining all these offices, the Provincial Governments were far from being enamoured of them. Downwards from the Bombay Government, which expressed open hostility, there was not one Provincial Government which did not find itself opposed to them, and expressed its opposition in more or less strong terms. The Commission makes various suggestions for limiting their activity to mere *reporting* and strongly deprecates all attempts on their part at *directing*. In fact, the only argument that can be advanced for their retention is that they serve, or ought to serve, as the eyes and ears of the Supreme Government; their designation then, if it is to correspond to the duties now expected of them, should be that of *Reporters-General*. But the main contention, that such officers are a costly, nay, even mischeivous superfluity, is scarcely met by a change in their designation and functions. For the purpose of keeping the Central Government *au courant* with all that is going on in the various Provinces in these different departments, can be far better served by having Annual Conferences of the Provincial Ministers and Departments combined with the Imperial Minister. An over great development of inspecting agencies inevitably tends to concentrate attention on the smooth working of the *machine* to the detriment of the *interests* that machine exists to serve. They should all be abolished.

SUPREME COURT.

To round out and complete the Imperial Government, it is essential that a Supreme Court of Law and a Central University be established at Delhi.

There has been for many years a demand for a Supreme Court both from lawyers as well as litigants. A few of the reasons might be summarised here. The Privy Council is much too far away not only geographically, but also from the consciousness of the people. A more accessible and, therefore, visible supreme dispenser of justice would appeal strongly to the imagination of the people and, at the same time, produce the solid good of lessened costs. Of course, it is not meant that the powers of the Privy Council ought or should be diminished in any way. What is meant is—to put it somewhat crudely—that it should be open to litigants to appeal to a nearer court. But for the heavy costs and uncertainties of a trial in England, a good many of the conflicting judgments of the diverse High Courts here, which produce confusion and even consternation, would get promptly unified. This would be possible only with an easily available Central Court. A Supreme Court would also be sufficiently high to serve as a sort of Hague tribunal for settling differences between the suzerain power and the vassal Indian States, and among these States themselves. From every point of view it seems desirable that such a Court with ample powers, almost co-extensive with that of the Privy Council, should be established in India.

Nine Lords Justices, including the Lord Chief Justice—to give them the necessary higher designation than those of the High Court Judges—would be ample, at any rate, in the beginning. The Lord Chief Justice should be selected from among those judges in England who hold judgeships of a rank not lower than that of a British High Court Judge. Of the eight Lords Justices, four must be Indians who have served for not less than five years on the Provincial High Court Benches, and four Barristers who have put in at least five years as Indian High Court Judges, or have held in England, Judgeships, higher than those of the County Court. Their salaries might be fixed at Rs. 5,000 for the Judges, and Rs. 6,000 for the Chief.

CENTRAL UNIVERSITY.

Without a *non-territorial* university *complete* in all its Faculties—which means not less than two-hundred Professors, Readers, Lecturers, etc., and ten thousand students—Delhi, the capital of India, will continue to be in intellectual darkness and a standing reproach to the Central Government. I lay stress on the non-territorial character of such a university, and in support of my contention and in reputation—complete and utter—of Lord Curzon's imposition of territorial limits under the plea of discipline which has so filtered down now that a boy finds it a very difficult task to transfer himself even from one District to another, to say nothing of from one Province to another, I need but cite two of the most eminent educational authorities in England, namely, Viscount Bryce and Viscount Haldane.

The Prussian Government founded the University of Bonn immediately after the recovery of the left bank of the Rhine from France in 1814, and the University of Strassburg immediately after the recovery of Alsace in 1871, in both the cases with the view of benefiting these territories, and, of drawing them closer to the rest of the country by the efflux of students from other parts of it, an aim which was realised. Indeed, the non-local character of the German universities, each serving the whole of the lands wherein the German tongue was spoken, powerfully contributed to intensify the sentiment of a common German nationality throughout the two centuries (1648 to 1870) during which Germany had virtually ceased to be a state. (Bryce: *Studies in History and Jurisprudence*, Vol. I, p. 280.)

The awakening has come to the old universities late. They are now doing very fine work, but they ought to have been able to develop it much sooner. Some stimulus has been wanting. Had their students lived under a national system, where there were many universities, and where the scholar was free to move from one to another to seek the Professor of his choice instead of being tied up in his academic domicile of origin, the teachers would have been stimulated, and things would probably have moved far more rapidly under the development of the rivalry of talent . . . . When I compare the state of things in Oxford and Cambridge with that in the universities of Germany, I am impressed with one point in particular in which the latter seem to me superior. In Germany, the student is free to go from time to time, in the course of his under-graduate career, to study under a Professor of his own choice in another university. (Haldane: *The Conduct of Life*, pp. 85-86.)

After two such powerful condemnations of the method, the spirit and the aim of education in England and the correspondingly high praise of the German system, no words of mine are needed for condemning the spirit that animates our educational arrangements—I cannot call it a *system*—and the bureaucratic methods giving rise to the hidebound rules and regulations. But to deal at all adequately with the question, education requires at least a long chapter, if not a whole book by itself, and so, after touching on one more essential point, I pass on to matters more germane to this chapter.

I have also laid stress on the view that the universities should teach every subject that is being taught in the universities of the West. There are a number of very important subjects, which are conspicuous by their absence from the curricula here. But I will rest content with mentioning one subject only, namely, the necessity of giving military training in all educational institutions. One more quotation from Lord Haldane's *Conduct of Life* will be enough for my purpose. He says:—

> The Officers' Training Corps differs widely from the old volunteer or cadet corps, which used to be all that our universities contributed to the defence of their country. Five years ago, when I was at the War Office, we came to see that it was waste of splendid material to aim at the production of nothing higher than this from among university students, and that what we needed most was to get from them a reserve of educated men who had had sufficient training as officers to be available in the event of war. We appealed to the universities new and old, but not until we had carefully prepared our plans. The officers' training corps of the modern university is wholly different from the old university volunteer corps. And the reason is twofold. It has now been shaped for the accomplishment of a definite end, the training for the duties of command in great emergency of educated young men who will, even in time of peace, put their obligations to their country before their love of ease and amusement. The second reason is that this training is given, not as of yore, under the drill sergeant, not even under the ordinary officer, but under the direction and supervision of the picked brains of the British army—the new General Staff. Such training based on the best scientific methods, therefore, takes its place *naturally within the sphere of work of the university, and expands and completes the work of that university.* (P. 93. The italics are mine.)

All the world knows now that, had it not been for this prescient action of Lord Haldane, England would not have been able to raise the enormous number of officers required for its armies, whose numbers had to be multiplied a hundredfold all of a sudden in face of the terrible emergency of the Great European war which burst out in July-August 1914. The impossibility of fully utilising the immense man-power of India—about which so much is talked of in England—is simply due to this one factor and one only, namely, the unwillingness of the Government persisted in for well-nigh three centuries to give us any military training beyond that of mere soldiers in the ranks, and that too on conditions that compare very unfavourably with those of the British Army.

FISCAL AUTONOMY.

Is India, "the brightest jewel in the British Crown," to remain for ever a mere Dependency or at once take her natural place as a Self-Governing Dominion along with the other Dominions of Great Britiain—this question has after well-nigh half a century of agitation become a 'burning' one now. It further profoundly hurts our self-respect that there is imminent danger of our being ruled in the future not only by Great Britain but,—and here is the dreadful sting—by it in conjunction with her adult daughters, the Overseas Dominions, every one of whom has been treating us so very shabbily.

Now, the only remedy for all this is self-government, government on colonial lines or, to give it its latest, most popular and convenient name—Home Rule; though the phrase that would perhaps most accurately indicate the situation is *Responsible Government*, and which might replace all the others. Our English rulers jib at the phrase when used in connection with peoples other than themselves, especially if they happen to be of a darker hue, so it might be helpful to the cause to use a phrase which will not act as a bogey. And what is Home Rule at bottom? The power of the purse, for the person who holds the purse strings rules the roost. The power to raise and to spend money in whatever way may seem best to us for our national interests. The power of the Secretary of State, whether with or without his Council, over Indian finance must be handed over, with certain political safeguards if deemed necessary, to our Imperial and Provincial Legislative Councils.

How jealously fiscal autonomy is safeguarded from even the remotest approach of the Secretary of State for the Colonies will be brought home to my readers by a quotation which I give below. A few explanatory words are, however, needed to make clear the situation. The British Government has always been averse to its colonies levying export and import duties even for revenue purposes, and much more so to a frankly protective tariff. The question came to a head, so far back as 1859, on Great Britain objecting to the Canadian customs tariff imposing very heavy duties. The Secretary of State, on the protest of the Chamber of Commerce, at Sheffield, calling attention to the damage which would result from such duties to trade in England, objected to the duties. The objection elicited this outspoken reply:—

The Minister of Finance has the honour respectfully to submit certain remarks and statements upon the Despatch of His Grace the Duke of Newcastle, dated August 1913, and upon the memorial of the Chamber of Commerce of Sheffield, dated August 1, transmitted therewith.

It is to be deeply regretted that His Grace should have given to so great a degree the weight of his sanction to the statements in the memorial, without having previously afforded to the Government of Canada the opportunity of explaining the fiscal policy of the province and the grounds upon which it rests. The representations upon which His Grace appears to have formed his opinions are those of a provincial town in England, professedly actuated by selfish motives; and it may be fairly claimed for Canada, that the deliberate acts of its legislature, representing nearly three millions of people, should not have been condemned by the Imperial Government on such authority, until the fullest opportunity of explanation had been afforded. It is believed that nothing in the Legislation of Canada warrants the expressions of disapproval which are contained in the Despatch of His Grace, but that on the contrary due regard has been had to the welfare and prosperity of Her Majesty's Canadian subjects.

From expressions used by His Grace in reference to the sanction of the Provincial Customs Act, it would appear that he had even entertained the suggestion of its disallowance: and though, happily, Her Majesty has not been so advised, yet the question having been thus raised, and the consequences of such a step, if ever adopted, being of the most serious character, it becomes the duty of the Provincial Government distinctly to state what they consider to be the position and rights of the Canadian Legislature.

Respect to the Imperial Government must always dictate the desire to satisfy them that the policy of this country is neither hastily nor unwisely formed; and that due regard is had to the interest of the Mother-Country as well as that of the Province. But the Government of Canada acting for its Legislature and people cannot, through those feelings of deference which they owe to the Imperial authorities, in any manner waive or diminish the right of the people of Canada to decide for themselves both as to the mode and extent to which taxation shall be imposed. The Provincial Ministry are at all times ready to afford explanations in regard to the Acts of the Legislature to which they are party; but subject to their duty and allegiance to Her Majesty, their responsibility in all general questions of policy must be to the Provincial Parliament, by whose confidence they administer the affairs of the country; and in imposition of taxation it is so plainly necessary that the Administration and the people should be in accord, that the former cannot admit responsibility or require approval beyond that of the local Legislature. Self-Government would be utterly annihilated if the views of the Imperial Government were to be preferred to those of the people of Canada. It is, therefore, the duty of the present Government distinctly to affirm the right of the Canadian Legislature to adjust the taxation of the people in the way they deem best, even if it should unfortunately happen to meet the disapproval of the Imperial Ministry. Her Majesty cannot be advised to disallow such acts, unless her advisers are prepared to assume the administration of the affairs of the Colony irrespective of the views of its inhabitants.

The Imperial Government are not responsible for the debts and engagements of Canada. They do not maintain its Judicial, Educational or Civil Service; they contribute nothing to the internal government of the country, and the Provincial Legislature, acting through a Ministry directly responsible to it, has to make provision for all these wants; they must necessarily claim and exercise the widest latitude as to the nature and extent of the burthens to be placed upon the industry of the people. The Provincial Government believes that His Grace must share their own convictions on this important subject; but as serious evil would have resulted had His Grace taken a different course, it is wiser to prevent future complication by distinctly stating the position that must be maintained by every Canadian Administrator, (A. B. Keith's *Responsible Government in the Dominions*, pp. 1160-1162.)

Every word of this wise and weighty pronouncement on the ultimates of true Responsible Government, and the limits of control by the Mother Country over the Daughter Countries, should be studiously meditated upon both by our leaders and by our British rulers.

SIMLA EXODUS.

Very little needs to be said against the abiding evil of this pernicious system of the Government of a vast Empire from an isolated hill eyrie, except to record the bare fact here. The matter has been discussed *ad nauseum* but the almighty Government continues obdurate. Simla should be only what it was meant to be—namely a place for a holiday resort for the tired Viceroys to spend a week in—

> On the hills like gods together
> Careless of mankind,

and not in reality *the* capital of India. The permanent location of the Military Department there and its resulting evils have been mercilessly dragged into light by the heart-rending muddle of the Mesopotamian campaign, as delineated in the pages of Lord George Hamilton's Commission Report. Let Delhi be the one and the *only* capital of India from which Secretariats are never moved and *where only* the meetings of Executive and Legislative Councils are held.

THE PROPER RELATION BETWEEN THE IMPERIAL AND PROVINCIAL GOVERNMENTS.

This subject belongs properly to the chapter on the *Provincial Governments*, where details will be gone into; but before winding up this chapter, it is necessary that the general principles that ought to govern the situation should be stated. It goes without saying that the Provincial Governments should be allowed as free a hand in the administration of territories under their charge as possible, consistent with the overlordship of the former. The supervision should not be close and minute, deadening all responsibility and killing out all initiative. The wish to interfere should be at a minimum, and no needless harassment should be caused by incessant watching and constant meddling on the part of the higher authority. It should be just enough to prevent harm to the wider interests of the country as a whole; which interests may have been overlooked in the intensive and, therefore, narrower outlook of Provincial patriotism. The example of New Zealand might be pointed out here, whose separate independent existence is an asset of such tremendous significance to the British Empire. If it had allowed itself to be swallowed up in the Australian

Commonwealth, all its powers for striking out new paths would have been suppressed by the iron laws of uniformity. At present it is always willing and ready to try all sorts of administrative, legislative and economic experiments, by which the outer watching world is only the gainer. If things go wrong, harm has not been done on such a scale as to cause widespread damage; but if any of the experiments succeed, they can be modified and adapted to suit the exigencies of other climes and different administrations. The United States of America is another case in point. *The American Commonwealth*, by Viscount Bryce, has some very illuminating remarks on the relations between the Federal and the State Governments, and they should be laid to heart by the people who hold our destinies in their hands. I would strongly plead, therefore, that the routine net of dull, respectable mediocrity be not wound tight round the Provincial Administrations choking out all initiative; but that the utmost freedom compatible with the safety of the Empire be allowed to these, to experiment unflinchingly and tread out new paths for themselves and for others.

It is also necessary that a clearer demarcating line be drawn than exists at present between the respective spheres of activity appertaining to the Supreme Government and to the Provincial Governments. A clear and precise Administrative Code should be compiled, which would lay down and define the sseparate spheres of the activity of each and put a stop to the eternal haggling and wrangling that goes on between the Subordinate Administrations, trying to safeguard some privilege, and the Superior Government trying to filch it away from it; and if there is any doubt or dispute after this, the final deciding authority should be the Supreme Court, as it is in Canada, in Australia and the United States, to which all such constitutional questions are referred for decision.

In any fixing of the respective spheres of action of the two, the fact should never be lost sight of, that the huge centralised Supreme Government cannot afford to make risky experiments; and that, by the very nature of its being it is forced to play a different rôle, namely, that of a regulariser, a controller; and that it cannot take up the other rôle of an experimenter, of a pioneer. This function is best left to the Subordinate Governments, who, in fact, should be encouraged to go ahead and try new methods and make experiments; in short, attempt to be as progressive as possible. Even if they make mistakes, these will not be fatal and, being confined to a small area, would be easy of rectification. The attempt to pin them all down within the straight-laced jacket of official uniformity, and reduce them to one dead level of mediocre respectability, is a serious and almost irreparable loss to living and progressive rule. Petrifaction and running into well-worn ruts should be actively discouraged and not fostered. Not respectability but advancement should be the standard for judgment. The innovations of a Local Government, if shown to be of wider applicability—

for conditions differ not only from Province to Province, but even within a Province (differing factors calling for different handling) and a centralized Government cannot take cognisance of differences and provide differential treatment — could be taken up and utilised by other Local Governments as also by the Supreme Government. By limiting the sphere of activity of these Governments, the Supreme Government deprives itself of a unique field of observation and experiment.

SUMMARY.

1. A Retrenchment Commission urgently needed with a strong non-official Indian representation upon it. Salaries and allowances under many and diverse heads are on a scandalously high scale. The number of practically sinecure appointments is also very large. There is a large amount of easily avoidable waste, for instance, in the Stationery and Printing Departments, in the Public Works Departments, in the Hill Exoduses, and so on.
2. The Governor-General's term of office should be four years, but open to a further four years' extension by the King-in-Council on a petition by the Governor-General's Legislative Council. His salary and allowances to be on the same scale as for those of Canada, Australia, etc.
3. The Executive Councillors of the Viceroy to be named Ministers, and to hold office for four

years only, namely, during the term of the Viceroy who has appointed them. Each Viceroy to appoint all his Ministers. They are to be responsible to the Governor-General and not to the Legislative Council. For our purposes the American practice is better than the British on this point. The salary of the Ministers to be Rs. 5,000 (£4,000 yearly) per mensem.

4. The Executive Council should meet as far as possible at least once every week. The total number of such meetings being not less than 52 in the year.
5. No Minister to receive any decorations or honors during his term of office, nor should he be eligible for any further paid appointment under the Crown within three years after relinquishing office. This is not meant to apply to their reappointment as Ministers, if the Legislative Council is agreeable.
6. The Home Department, which, to prevent confusion, should be named the Ministry of the Interior of the Government of India still controls a large number of sub-departments which do not properly belong to it, they should be handed over to their proper departments.
7. On the abolition of the Member for the Public Works Department, unfortunately the Department itself was not abolished. This ought to be done at once, and the Provinces, left a free hand in the matter.
8. The Governor-General should not be his own Foreign Minister. The Provincial Political

Departments should all be abolished. A *unified* and *reorganised* Indian Political Service to be brought into existence under the control of the Foreign Minister, who will be in charge of all those Native States also which are at present under Provincial control. The control of the Foreign Department over the Chief Commissionerships to be handed over to the Ministry of the Interior (Home Department).

9. The Commander-in-Chief should not be War Minister, or to call the office by its most appropriate name—the Minister for Defence. The Minister should never be one who holds any command but he may be a military man. It is not necessary that he must be a civilian. The Commander-in-Chiefship should be abolished as it has been abolished in England and other European countries. There should only be a Chief of the General Staff.

10. The Legislative Council should have some hand in the selection of the Ministers. Persons who are obnoxious to it should not be appointed. Not less than one half of these to be Indians. The Europeans to be selected from amongst the Parliamentarians.

11. Not less than one-fourth of the higher grades of the Secretariat of each Department to be manned by Indians.

12. Advisory Boards whose *personnel* should be selected

from the Legislative Councillors to be created for each Ministry.

13. Like the Railway Board there should be a Canal or Water Board to provide for water storage, and against havoc caused by inundations, and also to develop water-borne traffic—riverain, canal and coastal. There ought to be Indian members on all such boards.

14. The ubiquitous Imperial Officers known as Commissioners, Directors, Directors-General, and Inspectors-General, numbering about a score, should all be abolished forthwith.

15. Every High Court and Chief Court that is under the control of its Local Government should be brought under the control of the Government of India, as the Bengal High Court is, and removed from Provincial control. The Department of the Government of India in direct touch with these should, however, be the Ministry of Justice and not the Home Department (Ministry of the Interior).

16. A Supreme Court of Law at Delhi urgently needed. The Lord Chief Justice to be one who has held the rank of a Judge in England *not lower than that of a* British High Court Judge and given a salary of Rs. 6,250 (£5,000 yearly) per mensem; and eight Lords Justices on a salary of Rs. 5,000 (£4,000 yearly) per mensem each. Half of these to be Vakils and the other half, Barristers. The Vakil Judges to be selected from amongst the Vakil Judges of the various Indian High Courts

with not less than five years' service as such. The Barrister Judges to be brought out from England from amongst the K. C's. of not less than two years' standing.

17. The Law Department to be made into a properly constituted Ministry of justice. The statutory provision which limits the choice for the Law Member (Minister of Justice) to a Barrister to be modified to allow of a Vakil also being appointed to the post.

18. A *non-territorial*, all-India University, complete in all its Faculties—Engineering, Technology, Medicine, Law, Science, Arts, etc., etc.—to provide for ten thousand students to be established at once at Delhi.

19. The hill capitals to be abolished at once. No Departments, no Secretariats to be permitted in Simla.

20. Very much larger Financial and Administrative autonomy to be granted to the Provinces.

CHAPTER III.

THE INDIAN STATES.

It is not the purpose of this chapter to enter into a history of the relations of the British Government with the Indian States or enlarge on the methods by which foreign suppliants to the Native Courts gradually gained in power and prestige till the relations were inverted, and those who were suppliants became masters, and the masters of the old days reduced to vassalage, when not wholly absorbed into the rapidly growing extent of British India. (See Malleson's *Decisive Battles of India.*) Lapse and escheat; diplomacy and war; trade interests and scientific frontiers; necessity of linking up the isolated portions of British India—isolated by the existence of Indian States—have each, and all played their role in the disappearance of the Chiefs—Sovereign or semi-Sovereign—who have ruled India since the beginning of the seventeenth century. Well was it, however, for India that it was the English who gained the upper hand and drove out the Portuguese, the Dutch, and the French adventurers. For, it is only under the hegemony of the freedom-loving British that it may become possible for the future to see a prosperous, unified and united India, freed from the jealousies of caste and creed and race which have been our curse and our undoing.

Lord Bryce, writing about the work of Napoleon, has some very wise remarks, which are no less applicable to the condition of India in the seventeenth, eighteenth, and the first half of the nineteenth centuries, than they are to those of Germany and of Italy. He says:—

It was his mission—a mission more beneficient in its results than in its intention or its means—to break up in Germany and Italy the pernicious system of petty principalities, to reawaken the spirit of the people, to sweep away the relics of an outworn feudalism, and leave the ground clear for the growth of newer and better forms of political life. (*The Holy Roman Empire*, p. 408.)

It has only to be remembered that even to-day in India there are roughly 700 States, and some of them so ridiculously petty as to have barely an income of Rs. 50. (£3.) *per annum*. (Col. Malleson's *The Native States of India*, p. 375). What the condition must have been in the four centuries—16th to 19th with many thousands of princelings tyrannising over wee patches of the unfortunate land, plundering and fighting each other, may be safely left to the reader's imagination. From end to end the hapless land was honeycombed with the banded forces of Parsondom and Junkerdom, Ecclesiasticism and Landlordism, banded together to oppress the people.

It would be perfectly futile at this late hour to attempt to weigh in the balance the dealings of the British Government with the Indian Rulers of India. That long story of "force" and "fraud" (Sir Lepel Griffin's *Ranjit Singh*. p. 14) on the one hand and corruption on the other can serve no useful purpose for the guidance of Indian polity in the near future.

It may be matter for a treatise on the constitutional and political history of India, which has yet to be written. Aitcheson's *Treaties, etc.*, published under Government order, inevitably to some extent one-sided, cannot represent the other side so very impartially. If instead of taking the English versions of the treaties as authoritative, fresh tanslations were to be made from the originals in the Indian languages, perhaps many surprising revelations would come to light for those who now judge of the mutual relations of the Suzerain and his Vassals from that publication (the term Vassal States and Vassal Princes is taken from an official publication, *Afghanistan, the Buffer State* by Captain Lyons, with an introduction by Field Marshal Sir Douglas Haig.) A true and full history will be possible only when the secret archives of the India Office and of the Native States are freely ransacked. Here the practical necessities of the situation force me to confine my remarks within the four corners of 'settled facts,' and to take up the tale from the stage which the Curzonian self-glorification—miscalled the Delhi Durbar—displayed to all the world, when Lord Curzon dragged at his tail all these magnificent Feudatories through the streets of Imperial Delhi in the approved style of a Roman triumph of yore; and when, further the refusal to return their visits and the rigid limit placed on the numbers of followers they might bring with them filled up their cup of humiliation and fixed for ever the strictly subordinate position they are to hold in India. Not by insisting on their treaty-rights and raking up the ashes of a dead past can they hope to reap any benefit and to win back the position they have lost. That is gone to return no more; and good it is for India that it is so.

A new chapter, however, is now opening in the life of the country and these Rulers. If they once again desire to be respected and powerful in the land, and be the true sons of India, they must cast in their lot with the progressive spirit of the time and remain no more the self-indulgent laggards that alas! many of them have been and are yet, and must realise, as fortunately, some are beginning to do, that Rulers have responsibilities and owe duties to their people. The Indian Princes are apt to think with the pessimist philosopher that 'sufficient unto the day is the evil thereof,' and that it would not be the height of wisdom for them to trouble about progress and reform. Every interest cries out for the policy of sloth and 'let alone.' But does it pay? No. Nature's laws are inexorable. Stand still you cannot. Move you must. The only question is whether forwards or backwards. The policy of folding one's hands and sitting still, inevitably leads to degeneracy and its corollary, British intervention. If the Prince as individual, is not to be crushed beneath the ponderous wheels of the steadily and resistlessly onward marching car of the British Indian Government, he must betimes merge his individuality into his Princehood: convert the lands in his charge from a private domain into a public state: march not behind the British Government but in *advance* of it.

Let the Princes get the people to feel that their (*i.e.*, the people's) stake in the country is even larger than the mere dynastic stake of a family, and their responsibility not less for its good government. Let them cherish and develop patriotism in the breasts of their subjects and not look askance at it. Let them not call it 'disaffection,' nor stigmatise it as "sedition," as 'anti-governmental,' for unlike British India, there should not be any divergence between the aims and objects of the rulers and the ruled in Indian States. Here they are one and the same. The King and his people are one,

राजा प्रजानां हृदयं गरीयः ।
प्रजाश्च राजो ऽप्रतिमं शरीरम् ॥

not twain, (the King is the soul, the living heart of the people; the people are the matchless, irresistable body). The strength and greatness of the one is *interdependent* with the strength and greatness of the other. But where their relation is that of Autocrat and

नृपः प्रजा प्रियं द्वेष्टि ।
प्रजा द्वेष्टि नृपप्रियम ॥

Subjects, as in unfortunate Russia, where (the King hates the uplift of the people: the people hate the tyrant's ways) both come to grief. Whoever, even dreams of such a conflict of interests and duties in happy England? The safety and welfare of the Sovereign is bound up with the progress and strength of his people. The interest of the one is the interest of the other—identical—not exclusive, much less antagonistic.

The road leading to self-respect and self-preser-

vation runs straight through the gateway of a Constitution.

The Native States, being under home rule, to that extent resemble England rather than British India, and, therefore, I think they might conduct their local affairs *so far as may be practicable* on the English-model. (*Letters to an Indian Raja*, by a Political Recluse, with an Introduction by Sir W. W. Hunter p. 74.)

There being no chasm between the rulers and their subjects, and no feeling of alien domination, a policy of the fullest trustfulness and conciliation added to that of a paternal administration but on the strictest constitutional lives would *pay*.

The policy of resisting the pressure of the British Government is neither wholly desirable nor indeed possible. It deserved to fail and it has failed wholly. Irresponsible autocracy cannot safeguard alone and unaided its rights and privileges. To do so it must share its powers and privileges and thus make it the interest of the *many*, instead of only *one*, to safeguard its birth-right. Give the *people* liberty, raise *their status*, give *them* a stake in the permanence of the administration—thus only will you turn them into your supporters, for will they not be then, in standing up for *your* privileges, guarding their *own* homes and hearths, their *own* rights and liberties ?

If the Ruling Chiefs feel that their status as Sovereign Princes and their personal dignity are more and more on the wane under the overwhelming, incessant and minute pressure of the Suzerain working through the mysterious, omnipotent ways of the Foreign Office and its agents, they ought to realise that they cannot fight successfully for the removal of the pressure and all that it bodes as long as they persist in keeping up *personal* Government. The only way to resist it, and get the better of it, is to get beyond and *above* it; by doing better than the British Government of India. Autocracy necessarily implying selfishness is not a sufficiently powerful weapon with which to ward off attacks, much less to fight with. From being the 'led' they must become the 'leaders.' Instead of being dragged at the tail of the car of progress, let them make a spurt and win the dignified place of being in its van.

This is not an impossible ideal; if only all the resources of the States are bent to give all their subjects —high and low, men and women—the fullest educational benefits possible and merge dynastic interests into those of the State and make the people the bulwarks of their own progress and their liberty, by freely establishing full representative institutions and responsible cabinet government. In short, unless the people are trusted and treated as members of the same family, for whom no sacrifice is too great for the prince to perform, and whose smallest interests receive his fullest concern, there will not be present that feeling which would make for unity of action.

It is a well-recognised fact that constitutional governments resist pressure far better than personal governments; the individual autocrat easily succumbs to 'persuasions' of various sorts; while the united force of the community makes it stand firm.

FEUDATORIES AS CONSTITUTIONAL RULERS.

I hold that without doubt the straightest, surest, wisest, and worthiest course—one which combines duty with interest, and honour with policy—is for you and your brethren to turn their principalities into *States*, as I have already suggested, and thereby formally to create that identity of interests, or rather remove that apparent absence of such identity, between yourselves and your subjects, which is the main, indeed, the only excuse, for the Paramount Power for interfering with the affairs of the Native States. . , . . . If you and your brethren wish to obviate it, do adopt such constitutions as will place in the hands of your subjects peaceful and efficient remedies for all administrative wrongs they may be liable to, or may think they are suffering, and when this is done to the extent that is possible under the circumstances, the British Government will cease to concern itself with your internal affairs, because it will have no ground or excuse for it; and will see that then it will be acting in opposition not to the Rajas as *against their own subjects*, but against the *entire* state their Rajas *and subjects* together, and for such interference not only will it have no motive, but it will be contrary to its professions, its self-interest, its policy; and these causes together with its sense of righteousness and justice will always dissuade it from that course; in fact, in such a situation the interests or rather the attitude of the two parties will be identical. Then indeed the Indian Princes can fight with the British Government for their rights and interests on equal ground. (*Letters to an Indian Raja*, p, 58-59.)

Fighting for their own hands they are bound to be beaten, but, if for their people, and backed by a vigorous, enlightened and virile public opinion, success is sure, for then they will have the overwhelming moral power of the State to support them in their demands.

The present position of the Ruling Princes of India is an anomalous one, for neither does international law apply to them, nor are they under municipal law in many respects; the natural consequence of this undefined position is, therefore, fraught with mischief and peril for them. A direct subject of the British Government, however humble his station in life, is far better off—seeing that he is subject to well-defined law and courts of justice—than any Feudatory, however potent he may be. His independence is a mere name, utterly subservient as he is to the all-powerful, irresponsible and absolutely secret Foreign Department and its staff of "the politicals." There is no publicity, no court, no appeal, no persons before whom the cause of "Home-Ruled India"—its subjects and its Princes—can be brought forward. The policy of secrecy and of drift has produced terrible confusion and injustice. If there had been less irresponsibility to the public, joined as it is to autocratic power; and instead, full responsibility to the public and a limitation of their powers, like that of any other Governor of the British Provinces, the all-powerful Resident would not have been so largely a power for harm, instead of good, as he has been so often; then the administration of the Native States would not have been so defective, when not hopelessly bad, as it is to-day. The *nominal* ruler is responsible before the world for the acts inspired, nay commanded by the *real* ruler, "the power behind the throne," who keeps studiously in the background and can never be saddled with any responsibility or dragged into the glare of publicity before the bar of an enlightened, informed and powerful public opinion. Such an arrangement is an almost ideal one for tyranny and corruption to flourish in all the luxuriance of a tropical jungle.

RESIDENTS.

Even a Viceroy stigmatised the Political Agents as "dangerous officials" (*vide* p. 43. *Letters to an Indian*

Raja). John Bruce Norton no less famous in his day than his brilliant and equally pro-Indian son, Mr. Eardley Norton is to-day, has some very disparaging sentences about these in his book: *The Rebellion in India: How to Prevent Another*, (pp 116—117). He writes :—

> A word here on Residents—the most pestilent form of an Indian official. From the moment that Lord Wellesley subsidised his native allies, their fall was certain, however slow. The foundation of their independence was sapped. In the commencement, the Resident at the Court of a Native Prince was an officer of high importance. He had to watch carefully against intrigues with other powers hostile to the British interests. His was a diplomatic duty; he stood as the medium of communication between the court to whom he was accredited, and the company whose deputed servant he was. But as the power of the Native Sovereign crumbled insensibly away, the Resident imperceptibly encroached upon the proper bounds of his authority. Instead of being merely the servant of the company, he utimately became master of the Native sovereign. As the latter dwindled more and more into dependence, he crouched more and more submissively before the ambassador, on whose representations of his conduct to the Company he fancied the stability of his titular princedom to depend. He never rose to a tone of manly independence; he was too timid to remonstrate: the will of the resident became law: till at last an entire right of control was claimed over the most trifling items of expenditure. A Rajah could not buy a fowling piece without the sanction and approval of the Resident. Hence the presence of the Resident was a continual source of irritation and annoyance to the royal family; whilst on the other hand the Resident grew more and more arrogant, until his original and true character was totally forgotten. He is now a sort of Cerberus, uniting the three separate functions of spy, jailer, and dry nurse. His principal characteristic is the most overweening, fanciful idea of his own importance. I have seen a letter from one of these worthies, in which he distributes his approbation and disapprobation of the various members of the royal family with a condescension truly imperial; though the inflation led one to fear for the writer the fate of the frog in the fable, who puffed himself out until he burst.

Sir Henry Lawrence is no less emphatic about the system of appointing Residents. In his essay on *The*

Kingdom of Oudh first published in the *Calcutta Review*, in 1845, he says:—

> An able and virtuous despot may dispense happiness; the same ruler saddled not only with a Minister, but with a Resident, can only diffuse wretchedness. . . . . He is not master in his own country. . . . . If ever there was a device for insuring mal-Government, it is that of a Native Ruler and Minister, both relying on foreign bayonets, and directed by a British Resident. . . . . How rarely is the European officer to be found who, with ability to guide a Native State, has the discretion and good feeling to keep in the back ground . . . . . to be the adviser and not the master.

I have seen the heir-apparent to one of the most powerful of the Native States dismount to make his obeisance to the wife of the Resident, who was driving past and she most condescendingly nodded her acceptance of the lowly salute. When remonstrated with, the hapless young man replied that people in British India did not realise the vital nature of the question of keeping the Resident and his entourage in great good humour. His English governesses and tutors had evidently well drilled into his head and heart, during his plastic youth, the god-created subordinate position of the "natives" to the "white peoples." He could not understand that an Englishman may not like, but respects the man who will hit back. He loves not flunkeys however useful he may find them.

Every one knows that the Political Agencies are centres of intrigue and corruption; the Native State officials, the cadets of the Chief's family, the subjects of the Prince, and even the ruler himself have to keep doing incessant *Puja* to the Residency Staff from top to bottom to keep things going smoothly, or to gain special advantages.

M. Chailley too has something to say about the "politicals." He makes some of the really advanced Princes say :—

> And being what they are, why, they urge, should they continue to be subject to the minute guardianship, benevolent, it is true, but destructive of individuality, which the Government of India has so long imposed upon them ? The political officers who reside at their Courts are in truth (I reproduce here native opinion, which contains a material part, but only a part of the truth) their masters. That may not be true in the case of the Nizam who has eleven million subjects, nor perhaps in the State of Mysore with its five million ; the opposition of rulers of this calibre might be inconvenient, and they consequently escape from the annoying control of the political despot. (*Chailley's Administrative Problems of British India* p. 259.)

The author is misinformed. The "political despot" is as much their master as of the smaller rulers. The way the late Nizam was treated, for instance, by the late Mr. Chichele Plowden, the Resident, is so well-known that it is curious the facts never came to M. Chailley's ears. Blunt's *India Under Lord Ripon*, supplies a good many instances of the autocratic dealings of the Residents at Hyderabad.

> But elsewhere the attitude of the political officer, while ordinarily differential in form (though even that is sometimes lacking,) is the attitude of a servant, who directs his nominal master, haughty, polite, impertinent, and ironical. And what, say the observers, I am quoting, are these political officers save spies, whose words will be believed by the English in the face of all outside denial ? . . . . And the peoples of the States are not deceived ; they know that their rulers are thus subject to masters, and their attitude takes color from this. The respect paid to the chiefs decreases with their prestige, they are no longer kings. Will the Government of India, ask the chiefs, restore this respect and prestige ? How does it treat us ? In great durbars, for instance, the Viceroy addresses himself first to the Governor or Lieutenant-Governor and not to us. What must our subjects think of this ? And who has forgotten that atrocious circular of Lord Curzon which forbade us to quit India without his permission ? [They are even prohibited to go to Simla without the previous permission of the Viceroy.] . . .

Let there be less centralisation ; loosen the reins ; do. not force us to ask advice and permission for everything ; *do not behave like a schoolmaster with a cane.* (Italics mine.) Do not require us to treat nighbouring Princes like strangers ; recognise the necessity and advantage of our coming to understandings with one another. *In fine, do not keep us in fetters* (Italics mine.) . . . are you yourselves infallible, whether in your own territories or in ours ? Have the States always found themselves the better for your counsels, have our finances never suffered from your intervention ? Consider for instance, the case of chiefs who found themselves in deficit through having to visit the Coronation Durbar of 1913. (Chailley's *Administrative Problems of British India.*)

We might here call attention also to some other undesirable arrangements requiring urgent change. One of these is the not generally known fact that while every Feudatory has to incur considerable expense over Residencies, some like Kolhapur have even to pay the salary of the Resident and his entourage. The duties entrusted sometimes to the Resident are no less anomalous ; he is, for instance, in Junagadh, a tribute-collector for the Nawab from his subordinate Chiefs, and the British Government makes a charge of 25 per cent. for this duty ! This state of things, namely, the expenditure of Feudatory State money over Residencies is recognised as very undesirable by the British Government, and prohibitions are issued from time to time. A little while ago one such warning has again been issued by the Foreign Office but the same old fate of its predecessors has befallen it and it is more honoured in the breach than in the following. Paper anathemas are powerless before this evil, hoary with age.

The second anomaly is that while Indian Revenues have to pay for the political agencies in Kashgar, in Turkish Arabia, in Persia, in Muscat etc., etc , the officers are under the dual control of the British as well as the Indian Foreign Offices. It is the British Exchequer that ought to bear this cost.

This horrible fratricidal European war will probably see the disappearance of Turkey not only from Europe, but from Asia even. For the English and their Allies have stipulated among themselves that Russia's *quid pro quo* in this war will be Armenia and Constantinople; of Italy and France, Asia Minor and Syria; of England all the watershed of the Tigris and Euphrates from Baghdad to the Persian Gulf. Arabia under the Grand Sherif of Mecca will probably become an English protectorate like Egypt. Persia has also been parcelled out between Russia and England, with well-defined frontiers of their respective 'spheres of influence.' It will be realised how complex and onerous the duties in connection with all this enormous change will become, and how impossible it will be for the British Foreign Office to assign all this work completely to the Indian Foreign Office. So on all scores it seems best, that the Indian Foreign Office should not in any way entangle itself with all this work extraneous to itself but confine itself to dealing with those foreign states only which directly touch the Indian frontier, like Afghanistan and Tibet. It is to be hoped, however, that the land-grabbing policy of the vain-glorious Viceroyolties of Lords Lytton and Curzon will not be revived. Lytton was setting up three Amirs —in Herat, Kabul and Kandahar, and so by weakening them, would have brought them all under the same kind of protection as the Indian Chiefs enjoy. (See Lady Betty Balfour's *The Administration of Lord Lytton*). Lord Roberts was for annexing Kandahar outright, and he was right, for how, could he be Lord Roberts of Kandahar, if it were not British but Afghan territory! Luckily the attempt of the fire-eaters in India was scotched by the Government of Mr. Gladstone, (see the *Life* of the Marquis of Hartington, First Duke of Devonshire). Lord Curzon's similar attempt over Tibet was foiled by a Conservative Ministry this time. And as neither of these two countries are so easy of digestion, as was Burma which Lord Dufferin grabbed with the sanction of the Ministry of the day and so the opportunist British Ministries, Liberal and Conservative alike, repudiated the handiwork of their local agents, the Government of India.

PRINCES.

It must also not be forgotten what stuff these rulers are made of. Bagehot has given an inimitable description of a hereditary European Sovereign and it can scarcely be improved upon for the purpose of applying it to these Indian "Sovereigns." He says :—

> An hereditary king is but an ordinary person, upon an average at best; he is nearly sure to be badly educated for business; he is very little likely to have a taste for business; he is solicited from youth by every temptation to pleasure; he probably passed the whole of his youth in the vicious situation of the heir-apparent, who can do nothing, because he has no appointed work, and who will be considered almost to outstep his function if he undertakes optional work. For the most part a constitutional king is a *damaged* common man; not forced to business by necessity, as a despot often is; but yet spoiled for business, by most of the temptations which spoil a despot. History, too, seems to show that hereditary royal families gather from the repeated influence of this corrupting situation some dark taint in the blood, some transmitted and

growing poison which hurts their judgments, darkens all their sorrow, and is a cloud on half their pleasures. It has been said, not truly, but with a possible approximation to truth, 'that in 1802 every hereditary monarch was insane' . . . . . . A man made common by nature, and made worse by life, is not likely to have either incessant industry or great statesmanship; he is nearly sure not to be *both* clever and industrious. . . . A monarch in the recesses of a palace, listening to a charmed flattery unbiassed by the miscellaneons world, who has always been hedged in by rank, is likely to be a poor judge of public opinion. (*The English Constitution*, p, 231.)

If this is true of European Monarchs, where there is no polygamy, where open concubinage is condemned, and education is fostered, what can then be the condition of things, where public opinion as in "Home-Ruled India" is simply non-existent, and the Chief is guaranteed his State by the power of the bayonets of his Feudal Overlord?

Tucker in his *Memorials* says :—

The Princes and Nobles of India are not prepared by education for the great business of public life—the civil administration of their country. . . . . They are brought up as boys in the Zenana. . . . . and they have little opportunity of acquiring that knowledge of men and things which is so essential to those who are called upon by their birth and station to superintend the interests of a great community, . . . they are indolent, and inclined to indulge in those sensual gratifications which tend to enervate the frame, and to indispose the mind for the difficult and laborious duties which the conduct of public affairs imposes upon public men. There are illustrious exceptions no doubt . . . . the ascendency of the British has unquestionably had the effect of checking the spirit of ambition, and of discouraging on the part of the natives of India, those impulses which prompt to heroic action or useful labors, and which lead to honor and distinction. In this state of things it has usually happened that the native Princes, our allies or dependents, when invested with power, have been found incapable of carrying on the business of the government. They have generally fallen into the hands of favourites, who for the purpose of preserving their influence, and of engrossing all power in their own persons, have been studious to encourage the indolence, the extravagance, and the vices of their master. Thoughtless expenditure necessarily leading to pecuniary embarrassment, the most ruinous expedients have been

resorted to for raising funds to command some momentary gratification—the people are surrendered to the ruinous exactions of unsparing creditors, or rapacious revenue officers—discontent is engendered—the country is made desolate—and nothing but the military force of the British Government, is sufficient to repress insurrection, and to maintain the deluded Prince in the possession of his worthless dignities (pp. 240-241.)

The above quotation taken from a book published nearly sixty years ago portrays a state of things which unfortunately still largely holds good, as the bitter experience of many a would-be progressive Indian Minister in Indian States testifies.

This age, sceptical of the Divine authority of anointed Popes and anointed Kings, regarding them as no more sacred than the chairman of a commercial concern, is not prepared to put up with their 'Divine right to rule like the Devil.' The Hierarch and the Bureaucrat both must learn the bitter lesson of self-effacement, and treat the people not as *subjects* but as *citizens*. They must realise that the reverence and the obedience that the people yield to them are not yielded because of any belief in the myth of sacrosanctness attaching to them, by the mere accident of birth and position, as the Vicegerents of God on Earth; but because they are the transient depositaries of an authority that issues from the people *themselves*, so that in obeying, whether the spiritual or the political head, they are but obeying their own best nature. The old ideal of the days when the world was less progressed, of a Theocratic State (whether in the East or in the West) with the Political ruler exercising his powers only as a delegate of the priest has passed out of the consciousness of a progressed world. Maharshis (Popes) and Maharajas (Kings) are as much mortal flesh and blood as the lowliest untouchable Pariah. Their arrogance of sacrosanctness is the evil legacy of a rotten social system, that is being rapidly buried all the world over. The *modern* deduction from the eternal truth of the unity and supremacy of the spirit is not an eternal gulf of a soul-destroying caste and class system, but that of a common humanity, of brotherhood, of cessation of all strife and the promotion of co-operation among the many organs of the one body.

Nearly 1,400 years ago a great Indian King Bhartrihari—famous for his learning, made some very shrewd observations on the environment in which rulers were brought up. He makes an interlocutor say :—

> Who are we that we should have the *entree* of a Royal palace; We who are neither mimes nor pimps, nor singers, nor large-bosomed ladies of easy virtue.

No less pathetic and bitter is his delineation of the atmosphere of fulsome flattery surrounding such personages :—

> He who has power (wealth) he is high born, he is an orator, he is beautiful, he in short is everything that is great and good and noble,

however much the contrary of all this he may be.

Royal Courts whether in the East or in the West, whether in the 20th century after Christ or the 20th century before Christ are ever the homes of insincerity.

> The future ruler of a country is brought up without education without a knowledge of the world, under the care of women. He is through the jealousy of his father excluded from all interference

or share in public affairs, until the time of life for attaining habits of usfulness has passed away. Whether suited to govern or not his succession is secured through the introduction of our deadening laws of primogeniture . . . . . . Neither is an ignorant or jealous despot the least likely to give the reins to others which his own fingers have so long itched to handle . . . . . .

Such is the testimony of Captain Sutherland about the incompetence of the Native Princes, and he ascribes it to its true reason:—

The paralyzing effects produced in these independent states by their reliance on foreign power for protection, and which had the effect of the severing of that sympathy which binds the chief and his people together when they have to struggle against other power, either for their liberties, or for their individual or national advancement . . . . who would have expected to see anything virtuous or heroic in the character of the people of Greece whilst under the domination of Turkey, or in the character of the Poles whilst under the yoke of Russia, except what might arise in their exertions to free themselves from the dominion of foreigners (p. 184.)

That things are not so black now as they were seventy or eighty years ago may be the general belief, but such popular belief is very far from the truth. Neither of the two supreme factors in the case—the foreign Resident and the Native Ruler—have, in the vast majority of cases, come into line with what this twentieth century would regard as their true and proper functions. The Foreign Department shrouds its doings in a most impenetrable veil and so the above statement may seem to be at least very exaggerated, but two quotations will prove the contention to the hilt. M. Joseph Chailley in his book, *Administrative Problems of British India*, which has been translated into English by our present Finance Member, Sir William Meyer, by official permission, and the dedication of which was accepted by Lord Morley, then

Secretary of State for India, and whose presentment of *facts* may, therefore, be taken to be authoritative, says:—

> We may divide the chiefs of India into three classes (1) the *very few* (italics mine) who govern according to European ideas . . . . (2) Those who have introduced the elements of a reformed organisation . . . . . (3) Those who still imagine that they are the State; that its resources are their private property, and its inhabitants their slaves; that their affairs should take precedence of all others; and that their *chief business is pleasure. This last class is still the largest* (italics mine) . . . . The chief of such a state is a despot. He lives in his palace surrounded by his wives and his concubines the members of his family, courtiers, mounte-banks, jugglers, and astrologers. Sometimes he has no minister, but that does not lead him to work for himself, or prevent him from occasionally leaving the state, and allowing its affairs to look after themselves. What does it matter, so long as the chief has a good time? In his little court intrigue is rampant. Parties form round his favourites, his wives, and his concubines, and denunciation and calumny are their usual weapons in the struggle for favour. . . . . . In spite of so many intrigues life is monotonous, and it is not, as might be imsgined, wholly filled by women. . . The wives are generally (and this is especially the case with the first one) of good, and sometimes of high birth. The concubines are of low caste, and lack education and morals. Their presence, their talk, and possibly their actions exercise an evil influence over the children of the legitimate wives, . . . The State money which they treat as their own, flows out on every side, and, in the first instance, to those around them, to their relations, their courtiers, and their flatterers. They distribute the State property as our absolute Kings used to do . . . The taxes offer, as may be imagined, an infinite field of abuse. (Bk. II, Ch. I.)

Hear now what the present Lieutenant-Governor of Punjab, Sir Michael O'Dwyer, then Political Agent in Central India, said in his speech in Datia:—

> In circumstances which it is not necessary to detail to-day, the Supreme Government was compelled in 1911 in the interests of the Chief, of the State and of the people of Datia to intervene and assume a direct superintendence of the administration. Speaking from a fairly wide experience of Native States I have no hesitation in saying that for corruption, inefficiency, and general misrule, Datia then surpassed anything which has ever come under my notice. Life and property were notoriously insecure;

suicides, to call attention to unredressed grievances or to anticipate oppression or disgrace, were appallingly common. The State and the capital were being abandoned by their inhabitants. In the decade 1910-11 while all the surrounding districts and States showed a great increase of population, that of Datia fell off by one-seventh and one of the saddest spectacles that ever met my eyes was the sight (in September 1911) of the picturesque city with its empty streets and deserted houses. When I first visited Datia a few years ago, the chief justice was, I think, a palace-official on a salary of Rs. 15 per mensem and it was not surprising to hear the general complaint that justice was bought and sold, (Reported in the *Leader*, March 26-1913.)

When it is remembered that it was a public speech made by one of the most highly placed and responsible officers of the Government, and so naturally very restrained, things must be bad indeed to require so much outspokenness.

The frightful misgovernment of Datia is not so very exceptional ; if the confidential annual reports of the various Residents saw the light, they would fully bear out M. J. Chailley's remarks.

After the above statement of the case as against Residents and as against ' Native Chiefs,' it will be clear that it is not so much the *men* as the *system* that is to blame. It is true though, that the evil results that have accrued would not have been so disastrous if the men had been capable, sympathetic, honest, keenly alive to their duties, tactful and able, in short, not what they have, as a rule, been so far.

Even where the British Government does not interfere directly in the management of a State by taking it over bodily, as for instance in the case of Mysore ; its interference even when only partial and limited, and not direct and peremptory, by ' friendly counsel' through the Resident, makes for mischief.

For at the very outset the necessity occurs for supporting a particular Minister, who is considered to be favourable to our views of policy, and of sufficient talent and energy to govern the country. Here the seeds of jealousy and discontent are immediately sown in the mind of the Prince, who finds his authority superseded and his dignity infringed, and who becomes indifferent to the concerns of his country, and the welfare of his people. He confines himself to the retirement of the Zenana—engages in low pleasures and puerile amusements—dissipates his treasures or his income—contracts debts—and soon sinks into a state of humiliation and distress. The British Resident is looked up to as the real ruler, for he appoints the ruler. Whatever may be his vigilence or the authority of his virtue, his officers and dependents are prone to interfere and eager to establish a double authority or influence in the country. The ostensible Minister must provide resources for the payment of subsidy or tribute, as well as for defraying the public charges ; and being assured of support, he is reckless and careless about the means, and often resorts to the most mischievous expedients for raising supplies ; the people are impoverished and discouraged by endless exactions ; the country falls into a state of decay ; and the whole obloquy attending this course of maladministration falls upon the British name. Nor is it unreasonable that it should do so. We are accessory and mainly instrumental in the establishment of an anomalous administration—a nominal government without authority—an unavowed ruler without responsibility. And after all, this system leads to direct interference; for when the revenues fail and debts contracted under our guarantee accumulate, the country (as in the case of Gaekwar and others) is placed under sequestration to redeem the pledge. (*Memorials of Indian Government*, by Henry St. George Tucker, p. 244.)

The student of modern Indian conditions should carefully study and ponder over each word of the above extracts, taken from the work of one who spent the best portion of his life in the country and passing through every official stage became finally one of the Directors of the East India Company. They are not the words of an irresponsible outsider, an Indian, or an English globe-trotter, but of one who knew what he was about, and carefully weighed each word of the indictment before putting it down on paper. What more scathing criticism and exposure of the system and its utter hopelessness than this? The restless ambition of a generally military and dictatorial Resident only too willing to impose his irresistible personality backed up as it is by the whole power of the British Government, always works for mischief. If he is not dealt with discreetly or if his particular hobbies or notions are thwarted, there is instant trouble. He must be kept in good humour, whatever it might cost.

All this has had naturally a most deleterious effect on the character of the Chiefs and productive of much harm to the subjects of these States. The latter-day Rulers having been moulded under the Residential system and relying upon the help of the British bayonets—provided they are in the good books of the Resident—can pursue their reckless careers unchecked. There is neither the fear of an invasion from without, nor of a successful insurrection (the latest known instance is that of Mandi, a small hill State near Simla, and which was put down by British bayonets) of their own long-suffering and broken subjects, (which would, in other conditions, have probably rectified matters in a case like that of Datia, above-mentioned), nor that of a palace-intrigue, or even of the nobles or military Chiefs, for they can always be locked up if at all troublesome. Even more potent than the Deportation Regulation of the British Government is the autocratic will of the 'Swadeshi' Ruler. Secure on the throne of his ancestors, through the favour of the British Government, he need fear nothing, and instead of treating his State as a sacred public trust which he is bound to administer in the best interests, and with the advice and co-operation of his people, he treats it as a private domain from which an ever-increasing revenue is to be squeezed out, to minister to his magnificence and his pleasures. The training in the Rajkumar Colleges and by private English tutors that they are receiving these days, and even in England in some cases, only helps to denationalise them all the more. Instead of having feelings in common with their subjects, sympathy for their misery, being alive to the charms of praise and renown and sensible of the value of those qualities which command them ; they are only open to the praises of the English rulers of the country and work hard to acquire those foreign social accomplishments by which they might shine in that society.

All that has gone above will have helped to make clear that the Feudatories are not sovereign and not even semi-sovereign as the Foreign Office still tries to make them out to be. It may be worth while to try to define here what is the status of a "Native Prince" and his administrative means and methods.

The Feudatory Chief is a *reigning* prince and it is only a fiction which calls him *Ruler*; he has besides an army, of which he can make absolutely no use, but it is one of his toys over which he is allowed to waste the hard-won earnings of his subjects. How truly beneficial it would be for the State and its subjects if this were replaced altogether by an *industrial* 'army' organised with the same loving care and forethought, and the same minute attention to details and lavish expenditure which for so long, and to so little purpose, has been wasted over the fighting armies! His prerogatives of Coinage, his Post, his Telegraph, his Railway jurisdiction, his power to levy customs and imposts, his power to create monopolies in the interests of his own people, are all gone, or going. British cantonments are or can be located any where within his territories. Further, being a sovereign he is 'above law.' Herein lies the bitter irony of fate. While not subject to any court of justice or any well-defined law he is nevertheless in the nebulous but all the same iron grip of the Foreign Office. He cannot protect himself by appealing to any recognised public legal tribunals, but must do so by other means, which however are not always ineffective. Within his own territory and over his own nobles and subjects his power is uncontrolled and unlimited.

Official apologists are not wanting in their emphatic approval of the relations of the British Government with its Feudatories. Sir Charles Lewis Tupper says :—

> I believe the existing system of relations with Native States to be thoroughly sound, thoroughly beneficial, and capable of much useful development. (*Our Indian Protectorate*, p. vii.)

Not less rosy and optimistic is the belief of Sir William Lee-Warner.

Anglo-Indians of the type of Sir John Strachey and Sir Lepel Griffin can see nothing that is good in a 'Native State' and wait impatiently for the day when they all would be absorbed in the British possessions and the large patches of yellow would be replaced by red in the map of India. The only consideration which has any weight with officials of this stamp, which makes them hesitate before plunging headlong into a policy of wholesale annexation, is the feeling, voiced clearly by Sir John Strachey, that they served as breakwaters in the storm of the Mutiny "which would otherwise have swept over us in one great wave" (*India*—2nd ed., p. 366,) and may serve again the same purpose in the event of another mutiny. But as such an event is altogether impossible now, little consideration need be shown; and as diplomacy whether in the East or the West—especially when dealing with a weaker power—is seldom afflicted with the disease of honesty and straightforwardness, the Residents might well be employed by the Foreign Office as *agents provocateurs* to bring about the complete disappearance of the remains of Feudal power and prestige. That such a view is very narrow, prejudiced and wholly unfair to the Indian Princes is admitted by all officials who have the welfare of India at heart and see the possibility of re-infusing into these Rulers self-respect and the ability to govern themselves and their people once again. They rightly insist on regarding Feudatory India as an integral portion of the British Indian Empire owing well-defined duties to the British Sovereign on the one hand, and equally well-defined duties to their people on the other hand whilst themselves possessing no less well-defined rights and privileges.

M. Chailley is no less clear on the part played by the Native Rulers in 1857. He says :—

> Curiously enough, it was the surviving princes who restrained this movement, and thus contributed to save the British power. Before they had had time to act in concert for its overthrow they began to think that the British power would resist the assault made on it; and the most clear-sighted among them thought it desirable to remain loyal; and their loyalty saved the situation. Interests, if not gratitude, opened the eyes of England which realised the part which the Princes and the States had played during the Mutiny. Had they not existed, a huge wave of insurrection would, in an India entirely British, have swept over everything.

Another reason for the keeping aloof of the Indian Princes from the rising of 1857, was told me by an old Indian diplomat now dead. What element of truth there is in this it is impossible to discover now. It was this. One of the biggest rulers on being sounded asked who would "occupy the Imperial throne of Delhi" after the British were driven out? To this poser there could be no reply in those days, Federalism not having yet been born; so the scheme of joining the rebels in the British territories fell through. This wise and strong Hindu ruler, the master of eighty-thousand troops, knew as some of the hot heads did not, the marvellous tenacity of purpose of the English race, and the good that would accrue to the country as a whole by the overlordship of England. Even dynastic interests would not suffer to the extent that they were bound to suffer if India continued much longer to be a congeries of jarring units. If these were to be fused into a homogeneous nation, it was Divine dispensation that gave the control of the destiny of India into the hands of these freedom-loving, democratically-minded foreigners from a distant land.

After all that Strachey, Chailley and many others have said about the Mutiny of 1857 being really the turning point in the fate of the Indian Princes is nothing new. It is only a repetition of what "clemency" Canning (as he was stigmatised by the fire-eating Anglo-Indians of those days) wrote in his despatch of 1860 upon the subject of adoptions in Native States :—

> The safety of our rule is increased, not diminished, by the maintenance of Native Chiefs well affected to us. . . . in the Mutiny these patches of Native Government served as breakwaters to the storm which would otherwise have swept over us in one great wave. . . . . And should the day came when India shall be threatened by an external enemy, or when the interests of England elsewhere may require that her Eastern Empire shall incur more than ordinary risk, one of our best mainstays will be found in these Native States. . . . It was long ago said by Sir John Malcolm [Governor of Bombay and author of a book which is still valuable after the lapse of 90 years.—*A Memoir of Central India including Malwa and adjoining Provinces* 2 Vols. *3rd ed*,, 1832] that if we made all India into Zillas [British Districts] it was not in the nature of things that our Empire should last fifty years ; but that if we could keep up a number of Native States . . . . as royal instruments, we should exist in India as long as our Naval superiority in Europe was maintained.

But all this political wisdom is only a repetition of old Bacon of the 16th century. In one of his essays he says :—

> It is well when nobles are not too great for sovereignty nor justice, and yet maintained in that height as the insolense of inferiors may be broken upon them, before it came on too fast upon the majesty of Kings.

Further, there should be greater and lesser nobles

to balance each other. All this is nothing else than the world-old divide and rule policy, now newly and more euphemistically described as maintaining the balance of power, of securing adequate representation to all the various interests within the realm. It should be noted, however, that the observation of Bacon ascribing the duty of serving as breakwaters to the nobles nearest the King requires to be supplemented by the further observation that while they so serve as breakwaters against attacks on the king on the one hand, on the other hand they also serve as placers of curbs upon the license of those kings. It was not the "insolense of inferiors" that wrung the *Magna Charta* from the hands of a cowed king, but that of the "Barons bold" of "Merry England."

Sir John Strachey's chapter on the Feudatories is a deplorable blunder even from the official standpoint, tending as it does to create mischief, where none exists. For such a high-placed official to cast aspersions on the good faith and loyalty of the Indian Princes and to abuse persons who simply dare not resent or even reply, does not speak much for his sense of chivalry. If their lips could be opened they too could unfold a tale of wrong and woe which would amaze the world. Even Sir John Strachey, official apologist and intense bureaucrat that he was, confesses in an outburst of frankness that the relations are unsatisfactory. He says :—

> I have always thought that no part of our Indian administration has been so often unsuccessful as the management of our relations with the Native States (p. 367.)

He further prudently lays the blame on the wretched Indian Prince:—

> No real progress in such States is possible while their governments remain purely personal, and while the authority of the Paramount Power is exercised on no fixed system, but spasmodically, by special acts of intervention as necessity arises. (p. 379.)

He also quotes at p. 382, a despatch of the Government of India to the Secretary of State which wishes "to obviate the necessity for frequent and arbitrary interpositions by the Supreme Government." Such Platonic good wishes deceive nobody—not even their creators. As against these "wishes" we have to see what are the actual facts. Is it really possible for the British Government to fold its hands and not only to declare its firm faith in a policy of *laissez faire*, but actually to practice it? The policy of "non-interference" inevitably leads to the necessity of annexation as every reader familiar with the political history of India knows. It is never again likely to be revived. Intervention there has been and there will be, but spasmodic and ill-informed as it is, its benefits will never be lasting, while it always will give rise to a crop of evils.

Sir William Lee-Warner cherishes no illusions about the profession of "non-intervention."

> Native States, he says, give shelter to those enemies of civilisation and order, who, descended from the criminal tribes and predatory castes of India, practice their infamous trade in the Native States, and seize every suitable opportunity of crossing the British line. The Police administration of frontier districts consequently entails greater expenditure than that of districts in the interior, because the duties of guarding the frontier of a foreign State are so much heavier, The facilities afforded for the escape of criminals, in the intricate patch work of jurisdictions which

exist in the Presidency of Bombay, require special measures of prevention, and courts of law are subjected to grave inconvenience from the difficulties of securing the attendance of parties or witnesses from villages where the Queen's writ does not run. The collectors of British Revenue often experience the impossibility of excluding untaxed opium or illicit spirits from their districts, when an open frontier interposes no barrier to the free-commerce of their villages, with a foreign State, into which the British Inspector cannot carry his authority or his law and regulations. Again, where the necessity arises for sanitary measures, the spread of cholera or smallpox is dangerously assisted by the absence of precautions, such as vaccination or drainage, in close proximity to British Cantonments or to the capital towns of British Districts. (pp. 17-18.)

The condition of affairs has reached the stage where it has become inevitable for the British Government to continuously interfere with the administration of its Feudatories; so the question now is, whether it is possible to so adjust relations of the Sovereign with his Feudatories as to allow of a definite amount of autonomous control to them over their own governments, and regularise, so to say, the cases for intervention.

POLITICAL CODE.

After all that has gone above, it scarce needs saying that an idyllic happy-family relation does not exist between the Overlord and his Feudatories. If the future is not to be one of anguish and tribulations on the one side, and meddlesome interference and despotic dealings on the other, it is essential that the antiquated and rusty procedure governing the relations of the vassel Princes to the Paramount Power be displaced by a more adequate, fair, and up-to-date method. Apart from the bare justice of such a demand it would save the name of the British Government from much odium. As it is, the unenviable quadruple position of accuser, prosecutor, judge, and executioner occupied by the Foreign Department, is neither defensible nor desirable. Sir George Campbell in his *Modern India* advocated the necessity of a *Political Code* and so has Captain J. Sutherland in his *Sketches of the Relations subsisting between the British Government in India and the different Native States.* In one way or another all the old treaty obligations have gone, and no new definite instruments have taken their place, resulting in endless friction and trouble for want of a clear unimpeachable understanding. It has been mostly a scramble, the Suzerain trying—only too successfully—to grasp all it could, and the Feudatory trying—only too unsuccessfully—to retain all it could. A Political Code would have the supreme merit of definiteness and unambiguity ; it would fix the British Government to one system of measures which all would be prepared to act up to, and the mutual obligations of the two would be impossible to be misunderstood. For would it not be 'self-willed' to a very large extent, prepared as it would be by their representatives and those of the Suzerain in collaboration—embodying as it would not the temporary aberrations caused by the gusts of passion and of prejudice, but the calmly-considered higher will, intelligence and ethics of all concerned in the pact.? Obedience to it would not be through the fear of the master's lash, but because infraction of its rules would be like the contradiction witnessed in a teacher's high professions and low practices, bringing him to shame, thence repentence and regeneration. Such a code would bring about the already too long-deferred establishment of the *reign of law* in a sphere where individual caprice and arbitrariness, passion and prestige, pride and prejudice have caused no end of mischief and still continue their nefarious work. With a Supreme Court to interpret such a Fundamental Law of the Realm, as for instance in America, there would be the farther guarantee that its clauses would be fairly construed and enforced.

It is essential, therefore, that for a step so drastic and far-reaching in its consequences, a Royal Commission to go into the case thoroughly and impartially be appointed, on whose report such a code would then be built up. But the Commission must be such a one as to command the confidence not only of the officials but also of the Indian Chiefs, their nobles and subjects as well. A Commission composed only of British officials without a strong representation of the Indian States and of a few independent members, both Indian and British, would not meet the urgent needs of the case nor command any respect or confidence.

I, for one, believe that it is neither impossible nor very difficult to arrive at an understanding which would put the relations of the two on a firm, lasting, and satisfactory basis—while, what is imperatively necessary, it would make for an increasingly civilised and progressive administration of these States to the benefit and happiness of their subjects.

The policy of isolating the Vassal States that had been adhered to all these many years, should now be given up wholly. Even down to so late as 1881, and in the Viceroyalty of Lord Ripon too this policy of diplomatic isolation has been insisted on. Clause 11 of the Instrument of Transfer which handed back Mysore to its Indian Ruler, expressly lays it down. Now that the loyalty of the Indian Princes has been so convincingly proved, it is time that they were *fully* trusted and not forced into obedience to the highly derogatory and irritating rules prohibiting private correspondence even on such delicate matters as those of matrimonial alliances, except through the Political Agents. The definitely accepted newer policy of subordinate alliance, should be allowed full and free play. The conditions prevalent not only in Modern India but all the world over are in favour of Constitutions, Fundamental Laws, Federations. Why should not, then, an earnest and serious attempt be made for a Federal Union of the Feudatories, and light let into the present chaos ?

The Fundamental Laws of the German Empire, the United States of America, of the Commonwealth of Australia, of Switzerland supply models which with a little tact and patience, and some little changes could be enacted to meet Indian conditions.

It will be noticed that the models I have suggested are not those of the Union of England, Scotland and Ireland into Great Britain ; or of the Provinces of Canada, into the Dominion of Canada ; or of the

Italian Principalities, into the Kingdom of Italy. In all these cases the Union has been *complete* and uniting bodies have merged so to say into each other —thus not only losing their distinctive characteristics but their autonomy also. Here in India we have the example of the relation of the Supreme Government with the Provincial Governments in varying degrees of closeness or aloofness. But these cannot serve as models for the proposed Federation. In all these cases the subordination is much too complete to allow of the "Semi-Sovereign," Princes of India to accede to any such scheme. If the proposal is to be something more than a mere dream, these prejudices will have to be respected, and, a *quid pro quo* given for all the rights and privileges—however shadowy—which they will have to yield up. The *basic* differences that ought to govern such cases will lie in the fact that while the British Provincial Governments exercise only those powers which have been *delegated* to them by the Supreme Government, in which lies all the *residuum* of power, so that the latter has concurrent jurisdiction in *all* matters ; in the former it will have to be the other way. The Supreme Government will exercise *only those powers* which have been delegated to it by its Feudatories and the *residuum* of power will remain with them ; further, to avoid friction there must be no concurrent jurisdiction excepting in those cases where the permission of the Supreme Government has been obtained. The Princes retaining all their "Semi-Sovereign" powers and dignities—excepting those which have been expressly assigned to the Suzerein.

Herein arises the question of the conditions under which such a system of autonomy and dependence at the same time, can work with satisfaction and benefit to all concerned.

FOREIGN DEPARTMENT.

I will try to sketch briefly here the necessary—in fact indispensable—reorganisation of the Foreign Department of the Government of India and then deal with the question of the improvement in the internal administration of the Feudatory States. Only after such reorganisation will become possible the establishment of that intimate and close relation of trust and responsibility between the Sovereign and his semi-Sovereign Vassals which should be the goal of every earnest well-wisher of the Indian Princes.

There are roughly 700 Feudatories. Of these only 170 are under the direct control of the Supreme Government, and the rest under the Provincial Governments—Bombay having the largest number of these namely, 361, then Burma with 53, Bengal and Punjab with 34 each ; the rest of the Provinces have only a few under their control. All this is due to mere historic causes and not to any settled policy or well-defined scheme. It is an arrangement which has grown into existence in a haphazard way ; and there is no reason why such an ill-defined chaotic state should continue. Changes on a small scale have occurred in the past, for instance, Baroda was removed from Bombay control to Imperial control. Why should an equally important State like Travancore, for instance, not be similarly dealt with, instead of remaining under Madras control. The grouping of the States under 'Agencies' will also have to be abolished in a complete carrying out of the principle of concentration of control in the hands of the Government of India.

I would urge the advisability of concentration of of control, with its inevitable self-evident corollary the abolition of the Political Departments of every Provincial Government and the enlargement of that of the Supreme Government and its reorganisation. I have already advocated in my chapter on the Imperial Government the creation of a Minister of Foreign and Political Affairs and the freeing of the Viceroy from the responsibility of administering this department under his own immediate control.

THE VICEROY HIS OWN FOREIGN MINISTER.

This is if possible an even more vicious arrangement than that of the combination of the judicial and executive powers in British India. For here, there is not even a semblance of law or the shadow of publicity The Viceroy, as the head of the department, is directly identified with the actions of the Residents who are his subordinates and who, in fact, take their cue from their august head or are at least believed to do so. To whom is it that the poor Prince complained against can appeal ? To the accusing Policeman with plenary judicial powers ! The grim humour of the position might appeal to a Lytton or a Curzon, but can a conscientious and God-fearing Ripon relish the situation when, in pronouncing the doom of an Indian Prince, he addresses him as " My Honoured and Valued Friend"!

It is further absolutely necessary that the Minister must have been in close touch with the British Foreign Office and command its full confidence; seeing that he has to carry on relations not only with Asiatic States under International guarantees or of International importance—but also European powers, Russia, France, Portugal, Holland, Turkey, &c. These conditions cannot be fulfilled by any merely Indian Civilian and so he should either be a member of the British Diplomatic Service with wide and varied experience, or one with first hand knowledge and Parliamentary experience. As far as possible he should have put in some years of work, over and above his European experience, in Persia, China and Japan as well. He will thus inevitably be a man of over 50, wise, tactful and sympathetic; not likely to treat brusquely the Indian Princes and Chiefs as the generally young and often military officials of the department do—wanting in the knowledge of secretariat and civilian experience. Such a man will inspire real confidence in the Princes and Chiefs which can scarcely be asserted of the present *de facto* Minister who is almost always an Indian Civilian, imbued with all the prejudices imbibed in his Indian career.

The burden of social functions and of the supervision of an administration ever growing more and more complex and onerous, devolving upon the Viceroy, is so heavy that inevitably the business of the department which is his especial charge gets disposed of by irresponsible Secretaries who act in his august name; and behind his broad back they are effectually sheltered, while either the uninformed or misinformed Viceroy has to bear the public odium. The evils of such a condition of affairs are much too notorious—especially in the Native States—to need much expatiation upon.

It is obvious to all but those with vested interests that the Foreign Minister must not be taken from among the ranks of the Indian Political Service. The reasons that militate against the I. C. S., men being made the heads of Governments in British India whether as Lieutenant-Governors or Executive Members apply with tenfold greater force here. Mr. C. E. Bunbury, C.S.I.,—who is probably himself a 'political'—has but voiced the service aspirations in his cool advocacy of such selections in the pages of the *Contemporary Review* for February 1913. He naively remarks :—

> Moreover, a Foreign Minister and a Foreign Secretary so selected would naturally have the interests of all officers of the Political Department at heart.

In his angelic innocence he has failed to grasp the sinister import of his statement. It is the interests of the Service that really matter and not those of the poor 700 odd Princes and their 63 millions of subjects ! It has also to be remembered that in any such appointment the *amor propre* of the "Native" Rulers has to be given its full weight, and it is sure to be seriously hurt if the Minister is not of a commanding social position at "home" almost like that of a

Viceroy which can seldom if ever be the case if the choice is to be restricted to the cadre of the Indian Services.

The Indian Political Service should also be re-organised. There are over 150 officials of various grades, all Europeans. Lord Reay while he was Governor of Bombay—and be it remembered that the number of Feudatories under that Government is larger than that of the rest of India—was strongly impressed with the undesirability of the military element of its *personnel*. His views are lucidly set forth in Hunter's *Bombay*. For the present, at any rate, the Service should be made a preserve of the I. C. S.—but must be distinct from it. It should be composed of civilians of at least 20 years' standing out of which they must have had at least 10 years of District experience and at least 5 of the Secretariat. They should be given one year's training at the Head-Quarters of the Foreign Department and then only drafted off to their respective spheres of work. As a rule, they should be kept in one place for 10 years, and not be moved about every few years. Their work in the States should not be secret but public and they should be responsible for the advice they give, which should always be in writing; and copies of which with the notes of the Chief concerned and his Minister should always be forwarded to the Foreign Minister. While he is to preserve his character of 'Reporter-General' to his own Government and Adviser-General to the Court he is accredited to—his powers of *dictation* must be curbed; thus keeping full and intact the responsibility of the Princes and their Ministers.

It should be given out clearly that no Resident is to allow himself to be made a centre of intrigue, as he very often has allowed himself to become. He must keep aloof from the local politics of the State to which he is accredited.

SUPREME COURT.

The Government of India should, on its side, create a Federal Supreme Court of Justice, before which al. questions about the proper interpretation of the Political Code and of the Constitutions would go and before which only the Feudatories could be prosecuted, and not before special commissions and tribunals created for the occasion, every Chief being allowed the right of appeal to this Supreme Court against the executive orders of the Government of India.

There should be Federal Courts, subordinate to this Supreme Court, within the dominions of each Feudatory where all kinds of cases arising between subjects of different States or between Europeans and Indians could be tried.

Before these Courts should also go those cases in which the State and its own Tributary nobles are concerned. It is important to safeguard the rights and privileges of these as, under modern conditions, when their military services are no longer indispensable and their power broken, they are likely to, and do meet, cavalier treatment at the hands of their over-lords. The

Provincial Governments have had over and over again, as various Tenancy Acts testify, to safeguard the rights of the ryots against the encroachments of the Zemindars. The case of these sub-chiefs is not often much better.

The writs of these Courts should run all over India —British and non-British alike. This will solve the difficulty of extradition, without the necessity of extradition Acts and treaties with each separate State.

It might be thought very derogatory by the Ruling Princes etc., that there should be such a Court and that it would be a flagrant breach of their privileges to make them submit to its Judgment. But common sense generated of bitter experience should prove to them that this is the only way of safety to them. They cannot now assert their rights to be above law like Sovereign Princes, for in that case in all cases of misuse of their powers and maladministration swift annexation will be the only remedy left, as of old. For the safety and permanence of their dynasty their forefathers wisely yeilded up this position, and accepted the principle of bring judged and punished by their Suzerain in their own persons, so that the Principality was secure in the family. Would such a case as that of the late Maharaja of Baroda, Mulhar Rao, be thinkable even in a properly constituted Law Court? The charge brought against the Gaekwar was an attempt to have the Resident poisoned. It broke down completely, even before the special tribunal got up for the occasion. And then what did the almighty Foreign Department do? It *shifted* its ground and deposed the Ruler on grounds of maladministration ! If the case had gone before one of the regular tribunals, there could have heen no such shifting of grounds, and the Resident would have been heavily punished for bringing a false charge. To add insult to injury, though the charge of poisoning fell disproved, the black lie still continues to be repeated *ad nauseum* in authoritative writings by high political officials like Sir William Lee-Warner. The latest instance is that of the late Raj Rana of Jhalawar, who was kept as political prisoner in Benares. In this case the Foreign Office took such an extremely unjustifiable step as that of dismembering Jhalawar in flagrant breach of treaty rights entered into with Madan Singh, the son of the founder of the family, Raj Rana Zalim Singh, *perpetually* guranteeing the integrity of the newly created State. With such a Court in existence, the Foreign Office will have to be far more careful than it is at present. Of course it is understood that for the trial of every case in which a Prince as Chief is involved personally as defendant or accused, the trial will be by jury composed of his peers, before a full bench of the Supreme Court.

It may be pointed out that Sir William is not a very reliable or impartial guide, as one may suppose him to be because of the very high offices he held while in India, and in England as the Secretary in charge of the Secret and Political Department of the India Office. In his *The Native States*, under a great show of fairness, and 'hear both the sides' attitude there is mixed up a good deal of specious pleading against these States and their Rulers also. It is necessary to give this warning to prevent the work from being accepted as 'Gospel truth.' I will just give one more instance. According to him the Raj Rana Zalim Singh was a "notorious" person, who "was called by Todd, the Machiavelli of Rajasthan." Hear now what Major-General Sir John Malcolm says about this very person presumably on the information supplied by this very Todd, the Resident with the Western Rajput States (p. 306.) :—

> **Kotah the actual ruler of which is the Raj Rana (or Regent) Zalim Singh, one of the ablest Native Chiefs of the present day, who by his prudence and policy has continued to flourish in most eventful times, although placed in the very centre of the predatory hordes (p. 501).**

For another equally eulogistic reference to him, this time in connection with town-planning, see under Patun (p. 510). Such was the man whom Lee-Warner would blacken, may be, because he all too successfully succeeded in keeping Kotah a yellow patch, instead of allowing it to be colored red by British administrators not so "notorious" or "Machiavellian" as the Raj Rana.

A reversal of the policy of the suppression of the rights and dignities of the Indian Princes which found its culmination in the notorious order of Lord Curzon that they were not even to leave their States without Viceregal permission, has been inaugurated by Lord Minto. He believes in trusting the Princes, as is well shown by the 'Sedition-correspondence' between him and them, the Foreign Office for a wonder, for the first time allowing such outspoken and wholly admirable replies as those of the Gaekwar and the Nizam to be published unedited! His speech at Udaipur in November, 1909, has still more emphatically announced that fact, and it is fully worth while making a few extracts from it. He said :—

"It is sometimes asked by Ruling Chiefs, as well as by the public in India and in Europe, what our policy towards Native States is. I can only tell you that the basis of that policy was laid down in Queen Victoria's Proclamation of 1858, and repeated in the Coronation Message of His Majesty the King-Emperor. In 1858, Queen Victoria addressed the Princes of India as follows":—

> We hereby announce to the Native Princes of India, that all treaties and engagements made with them by or under the authority of the Hon'ble East India Company, are by us accepted and will be scrupulously observed, and we look for the like observance on their part. We desire no extension of our present territorial possessions and while, we will admit no aggression upon our dominions or our rights to be attempted with impunity, we shall sanction no encroachment on those of others. We shall respect the rights, dignity, and honour of the Native Princes as our own, and we desire that they as well as our own subjects should enjoy that prosperity and that social advancement which can only be secured by internal peace and good government.

"And 44 years later, the King-Emperor wrote :—

> To all my Feudatories and subjects throughout India, I renew the assurance of my regard for their liberties, of respect for their dignities and rights, of interest in their advancement and of devotion to their welfare which are the supreme aim and object of my rule and which, under the blessing of Almighty God, will lead to the increasing prosperity of my Indian Empire and the greater happiness of its people.

"In pursuance of these pledges, our policy is, with rare exceptions, one of non-interference in the internal affairs of Native States. But in guaranteeing their internal independence, and in undertaking their protection against external aggressions it naturally follows that the Imperial Government has assumed a certain degree of responsibility for the general soundness of their administration, and could not consent to incur the reproach of being an indirect instrument of misrule. In a word, the object of my Government has been to interpret the pronouncement of two successive Sovereigns as inculcating, in accordance with the eloquent words of His Royal Highness, the Prince of Wales, in his speech at the Guildhall after his return from India, a more sympathetic, and therefore a more elastic policy. The foundation-stone of the whole system is the recognition of identity of interests between the Imperial Government and the Durbars, and the minimum of interference with the latter in their own affairs."

But this easing of the pressure must not be misunderstood, and attempts made to take sinister advantage of it by sliding back into the bad old ways. The advice of Lord Mayo, given in his speech at a *Durbar* held in Ajmere in 1870, should never be lost sight of by the Princes:—

If we respect your rights and privileges, said Lord Mayo on that occasion, you should also respect the rights and regard the privileges of those who are placed beneath your care. If we support you in your power, we expect in return good government. We demand that everywhere throughout the length and breadth of Rajputana justice and order shall prevail; that every man's property shall be secure; that the traveller shall come and go safely; that the cultivator shall enjoy the fruits of his labour, and the trader the produce of his commerce; that you shall make roads and undertake the construction of those works of irrigation which will improve the condition of the people and swell the revenues of your States; that you shall encourage education and provide for the relief of the sick. . . . . Be assured that we ask you to do all this for no other but for your own benefit If we wished you to remain weak, we should say: be poor and ignorant, and disorderly. It is because we wish you to be strong, we desire to see you rich, instructed and well-governed.

How valuable the Native States could be made if they under proper guidance were permitted real self-government, and allowed to take on the role of experimental stations is well put in one of the Oxford Pamplets, *The Value of Small States*, by Mr. H. A. L. Fisher, Vice-Chancellor of the Sheffield University, and the present head of the Education Board of the British Government. He says :—

Indeed, one of the advantages flowing from the existence of smaller States consist in the fact that they serve as convenient laboratories for social experiment—a point likely to be appreciated in America, in view of the great mass of materials for the Comparative study of social and industrial experiments which is provided by the enterprise of the American State Legislatures. Variety may often be troublesome, but to regard it in itself, as injurius, bespeaks the narrow bureaucratic, regimented mind. Indeed, one of the principal arguments in favour of the preservation of the small States of Europe (and the same argument applies to the preservation of the state system in America) lies in the fact that these small communities do vary from the set type which is imprinted by steady and powerful governments upon the life and behaviour of the larger powers. The mere fact of this variety is an enrichment of human experience, and a stimulus to self-criticism and improvement. Indeed the existence of small states operates in the large and imperfect economy of the European system very much in the same way as the principle of individual liberty operates in any given State, preventing the formation of those massive and deadening weights of conventional opinion which impair the free play of individuality, and affording a corrective to the vulgar idea that the brute force of organised numbers is the only thing which really matters in the world.

This eloquent plea of the Rt. Hon. Mr. Fisher, M. P., for the integrity of the smaller Western States, applies no less forcibly to the Eastern States. Only care has to be taken that liberty does not degenerate into license, and misgovernment does not raise its head high under the banner of freedom.

LAW AND LAW COURTS.

The system of administering Justice where either 'inter-statel' subjects or interests are concerned or where British Indian subjects or Europeans are concerned has to be put on a really satisfactory footing.

For this purpose it is essential that every Indian State should have a well-drafted, properly enacted and complete body of Laws, besides properly constituted Courts of Justice to administer them.

The Court of Vakils at Mount Abu under the control of the Rajputana Agency, or the Residency Courts are all an anomaly, leading to much trouble and injustice, and should be replaced by *really* legal, responsible, and properly equipped tribunals where *justice* would be dispensed and not *favour*. All such Courts are kept up under the ostensible plea of "extra-territoriality" and the fiction of the sovereign rights of the "Native States"—as if they were on a footing similar to that of Turkey, Persia, China, Siam, &c., The Residents are not Ambassadors and they with their following should not be above the law of the land; and the judgments they dispense to themselves and to their staff and hangers-on, as well as to the inhabitants of the States in their dealings with or sufferings at, the hands of the Europeans, should be appealable. A regular system of appointing Justices of Peace, who only are able to try in British India—under certain restrictions though—European offenders should be extended to these States as well. That is to say, selected judicial officers of those States which have remodelled their Law, Law Courts, and Jails on modern lines should be invested with this power, as they are in British India. Further, the present travesty of justice going under the name of appeals from the Residency Courts to the Foreign Offices—Provincial and Imperial—should be entirely done away with, the appeals going before regular and properly constituted Law Courts. All this, of course, means that an Indian Prince must cease to exercise *personally* his judicial functions and delegate that power as in all constitutional monarchies to public tribunals.

EDUCATION OF THE PRINCES.

With regard to the education of the Chiefs, the present arrangement of perpetuating their isolation by herding them in specially designed Colleges for themselves alone, or putting them under the tutorship of European governesses and tutors, has not worked to the satisfaction of their subjects. The Imperial Cadet Corps too, which was ushered in with a great flourish of trumpets by Lord Curzon, is, it is clear only for the purposes of providing a showy guard of honor on regal occasions from the ranks of "Semi-Sovereign" Indian Princes and not for any purpose of giving them a genuine military training or providing them with commissions in the Army. Lord Kitchener, in answer to an interpellation in the Imperial Legislative Council, definitely stated that there was no idea of utilising the talents of these young noblemen by providing them with responsible work and implying that the hobby of Lord Curzon extended only to creating an ornamental corps for Viceregal glorification—and Feudatory humiliation!

The education of the future Chiefs and their kith and kin, who will be their future advisers, helpers and administrators, should be such as to fit them for their future duties and that goal should never be lost sight of in arranging the courses of study and their surroundings.

Instead of being sent to special schools from which the middle classes are excluded, they should as a rule be sent to ordinary schools and made to mix with boys who will be their subjects. A common school education in the early years, say up to the 16th year, is the best and truest that could be given. It will teach them that sympathy, which comes only of an intimate acquaintance with the daily life of the people at an impressionable age and when neither side has yet learnt any other behaviour than that of boyish frankness and class-fellow equality.

Education must be. . . . not the sickly and dry acquisition of the elements of knowledge gathered within their own homes with the aid of obsequious teachers who have to wait on their pleasures and whims, and amidst pandering parasites. (*Letters to an Indian Raja*).

Their general education must be a manly and vigorous prosecution of studies *carried on in the class rooms of public schools and colleges in competition with the intellect of the commonalty.*

Baron Stockmar's advice to the Prince Consort as given in Sir Theodore Martin's *Life of the Prince*

Consort, when asked about the education of the Royal children is clear and distinct, that the system must

> **not admit of dividing lines in educational institutions which are not the natural result of brain-power, and *all aristocracies are the better for a common struggle with those whose studies must be taken up in right earnest***

and this was acted upon to the great benefit of the dynasty and the British Nation.

The best mode of impressing those who are born to wealth and power with the insistent responsibility of their station in life is to

> **educate them under conditions which would imperceptibly lead them to compare themselves with the sons of the middle classes as men, and to feel that *their true worth must depend* on their *mental* and *moral* attributes.**

and not on the factitious accident of birth. They must be made

> **to realise that outside their home they are no better than ordinary men, and that it is their behaviour as such that alone can reflect lustre or shame on their birth or their fortunes.**

What can be said of an education which would surround them from their very birth onwards "with the divinity that doth hedge a king." The fruits of such an education turn inevitably to wormwood and ashes in the mouth and spell ruin and misery to the subjects of such Princes as is but too well exemplified by history.

The next five years after the age of 16 above-mentioned, might be spent in the company of their social equals in special Chief's colleges for the study of such subjects, as—Politics, Economics, Jurisprudence, Constitutional History and Law, Industrial and Commercial Law, Public International Law,

Public Administration, Accountancy and Business Organisation—(this is very important),—Banking and Currency, finally, Sociology and Psychology; Forestry, Agriculture, and Mining should also be included, as also Biographies—legal, political and military. After getting a sound grounding in the *elements* of all these subjects they should be taken out for a year's tour in India under competent guidance, studying the application, in daily life, of the subjects which they have been studying theoretically, these last 5 years. After the Indian tour there should follow a European tour through the smaller countries, Holland, Switzerland, Scotland, Ireland should have special attention, nor is America (both North and South) to be neglected, with a similar purpose in view, winding up with Japan, and other Asiatic countries like China. Then a year at the Head-Quarters of the Government of India learning the daily work of administration of every department. Then 2 years in their own States thoroughly learning the work of every department. Each Chief should have a sound colloquial command of at least 2 Indian vernaculars besides his own mother-tongue and either French or German besides English. Education in Arts cannot with impunity be neglected either. Sculpture, Architecture, Painting, Music, have all to be cultivated, for the artistic and emotional is no less important in the life of a person than logic chopping or the severely practical. No Hindu needs reminding that Arjuna who was one of the mightiest warriors of his age and had inherited philosophical aptitude from his grand-father, the Holy Rishi Veda Vyasa and so was fit pupil for the lessons of the Gita, was also such an accomplished dancer and musician, having learnt the arts from the famous heavenly *hetaira* of his father's Court, Urvashi, that he could teach those arts to his future daughter-in-law, the beautiful but unfortunate Uttarâ.

Any arrangement which would sever in early life this connection with the traditions of the people over whom they will be called on to rule is wholly mischievous. *They should in no case be sent out of India before their twenty-second year.*

The benefits of an English education even in India would be too dearly bought if the Chief and his future Councillors were to grow up to manhood devoid of sympathy for the people of their country or bereft of their affection and confidence.

Lord Reay, the experienced and sympathetic Governor of Bombay, held to these principles and gave effect to them as far as lay in his power in his dealings with the Feudatory States who were under his charge. Wise Governor that he was, he insisted on the solid acquirements as against the frivolities of superficial foreign social graces, which only helped to plunge the Feudatories into ruinous expenditure besides alienating the sympathies of their subjects and their brother-rulers and colleagues of an older generation.

A great deal is being done by the Government of India for the education of the children of the Princes and their nobles, but so far the results obtained have been very incommensurate to the money and energy spent upon the purpose when they have not been actually mischievous. The reasons are not far to seek. It has been education on *alien* lines.—English nurses, English governesses, English companions, English tutors, and finaly English ideals. As M. Chailley truly remarks :—

> The fact remains that hitherto the Chief's Colleges have not fulfilled the hopes to which they had given rise (p. 225). Whether it be that the minds of the pupils were not sufficiently developed, or their work not sufficiently arduous. or whether . . . . the teaching staff was inferior, the results obtained satisfied neither the parents of the pupils, nor the Government of India. It was alleged that the pupils received no solid instruction and acquired no taste for reading beyond illustrated papers. (p. 223.)

From 1902 onwards Lords Curzon, Minto and Hardinge have called together from time to time conferences of the Indian Rulers for tackling this grave problem, but so far the outside world sees little headway made in the proper direction. No doubt a solemn adjuration was addressed by Lord Curzon to the students in the Rajput Chief's College in 1900, that they were not to regard themselves as

> a privileged body to whom God has given a *sanad* of perpetual idleness. Their States are not their private property ; the revenues are not meant to be swallowed up by their privy purses Providence has destined them to be the working bees, and not the drones of the time. They exist for the good of their peoples, and not their peoples for them, and they ought to be models, examples and guides. (*Lord Curzon's Speeches* edited by Sir T. Raleigh p. 221.)

But alas, the advice, the warning, still remains largely unheeded. A sifting *public* enquiry as to how the Principals in charge of these Chiefs' Colleges have been and are discharging their duties towards their wards, and whether they have been and are *sincerely* endeavouring to train their pupils along the lines of the ideals so grandiloquently laid down by Lord Curzon in public profession—would probably disclose a very remarkable State of affairs.

One wonders now how many of the 700 Chiefs have truly and honestly separated the *State revenue* and their *privy purse*, how many have become really qualified working bees, how many regard themselves as *servants* of their subjects and not their subjects as their *slaves* ; probably not even 5 per cent.

EDUCATION OF THE PRINCESSES.

No less important is the question of the training and education of the Princesses. Unless the girls of the ruling families and of those also with whom they intermarry are properly educated, it will continue to be a difficult problem—the supplying of the proper environment to the boys of the ruling families. The vital importance of the subject is so thoroughly clear that it needs no dwelling upon. But, unfortunately, it is a question of such extreme delicacy that the British Government has wisely kept very aloof from it. Will the newer race of Princes tackle it in right earnest ? Will not the part that the English women from the highest to the lowest are taking in this terrible European war open their eyes ? But for this splendid backing of their womenfolk, could England have hoped to win this war ? It is only high-souled and well-trained mothers that can produce heroes.

THE AGE FOR FULL POWERS.

All this training necessarily postulates that the age of majority, of investiture with full ruling powers, must be higher than it is in the case of ordinary mortals. The greater the responsibility, the longer the period of training and dependence is the well-known rule of Nature, and it may not be broken in the case of man, without bringing him to pain and trouble. The Government of India has therefore been wisely advised in advancing the age of majority of a Ruling Prince from 18 to 21 years but this is not enough. When it is remembered that the well-being, the prosperity, of millions of human beings—nay their very life and honour will have to be committed to his charge, it is but fair that the rules that apply to average humanity should not apply to him, but that a much higher standard should be exacted from him. Not till he has passed his 25th year, as it is expressively called in Hindustan, *gadah pachisi*, (the *pous asinorum* of the first 25 years of life) should he be entrusted with the lives and destinies of peoples. This of course does not mean that the installation ceremony is to be deferred to this age. The succession ceremony should take place as a matter of course on the demise of the previous Ruler.

INSTALLATION.

There is a good deal of feeling among the Indian Princes and Chiefs over the procedure adopted by the Government of India with regard to this subject. They hold that it is against their dignity and against their rights as semi-Sovereign Princes that they should have to suffer the humiliation of being enthroned on their ancestral *gadi* by any outside power, be it as high as a Governor-General, or lower in the official scale, a provincial Head, or still lower, an agent of either. Their contention is, that they hold their States in their own rights, and their admission of British Protectorate over them, does not give the Government of India the right to treat them in the manner in which a Suzerain may treat his Feudal nobles who had received grants of Fiefs *from* the Over-Lord. This point ought to be conceded, and the Princes and Chiefs should be installed by the chosen representatives of the people whom they are to govern. This was the goodly ancient custom, and it is in the fitness of things that modern democratic sentiment (which on this point is in full consonance with ancient Hindu practice as well as Western) demands that the Ruler should be handed the insignia of his high office by those over whom he is to rule, and after he has been made to take the coronation oath of protecting the rights and liberties of the people in accordance with ancient traditional forms. On this point of installing their king by the *people*, the *Mahabharata* says :—

असंत्यक्तमनुष्यं च तं जनाः कुर्वते नृपम् ।

(Him who is ever accessible and sympathetic, the *people* instal as their king.)

The Coronation oath as exacted by the *Rishis* from Prithu, whose father, King Vena, they had condemned to death because of his manifold misdeeds ; as given in the *Mahabharata* runs thus :—

प्रतिज्ञां चाधिरोहस्व कर्मणा मनसा गिरा ।
पालयिष्याम्यहं भौमं ब्रह्म इत्येव चासकृत् ॥
यश्चात्र धर्म इत्युक्तो दंडनीतिव्यपाश्रय : ।
तं अशंक : करिष्यामि स्ववशो न कदाचन ॥

(I swear in thought, word, and deed to unceasingly foster and protect the good, and to punish the wicked : to act unhesitatingly according to the law, and never to behave, autocratically, despotically or wilfully.)

Unfortunately all this was not always acted up to. It was only when the hereditary hierarchy fell out with the hereditary bureaucracy, then only the people, the masses, came into their own ; then only could the Rights of Man, as against the Right of Might be successfully asserted.

NAZARS.

Another sore point is the rule that the Feudatories are to present *Nazars* to the Governor-General and the Provincial Heads. Now this presenting of *Nazars* is a relic of the barbarous days of military autocracies, and it subserves no useful purpose to keep up ceremonials fit only for those Dark Ages. But the evil is ubiquitous. The acceptance of *Nazars* is practised by every one who gets the chance throughout the whole of India, British and non-British. While the Native Chief feels his dignity hurt by having to present *Nazars* to some British official, he does not scruple to inflict the same humiliation himself on his own people. In British India also *Nazars* have to be shown to the Provincial Heads in *Darbars*. Now the observance of all these antiquated formalities which have no living significance left, becomes ludicrous in British India. Still lower come the Zemindars in British and non-British India, whether holders of broad acres, or of a trifling patch of land, they all insist on exacting *nazars* from their tenants and their servants. All this ridiculous and exasperating system reminiscent of the dark days of Feudalism should be made a clean sweep of.

HONOURS.

Now, that the vital question of self-preservation is no more the concern of the Indian Princes as far as aggression from without or insurrection from within is concerned, but is that of the Sovereign power, it behoves the princes then to push on with all the vigour and earnestness they are capable of, the imperative duty of Progress and Reform in their States, and of welding the 'isolated' chiefships into a Federation of enlightened and civilised States.

This can be helped on by many methods—one of them—the most potent one—by proper education has been delineated above. Another is by the method of judicious bestowal of honours.

Of the two that would appeal most strongly would be the increase in the Salute. Two more grades of 23, and 25 might be formed and the bestowal of some higher designation than that of H. H. Many of these style themselves *Farzand-a-Englishia*, etc., which can only mean "Child of the English Royal Family."

Why not then utilise this and give to a select few the rank of the Princes of the Blood-Royal and style them H. R. H.? How highly it will be valued and how much more it will help to bring them nearer the British throne, may be realised by seeing how tenaciously the Princes cling even now after the utter disappearance of the Mussalman Empire, to the windy, bombastic titles bestowed by the Great Moghal. Similarly, greater honours and more profusely, might be bestowed on the officials of the Indian States. In fact, they might be put on the same footing as the officers of the British Government with regard to questions of precedence and decoration.

One thing more. The power of bestowing titles on their own subjects exercised by the Princes of first rank should be put on a proper footing by those titles being recognised by the Government of India. But if this is to come about, a definite understanding will have to be arrived at, regulating the numbers and conditions of bestowal, of public notification, of office record, etc., etc., with the Government of India by the Princes desirous of such recognition. They might also be allowed to distribute a certain fixed number of British decorations and invest the recipients themselves in public *durbar*—as do the Provincial Governors.

Finally, the important questions, namely, that of the rank, and precedence, and the mode of address for the heir-apparents and of the brothers and sons of the Ruling Princes and Chiefs has so far never been settled. It is manifestly absurd that the heir should be addressed as H. H.; it is decidedly derogatory to address him or his brothers as commoners. The official mode of address is a sore point in every Native Court. There was much sulking and quite justifiably when the Residency refused to address the heir-apparent of the premier Vassal State as *Shahazada.* Will the Princes themselves send up a united suggestion as to the proper forms to be observed when referring to the members of their families ? No such confusion and uncertainty exists with regard to the social proprieties, that should be observed in dealings with the scions of the British Royal family or those of the British nobles, then why cannot this be settled for these also, to the comfort of every one concerned ?

The other ticklish question is that of precedence. It is not possible in the 20th century to revert to the ceremonials observed a 100 years ago, where a Maharana of Udaipur could sit enthroned while the bare-footed British Agent was kneeling *dozanu* among his courtiers below; nor is it desirable that these Ruling Princes should suffer the indignity of having to go to receive the Residents at Railway Stations, or to allow them to sit side by side with them on their thrones,—as if both were the *joint-sovereigns* of the State—in public Darbars, or be invariably accompanied by them side by side in Imperial processions, and undergo the further humiliation of having the Resident presented *before* them. Tact and commonsense ought to find a *via media* between the two extremes. For one thing, every Ruling Prince should be accorded the ceremonial due to a "semi-Svereign" and so should have precedence of every British official below the Viceroy, in India; and in England they should, as naturally, be accorded precedence over the Foreign Ambassadors, and just after the Royal Family.

The Indian Princes, like the Indian people, are becoming self-conscious, and are no more inclined to give up tamely their rights and privileges than the latter are. While courtsey costs nothing, and is in fact the lubricant, of the social machine, want of it generates heat and conflagration. But while pleading for full social consideration for the Indian Feudatories, they too need reminding that their social behaviour towards Indians, who are not of their own exalted rank leaves very much to be desired. Most of them insist upon keeping up absurd, antiquated Court customs in this democratic century, in which insistence on the privileges of birth and of caste, look foolish and ridiculous, when not downright idiotic. When the veneer of shams and of mere gilt and tinsel is being so ruthlessly torn asunder, is it right, is it politic, for these Princes to behave in such stuck up fashion, as unfortunately—with a few bright exceptions—the great majority of these do? The pitiable part of it is that none of them dare behave in those discourteous ways towards an European, however lowly his social status may be. It is the observance of this racial distinction as galling as that of the Arm's Act, which still more lowers the Native Prince in the eyes of the people and makes it impossible for self-respecting Indians to come into touch with them. Lest I might be thought writing at random, I will give concrete instances. The Maharaja of Travancore, while he will accord a proper seat and receive any and every European with due courtsey, will do nothing of the kind for an Indian, be he his own subject or British. His highest officers—Chief Minister, Chief Judge etc.,—must stand all the time they are in his presence, even though it be a business interview lasting for hours. On public occasions, when Europeans and Indians are both present, the former are alloted seats, but the latter must keep standing, so that it happens that Europeans in the Maharaja's service, have seats while their Indian superiors have to keep standing! This may be an extreme case, but the less extreme cases require no less a change of attitude. For instance the latest Minto-created ruling Chief, while he himself sits on a chair, expects everyone of his 'native' visitors to squat down on the floor at his feet, among his servants and flunkies, his high officials—Chief Secretary, Chief Judge etc., all squatting there. All this must be replaced by modernised social behaviour, where the differences of mere rank do not count to such an extent that one of a lower social rank will not be forced to observe such humiliating social etiquette which would be lowering to his dignity as a fellow-creature, as a man. 'Do unto others as you would be done by' is a very useful maxim to remember by the Princes, when they are demanding proper social treatment for themselves. Let them treat their own people as men, and not as slaves; and *then only* will they themselves deserve to be treated as men by those who now treat them as if they were tame bears and themselves the keepers.

STATE BOUNDARIES.

Before going on to suggest the heads on which reform would be welcome, indeed urgently required, I would urge here the prime necessity of a well-defined boundary. Sir William Lee-Warner says:—"In the Bombay Presidency there is hardly a single district outside Sind in which one or more *enclaves* of foreign territory do not abound. Even in the case of a solid block, like the State of Hyderabad, the frontier is so irregular that British towns are surrounded by the jurisdiction of His Highness the Nizam, and his villages lie in the heart of British territory." (*Protected Princes of India*, p. 16.) Now, such a state of affairs is not very desirable, for it inevitably produces friction. It ought to be and can be rectified. The difficulties in its consummation are not insuperable. All the three methods possible (*a*) purchase, (*b*) lease, (*c*) exchange, could be employed by turns to secure clear, undisputed boundaries avoiding intermingling of different territorial jurisdictions.

STATE ARMIES.

Another thorny question which might as well be dealt with here is that of the armies of the Feudatories.

Modern British diplomacy throws a cloak over it and is not fond of publicly girding against this enormous rabble—more dangerous to its own masters and their subjects than to anybody else. Time was when the British officials minced not their words, but frankly and openly deplored and denounced the existence of this army—every treaty bears witness to the uneasiness caused by it. Even now British India has to pay for a large British army and huge cantonments located in or near the territories of Indian Princes, which burden has to be borne by us as long as the Feudatories continue to maintain large ill-disciplined armies.

Now, what use are these to them? They simply eat up their substance and snatch the hard-won bread from the mouth of their subjects. These armies cannot be employed either for aggression or for repression, neither can they be properly armed and equipped, nor provided with Indian officers trained in the Military Schools of Europe. Why then continue this utterly useless and costly waste? Everybody knows that even the British-officered and inspected Imperial Service Troops have to be maintained on a lower level of efficiency than the British troops. By the abolition of these armies—a large amount of money would be liberated both in British and Feudatory India for developing the capacities of the people and the country. All this saving might well be spent *on education, which is in a deplorably backward condition in all the States except two or three, and on the development of the economic resources of the State, and the financing of trades and industries. An expenditure of twenty per cent. of the State Revenue on education would be none too much under the present circumstances.* They would besides be able to win some especial privileges for themselves by such a step which under the circumstances would be far more useful than this sham of a show of sovereignty. For instance, the conditions of the Railways, Steam Navigation, Telegraph, Wireless and other such like concessions vary greatly from State to State—some being positively harsh—and they could all be made easier and more uniform.

Every one of them might well keep Imperial Service Troops as their share of contribution towards Imperial defence but only up to a limit of 3 per cent. of their income. In an interpellation in the Viceregal Council it came out that Alwar spent 14 p. c. of its income on the troops while the Nizam spent a bare 1 p. c. The burden on the poor revenue of Alwar is enormous in comparison to the rich one of Hyderabad. The squeezable capacity of the Ruler of the time should not be set up as the criterion of the contribution. For purposes of internal order a small body of well-disciplined Military Police would be amply sufficient—as an aid to the Civil Police.

The Native States may feel sore that while they are so rigidly "supervised and advised" in matters military even to the extent that they have to depend upon the sweet autocratic will of the British Resident for a rifle or a revolver for their own personal use, Afganistan is *helped* by a subsidy of 18 lakhs a year to arm not only its army, which, unlike that of the Indian States, may be as large as it chooses, but all its ferocious subjects even with arms of the latest pattern. The native Afghan Officer is not capable of merely leading his men into action, but understands strategy, is a capable artillery officer (which no Indian whether in British-ruled or Native-ruled India—is), knows all about aeroplanes even, in short, thanks to his Turkish teachers, is as up-to-date as possible. Further all sorts of military factories have been permitted to be established there and the Government of India has given active help for establishing such works, while the feudatories have to submit an annual report even on the amount of gunpowder they possess! They are prohibited from giving even simple infantry drill to their subjects at large. The Rajputana and Punjab Chiefs find it hard to forget that they ruled over Kabul as Governors in the days of the Moghal Emperors—and that it was as much a part of India as Sindh or Punjab to say nothing of those pre-Moslem days when it was as much Hindu as any other portion of India and ruled by Hindu and Buddhist Emperors. Even so late as 1885 when Lord Dufferin held a Durbar at Rawalpindi to receive *His Highness* the Amir of Afghanistan, and dragooned a number of Indian Rulers into being present at it to add *eclat* and magnificence to the function and show off the power of Great Britain, the late Ruler of Kashmir successfully resisted the pressure and declined to be a consenting party to his own humiliation. For at that Durbar the Viceroy and the Amir sat side by side enthroned on high, while the Indian *His Highnesses* had to take lower seats. Maharaja

Ranabir Singh whose armies had often chastised the Afghan as had before him those of the "Lion of Punjab," Maharaja Ranjit Singh, his father's Surzerain, and the name of whose commander-in-chief, Hari Singh Nalua, was such a terror to these strong-limbed and lawless people, that their wives used to frighten their howling children into quietude with Nalua's name, would not brook being given a lower place than the Afghan Chief. Such sturdy assertion of independence would bring condign and swift punishment now, and the Princes have to attune themselves to their present environment. Lest this be regarded as mere rhetorical exaggeration, one has only to remember the unhappy cry at the glorious Coronation of the Emperor in Delhi against the Maharaja of Baroda. How every Anglo-Foreign paper bursting with race-hauteur and race-hatred gave tongue throughout the length and breadth of the land against the poor Gaekwar, the *bete noir* of the bureaucracy, who it seems had had the temerity to make certain suggestions for the better ceremonial treatment of the Ruling Princes but which unfortunately were displeasing to the powers that be. Nothing short of drawing, quartering and hanging the Maharaja would satisfy Anglo-India and for months after the event which nobody knew exactly what it was, its press kept resounding with anathemas against His Highness, who barely escaped with the skin of his teeth, a sadder and a wiser man. The Maharana of Udaipur too had to break his hereditary family oath, in the spirit, if he was saved the humiliation of having to break it in the letter by the magnanimity of the Viceroy and his own timely surrender, and had to be present in Delhi. *His Highness* of Kabul has been raised to the dignity of *His Majesty* but let us hope that in the universal disappearance of every independent Islamic Kingdom before the march of the European powers, under the compulsion of their greedy traders ever on the look out for markets, under their own flags, his kingdom too, may not have reserved for it the fate of the "Kingdom of Oudh."

But the Sun of Kashmir has set, the sceptre fallen from the hands of that virile ruler into those of a weakling has suffered many an indignity, even to the extent of practical deposition. The powerful Governors of Kashmir and of Jammu who used to be addressed by the British Government as Excellencies, are now no better than the lowly *Tahsildars* of British Districts, ever genuflecting before the puissant Resident. While there is the Arms Act for His Highness's own subjects and other Indians, the foreigner enjoys the prestige and privileges of carrying arms freely! Not only many valuable rights of semi-soverignity have been handed over to the Resident, but worse still even a large slice of border territory towards Afghanistan (Chitral) had to be made over to the British. It is an old, old tale. The weakness and incompetence of rulers makes interference unavoidable. So low have some of these Princes fallen, that shameful to relate, they themselves intrigue against their own Sirdars. For instance, one Rajputana Maharaja is reported on his way back from England to have told the political officer who was bear-leading the party that some of his Sirdars had been surreptitiously purchasing rifles in England. Some few weak-kneed amongst these dropped their purchases in the Red Sea, for fear of a search of their baggage, as if they had been common thieves; but others of true Kshattriya mettle, bearded their Ruler before his 'boss' the Resident, and told the latter that the purchases had been made only after the Maharaja's permission had been obtained, to his confusion and discomfiture.

A brighter future, however, is dawning for the Indian Princes, the feeling of mistrust and suspicion is being replaced by one of trust and faith; they too are getting educated on modern lines, (though alas ! very, very slowly) and it is to be hoped that in the interests of all concerned—the sovereign, the semi-sovereigns, and the 300 millions of the peoples of India—they may be, before long, permitted and trained to help in the higher task of bringing to birth a Federated Greater India under the guidance of Great Britain. For this great birth it is very necessary that the military career in all its highest branches should be thrown open to them, and in fact to every Indian, as freely as it is to every Britisher. Capacity and not color, should be the sole selecting guide.

EDUCATION.

The Government of India under the specious plea of want of funds will not make primary education compulsory and free, nor elementary and college education more widespread and less costly. Some, alas, too few, of the Ruling Princes have risen to the occasion and are doing their best to educate their people. Baroda led the way. Indore has followed suit. The latest instances are those of the Begum of Bhopal and the Maharaja of Kolhapur, who have conferred the boon of compulsory and free primary education on their subjects. Mysore has taken the lead in establishing a University. More recently Hyderabad has started the *Usmania* University, with English *put in its right place*, as a second language, while all the subjects are to be taught in the language of the Court, namely Urdu; for not till the medium of education becomes our own mother tongue and not an alien tongue, can there be genuine education in this country. It is the primary duty of every Indian from the highest to the lowest to do his utmost for spreading the benefits of education in the country. If every Native Prince, Chief, Feudatory, Tributory, or Zamindar vowed that he would not rest till the peoples committed to his care were educated and prosperous, fifty years hence the whole aspect of the land would be far different from what it is to-day. But he must not slavishly copy the Anglo-Indian methods. The United States of America and Germany, the smaller European States—Switzerland, Holland, are the places to go to learn what education can do and has done, and *how to do it.* If Japan has done it, why not we? If the method has been so brilliantly successful for the Philippines—and that too within less than twenty years—then why not for us? It is all a question of the *will to do.* Let every Native State establish post-graduate travelling scholarships, in as large numbers as it can, and send out every year, in their scores and in their hundreds its brightest intellects to roam the world in the search of knowledge.

NUMBER OF FEUDATORIES.

The large number of Feudatories is due to the inclusion among them of numbers of chiefs owning only paltry patches of land, daily diminishing under the stress of the law of equal division, as, for instance, in Kathiawar, in the agencies of Rewa Kantha, Mahi Kantha, &c. Wherever there has been no primogeniture, no Feudatory rights should be recognised. In fact, it would pay to confer Feudatory rank and insignia on some of the Zemindars of British India with impartible states and incomes running into millions of rupees. Why need it be forgotten that many of these nominal Rajahs and Maharajahs were real ones in their day, exercising ruling functions. A certain definite standard of size, income and population ought to be fixed and only those States which conform to it ought to be recognised as Princes and the rest to be given the rank of premier Zemindars in their respective provinces. This is, of course, a very delicate matter, and will require as great *finesse* as that of Lord Curzon, who got the late Nizam to come to a permanent understanding with the British Government over the long open sore of Berar. The G. C. B. he got in exchange being interpreted by flippant wags to mean—Gave Curzon

Berars! But the situation has got to be faced with courage and with pertinacity, and of course with great sympathy. I would suggest that only those Feudatories be recognised as *Ruling* Princes and Chiefs whose revenues are not less than fifteen lakhs a year (£100,000); and territory not less than one thousand square miles. This would limit the numbers of the Feudatories, who really deserve to be ranked as such, to something like one-third of their present number.

FEDERATION SCHEME.

Now for the tentative scheme of Federation and the conditions by fulfilling which the Feudatories are to be admitted into it:—

1. Every Ruler, to grant a Constitution under the guarantee of the Government of India against its being withdrawn.

2. To appoint Legislative and Executive Councils with Ministerial responsibility.

3. To enact a *complete* body of Codified Laws; Civil, Commercial, Criminal, Labour,-Agrarian etc, etc. The British Acts, the Anglo-Indian, the British Colonial, the American, the Swiss, the German, the French, the Italian, should all be utilised in building up these codes, with the necessary modifications due to all that may be best in the indigenous, Hindu, Mussalman, and finally Customary Law.

The Indian States having a much freer hand than the Government of India, could be of immense help to the latter, if groups of States were to appoint Law

Commissions to compile digests of Customary Law which could be later codified into well-drafted Acts in the light of European experience.

It is not generally known though well worth knowing, that in Nepal it is a Penal offence to possess a copy of their nebulous regulations which are styled out of mere courtesy, Law. I wonder if there is a printing press or a newspaper in this rigidly "home-ruled" almost independant State. Such is the attitude of the only Native State where British influence is least —a relic of those barbarous mediæval days of India when none but a Brahmin may know the *Shastras*; a state of things not unknown to the aristocratic Roman Empire when a knowledge of the "Laws" was the heritage of the noble alone, and the *people* had to take it from the august hands of their masters, twisted and distorted to suit the patrician ends.

The publication of laws, full, clear and precise, has always been the outcome of the triumph of democracy.

With regard to law-making, it seems necessary to make one remark here. The Indian States must avoid enacting laws which emphasise racial cleavage, if they are not to lay up for themselves a store of bitterness and tribulations. The Travancore Arms Act of 1909, is a strong case in point. Similar is the import of the Kashmir Arms Regulations—the Foreigner shall not be required to take out a license—but not so the Native! The many Press Acts and Newspaper Regulations of diverse States are all equally bad and the whole lot of them have to be very carefully revised.

The making of laws is not half so important as the *observance* of them, and to secure this end no one, however highly placed, must be exempted from their operation: the king himself must not be above the law. Hear what Manu—whom nobody can accuse of an anti-patrician bias and according to whom a king is a divine being not an ordinary mortal — says on this point of the sovereignty of *law*, as against *personal* sovereignty. He says:—

> The Rod of Justice, the Sceptre of the Law, is verily the king the leader, the ruler, the seminal principle that vitalises the whole body politic. It is the living pledge that all the four types of men, in all the four stages of life shall do their Duty without fail. It governs all the peoples, it protects them; it alone keeps wakeful watch when all others sleep. It is Law (*Dharma*) *itself. It destroyeth the king who deviates from the path of Duty and of Righteousness.* (Ch. 7, Verses 17, 18, 27, 28.)

There is the famous instance of that powerful king, Venu having been done to death by holy Brahmins in the ancient days.

In short, autocracy, irresponsibilism, the personal will of the ruler, have all got to be abolished in favour of "limited monarchy," of the Reign of Law.

4. To inaugurate proper Courts of Justice.

5. Every ruler to take an oath, modelled on the British Coronation oath, publicly on his installation, to his people, pledging himself to do the utmost that lies in him to advance *their* interests.

The canker at the root of the Hindu Polity has been the centering of all the three functions of sovereignty, namely the Executive, the Judicial, and the Legislative, which are organically separate, and different, in the person of the monarch. There can be no stability, no permanence, no continuity, in a State where Government hangs on a single life. It may be cut off any moment by the assassin's dagger, by disease, by accident. And, after all, there is the fundamental psychological difficulty that there can never be a person, however Superman he be, who can properly combine within his single body such three diametrically opposed temperaments, as are necessary for the proper carrying out of the three functions. The inevitable result of such a centralisation of powers has been favouritism, dilatoriness, laxness, insufficient knowledge, in short inefficiency, and oppression. How, then, is the enormously longer and enormously more complete life of the State than that of an individual to be guarded from shocks which may weaken and even may kill it, and how is its health and strength to be promoted? By making its *Sutratman*, not a frail human creature, but a Constitution; with its fundamentally separate triple aspect of Brahma, Vishnu, Mahesha represented in the permanently independent activities of the Executive, the Judicial, and the Legislative and Fiscal authorities. Disturb their balance of power and you have *Pralaya*, destruction, chaos.

Even the oldest Hindu polity blundered here. While separating the Executive function, they mixed up the Judicial and the Legislative. It made still further trouble for itself, in the long run, by making the exercise of both these functions the monopoly of *hereditary* castes (the Kshattriya and and the Brahmin) and so sinister vested right divorced from duties, grew up with tropical luxuriance, and the *people* suffered.

The two weakest points in the administration of Native States are, their Financial and Judicial systems, while the Executive is their over-strong, mischief-making point which needs much curbing.

The judiciary higher and lower alike, has to be made as inflexible, as incorruptible, as independent, as jealous of outside interference, as it is in England.

Neither King, nor Minister, nor Parliament can exert the slightest influence over it, or modify, hasten or delay either its procedure or its judgments. (*The German Peril* by Frederic Harrison, p. 204.)

Alas! that this cannot always be said of even British India; for under certain circumstances instead of enforcing *justice*, the Courts enforce *policies*, as has been pertinantly remarked by Maitland about the doings of the notorious Star Chamber a few centuries back in England. (*vide* his *Constitutional History of England*).

The Legislature which will be representative of all varieties of class interests and industries in the State, has to be equally strong in the exercise of its functions. No amount of pressure should prevent its passing laws it deems necessary nor force it to pass laws that it deems hurtful; nor without its authority should there be levied any taxes, or State revenues distributed, nor should it be so accomodating as to vote all the monies that an Executive may want, against its own convictions of right and wrong. For "If the executive can control taxation, the result is tyranny." (*The German Peril*, p. 210).

EMPLOYMENT OF EUROPEANS.

The embargo laid on the Native States with regard to the employment of non-Indians without the special sanction of the foreign office should be abrogated. There is no danger now of their employing military adventurers to train their troops. Under the present conditions of service, every European servant of an Indian State regards himself more as a servant of the British Government than of the State employing him, and believes more in keeping the Resident in good humour than doing his duty. Naturally, there is a great aversion to employing foreign agency however skilled and helpful it might be, when there is always present the trouble of such an employee playing the master instead of the servant. With healthier conditions the relations are bound to be healthier also and lead to a greater utilisation of foreign ability and talent—till it can be safely and usefully replaced by a home-grown one.

The Egyptian system of having 'Native' Ministers and 'Foreign' Advisers is alleged to work on the whole fairly well. The initiative and responsibility remaining with the Egyptian—while trained advice—critical and constructive, is at the elbow of every Minister (*vide.* Cromer's *Egypt*). The Egyptain version of the state of affairs as it exists in *reality* is however very different. It has been voiced by Hall Caine in his very sympathetic treatment of the situation in Egppt, in his well-known novel, *The White Prophet*. It is shown there that the English Advisers are all-powerful, while the very-much-advised Egyptian Ministers non-entities; only there to register their decrees, and execute them as their own! All such Advisers—Public Works, Judicial, Financial, etc., if it be thought advisable to have such, to have the privilege of attending 'Cabinet' meetings with powers of speech and discussion but not of vote. The employment of Americans and Europeans in such capacities would, perhaps, be more useful than of employing them in actual Executive or Secretarial work as at present. They are apt to kick against the feeling of subordination which all such work naturally implies in Feudatory States with Indian heads of departments. Of course, this feeling would gradually diminish and vanish under a different system of recruitment and subordination and with a much superior set of Indian official heads than is generally the case at present.

MINORITY ARRANGEMENTS

The system followed in India—especially during minorities—of appointing a Council of Regency with the Resident as President is wholly mischievous. It always becomes in practice irresponsible autocratic rule, sheltered behind a Council. Neither has joint-administration much to recommend it. It may work well, as it is said to have done in the case of Bhavnagar; but in that instance it was due rather to an accident than to the policy. It is not easy to get hold of Europeans and Indians of the mental and moral quality of harmony which would make for smooth *joint* responsibility, without the former trying to domineer over the latter under the state of conditions as prevalent now in the Native States. In those States, however, in which through the liberality and wisdom of the Rulers, the people have been associated with the Government, and the eternally true principle of Government of the people, by the people, for the people, has been properly established, there will be no difficulties. There will be no break in the administration because of the death of the Chief; the impersonal Constitution never dies, it lives on for ever, meeting every emergency as it arises.

FINANCE.

The question of Finance is generally a thorny one on account of two special reasons.

The British Government brings pressure to bear upon the Feudatories for the abolition of Customs duties in the interests of foreign traders and manufacturers, and keeps generally a tight hold over their Budgets. *There is a steady tendency to absorb every Feudatory seaport and to encircle every frontier Feudatory with a strip of British red.* With ministerial responsibility and legislative control, complete financial autonomy must be allowed and proposals for levying a tariff for Revenue or even frankly protectionist purposes or the creation of monopolies should not be vetoed as they are at present, by the Government of India most illegally. The other difficulty comes from the Chiefs themselves who have been treating their States as if they were all crown lands or private domains—just like Zemindary property whose whole income is treated as private income.

The constitution should fix a separate Civil List which might vary between 3 to 6 per cent. in the *inverse* ratio of the State Revenues nor should the ruler be permitted *jagirs*, crown lands. Even where some arrangement for fixing a Civil List exists, it is on an enormously wasteful scale. To give one instance only. The Nizam has a Civil List of about 50 lakhs, besides Jagirs known as *Paigah* estates yielding over a crore which with better management, would yield half as much again, and with all this enormous sum in his privy purse—the late Nizam was heavily in debt! This is practically double that of the King-Emperor which is roughly £600,000 a year. Such fearful waste is nothing short of criminal and should be put a stop to, and the money thus saved to be utlised for State purposes—for Education, for Public Works, for industries and diverse other insistent calls.

It is a most culpable misuse of the surplus of Native State Revenues or of the private hoardings of the Chief that they should be invested in Government of India Promissary Notes or in any other Foreign securities, or deposited in Foreign Banks. A few years back the State of Travancore lost a huge sum of money through the notorious bankruptcy of the Madras firm of Arbuthnots. To begin with, it is very bad finance that the taxes should be so heavy as to allow of such surpluses, secondly it is still more reprehensible that the surpluses instead of being utilised for advancing the interests of its own subjects, in a hundred diverse ways, should be invested in interest bearing securities, as if the State administration was a banking firm! What moral justification can the Foreign Department of the Government of India plead for taking away six crores to invest in Promissory Notes, the late ruler's savings and that too during the minority of the present ruler of Gwalior or for similar investments during the minority of other Feudatories? Such transactions have almost as bad a flavour in the mouth, as those of the older days, when, 'benevolences' were accepted from the Native States. (*vide* Sir Henry Lawrence's article on Oudh, reprinted in his *Essays.*)

AUDIT.

In most States reckless extravagance and unaccounted spending is constantly going on—especially in the Public Works Department—to say nothing about the expenditure incurred under the immediate orders of the Rulers. To give one instance only,—take the Kashmir Electric Power Scheme, where it seems, from an original estimate of sixteen lakhs the costs have gone up to near a crore and a half! When the difference is so vast between the actuals and the estimates, naturally the possibility of the high return shown in the original, will be in the inverse ratio of the outlay. During the last days of Sir Sheshadri Iyer's tenure of the Chief Ministership of Mysore or perhaps just after his resignation, a similar fate befell the revenues of the State over the renewal of the Gold Mining Lease and the Cauvery Electric Power Installation. Can any merely 'native' Minister under the present condition of affairs hope to cope with this evil without getting an ignominious fall?

An *audit department* as a check on all unauthorised expenditure is necessary in the interests of the State itself. Nothing favours peculation and misappropriation of the public money so much as entrusting one and the same department with the power of collecting taxes, sanctioning or incurring expenditure and keeping accounts. Therefore, this function of keeping accounts and seeing that no department, however important, and no officer, however exalted, incurs the smallest expenditure that has not been previously sanctioned must be vested in a special department which shall have no hand or part in any branch of the work of administration.' (*Letters &c.* p. 64).

Where European experts are generally employed, these, though technically subordinate to the Indian Ministers, are really independent of all serious control, for over and above the prestige of expert knowledge the race prestige effectually cows the Indian controlling heads—the fear of the Resident and the Foreign office acting as a wet blanket on the enthusiasm of an indiscreet 'native' Minister.

This department to be really effective and powerful, will have to be manned by experts, who must be allowed full independence by express enactment and with whose rulings not even the Ruler of the State should be able to interfere so as to deflect them from the right course.

It hardly needs pointing out that the Financial condition of the Indian States and their Rulers would have been far different from what they are to-day if such a powerful brake on the spending departments as also on the wasteful whims of the Chiefs themselves had existed.

To enter into greater details of the *internal* management of the States would only mean the repetition to a large extent of all that I have already said with regard to the administration of British India in my other Chapters of the book.

Such in rough, and with many crudities, is the outline suggested for fixing on an equitable and stable basis the mutual relations of the British Government and its Feudatories, the relations of the Feudatories and their own subordinate chiefs and subjects and finally, the relation that should subsist between the subjects of British-ruled and "Home-ruled India." For the future of United India lies even more in the hands of the Native States and their Rulers than it does in those of the British and British-ruled India. Through acting and reacting on each other, learning from each other's failures and shortcomings, profiting by each other's successful experiments, may they all work in unison with a single eye to the progressive development of the Motherland and its 300 millions of poverty-stricken, God-loving, and law-abiding inhabitants.

SUMMARY.

(1) The Ruling Chiefs to be separated into two broad classes; namely, (*a*) those who do really exercise the powers of a semi-sovereignty, and (*b*) those who are rulers only in name and possess either very few of the attributes of this semi-sovereignty even or exercise these through the agency of British officers whether paid by

the State or States concerned or even by the British Government.

(2) All these latter—and they will number some hundreds—to be removed from the category of Feudatories and put on their proper and real level as Zemindars, with plenty of show and pomp and dignity about them but all their *show* of power and administrative independence shorn in theory also, as it is in actual fact. All such 'Chiefs'—a good many of whom do not even follow such an elementary self-preserving ordinance as that of primogeniture—owning only a bare few miles of India's land or a few thousands of rupees as their State income and exercising some shadowy 'civil' powers might well be humored and 'honored' into giving up these rights and privileges which, while devoid of all substantiality, effectually keep the Chiefs out of the pale of the protecting English law and keep them and their States under the thumb of a Foreign Office owing an account of its actions to none.

(3) All these States to be divided into 5 groups according to their size, population, income and their general importance.

(4) A Council of Princes to be established, which is not to be a sham like the "Imperial Councillors" of that administrative failure Lord Lytton, but to be a reality.

(5) The Council to elect annually from among its own members, one President and four vice-Presidents. These not to be open to re-election without one break

of term. The Council to have a properly organised office, with paid Secretary, Assistant Secretaries, Registrar, clerks etc. The Viceroy's duties to be confined to delivering the opening and closing speeches every session. All the members of his Executive Council and the Foreign and the Political Secretaries to be *ex-officio* full members. Each of the 5 groups of the Feudatories to elect for a term of 5 years 20 Councillors, thus making a total of 100. No Councillor to seek re-election without a break of one term, except those of the first 2 groups because of their very small numbers.

(6) The Council to hold a Session every year after *Depavali* (sometimes in November) in Delhi for not more than a fortnight and not less than one week.

(7) To start with, the business of the Assembly to be social, consultative and advisory. The Administration Reports of each State to be produced before it and special attention called to any new or remarkable feature of the year's administration in any of the States. Answers to be provided to questions arising out of these; the speeches to be mostly confined to suggesting better or improved methods of dealing with progressive administration. It is time and experience that will show in what directions its work could be most profitably enlarged.

Lord Chelmsford deserves the thanks of all India for having inaugurated such a Council in the last days of October 1916 ; and it is to be fervently hoped that no reactionary counsels will prevail either making it an impotent, mere show, affair, or suppressing it altogether. It is to be hoped that it will be given statutory recognition by an Act of Parliament, which will prevent its discontinuance, and that Secretariat influences would be so carefully provided against that they will not be able to make it a very showy but very empty shell as they have the wise action of Lord Morley in the case of the Legislative Councils, by enacting the thoroughly hampering and even mischievous Regulations against which the country has been ever since crying itself hoarse.

(8) The Viceroy not to be his own Foreign Minister.

(9) The Provincial Political Departments should be abolished, and every Feudatory State brought into direct relation with the Government of India. This would not only please the Ruling Chiefs and their subjects very much, for the sense of subjection is very much mitigated by a contemplation of the rank and high name of the person by whom power is exercised, but would also be of solid advantage in various ways. It would bring to bear on "Native State" administration high statesmanship instead of the mere petty administrative skill of the Provincial Political Agents. It would make for a more even-handed justice and uniform treatment of the States, which is not possible under many and divergent authorities, all equally autocratic.

(10) The Cadets of the Ruling Houses should be employed in large numbers, as honorary *attaches* to

every political agency and in the Secretariat, and be given real hard work to do. It is obvious that this would give invaluable training to the future Rulers and Ministers of the States, who will naturally be taken from these. This will, besides, help to break down the fearful isolation of the Feudatories, for as *attaches* they will have made life-long friendships, already begun in their Rajkumar College days.

(11) No ruling Princes or members of their family to hold *Jagirs* (crownlands). A cash Civil list is the only proper arrangement.

(12) All Indian States in the interests of a Greater India to yield up their Currency and Postal rights. One Coinage, one Post, one system of Weights and Measures are essential.

(13) Each group of the Feudatories to elect four members from among the nearest relatives of the Rulers that may be available for the purpose, to represent the group of States sending them, to the Supreme Legislative Council.

(14) The dual control over the Political Agencies beyond India should be abolished. If the British Foreign Office thinks it necessary to keep these under its control then their expenses must come out of the British Exchequer; India should not be saddled with them. But if India must pay, then they should be under the sole control of the Indian Foreign Office.

CHAPTER IV.

PROVINCIAL GOVERNMENTS.

At the very outset it will be well to realise clearly that the present system of administration in India is the result not of *fission* but of *fusion*. It was the Regulating Act of 1773 that created the office of Governor-General—or rather made the Governor of Bengal, the Governor-General of India, while retaining his direct control over Bengal as its Governor—and made him the supreme controlling authority in India. This control was extended by Statute in 1784 and 1793, and was rendered absolute by the Charter Act of 1833, and the instructions issued thereon by the Court of Directors. As the three Presidencies grew and grew and their political relations with the sovereign 'Native States' about them became more and more complex and a constant source of danger and of anxiety, even to the extent of sometimes menacing the very continuance of the British occupation of the country, it became necessary to check the waywardness of the Presidency Administrations—each playing for its own hand, unmindful of results to the others—by unifying for *political* purposes the different and conflicting administrations under a central authority. But the process once started, and its causes forgotten, it has gone on at an ever-accelerated pace till every vestige of real independence—and even of nominal for the matter of that—has gone, and Madras and Bombay have been reduced to the level of the other subsequently created Provinces. The Presidency Mints have gone, the Presidency Armies have gone, the Presidency Services have become merged into Imperial or All-India Services, and so on. But circumstances have changed, and it is to be fervently hoped that the three Presidencies will regain most of their early independence and the newer Provinces will approximate to *those* in their autonomous powers and *not* drag them down to their own level of subordination. Further, the grip of the Government of India over the Provincial throats has not meant the relaxation of the Secretary of State's grip. So these labour under a double thraldom.

WAYS OF CONTROL.

It is not necessary to go into the ways in which the Secretary of State controls the action of the Provincial Governments; here we are concerned chiefly with the control of the Government of India over them. The following excerpts from the Decentralisation Report will show the various ways in which the overlordship is asserted.

(1) By Financial rules and restrictions, including those laid down by Imperial departmental codes.

(2) By general or particular checks of a more purely administrative nature, which may (*a*) be laid down by law or by rules having the force of law, or (*b*) have grown up in practice.

(3) By preliminary scrutiny of proposed Provincial legislation, and sanction of Acts passed in the Provincial legislatures.

(4) By general resolutions on questions of policy, issued for the guidance of the Provincial Governments. These often arise upon the reports of Commissions or Committees appointed from time to time by the Supreme Government to investigate the working of departments with which the Provincial Governments are primarily concerned.

(5) By instructions to particular Local Governments in regard to matters which may have attracted the notice of the Government of India in connection with the departmental administration reports periodically submitted to it, or the "proceedings volumes" of a Local Government.

(6) By action taken upon matters brought to notice by the Imperial Inspectors-General.

(7) In connection with the large right of appeal possessed by persons dissatisfied with the actions or orders of a Provincial Government.

Summarising the general trend of *official* opinion on the above subjects, the Decentralisation Report (p. 26) says:—

> The Provincial Governments, with the exception of Bombay, are content with the general lines of the present system, but all hold that there has been an excessive interference by the Government of India in matters of detail.

The Report makes detailed suggestions for minimising in future this *excessive interference* by the Government of India. But, it is to be feared, all those detailed suggestions will prove merely temporary palliatives and the over-grown Imperial Secretariat, with the help of the Imperial Inspectors-General will, no sooner decentralisation has begun, find ways and means for tightening again their grip on the Provincial Governments.

The importance of the matter was so fully realised by the Commission that practically the whole of the bulky Report deals with the relations of the Central and the Local Governments. They realised that the state of affairs was far from what it ought to be. A few quotations would help to bring clearly to the reader's mind the attitude of the Commission to the question. They say that even over *ordinary internal administration*

> the Government of India exercise a general and *constant* control. They lay down lines of general policy, and test their application from the administrative reports and returns relating to the main departments under the Local Governments. (As already stated, the Local Governments also submit copies of all their printed proceedings to the Government of India.) They also employ expert officers to inspect and advise upon a *number* of departments which are *primarily* administered by the Local Governments, including Agriculture, Irrigation, Forests, Medical, Sanitation, Education, Excise, Salt, Printing and Stationery, and Archæology. These officers are commonly known as Inspectors-General. (Italics mine.)

The above is a truly formidable list and even then it is not exhaustive!

> The control of the Government of India is, moreover, not confined to the prescription of policy and to action taken upon reports and inspections. It assumes more specific forms. . . . . The practical result is that no new departure in Provincial administration can be undertaken without their preliminary sanction, or in important matters, without that of the Secretary of State also. . . . . The *essential* point to be borne in mind is thus that at present, *even* in matters *primarily* assigned to the Provincial Governments, these act as the *agents* of the Government of India, who exercise a *very full* and *constant* check over their proceedings. (p. 21).

Is it to be wondered at that the Government of Bombay strongly objects to this sort of absolute muzzling and manacling? See the very illuminating views of the Bombay Government on the subject (pp. 224-237 vol. VIII. Dec. Com. Report.) but which are too lengthy to be conveniently summarised here.

A few excerpts from the note of the Chief Commissioner of the N. W. F. P. which was created by Lord Curzon, in 1901, in the teeth of Punjab opposition, not only non-official but also official, printed in vol. IX of the Dec. Com. Report are no less outspoken—considering that it is an official document emanating from a Local Government *directly* subordinate to the Governor-General, and therefore bound to be more or less muzzled, unlike the Bombay Government, with its traditions of equality and of independence.

The Local Administration, while necessarily admitting that a considerable degree of centralisation is inevitable, and no one would wish it otherwise, go on to remark that:—

> There is, however, at times a danger of this centralisation being carried to extremes, and of the Foreign Department of the Government of India attempting to administer the frontier too much in details and from a departmental point of view.

When it is remembered that the Frontier Districts were created into a province by the autocratic Viceroy Lord Curzon, to save these from the bane of this very *departmentalism*, by bringing them through the Foreign Office under his immediate control, it will be seen how well-grounded was the Punjab opposition to its creation. The note has many such sentences:—

In this and other matters the influence of the departments of the Government of India, owing to excessive caution *due to ignorance of local conditions*, is apt to be too rigid and uniform. (Italics mine.) The Local Government may be sure of its ground and able and willing to push forward in a particular line of policy, but the Government of India Departments are inclined to look with doubt or suspicion on a step forward being taken in our province unless all other provinces are ready to advance in the same direction. *Hence the pace in matters of administrative progress is usually that of the slowest province.* (Italics mine.) The tendency is strong in the Finance, and Public Works, and Railway Departments, especially in the latter, where revenue and departmental considerations are allowed to stand in the way of salutary reforms, when suggested from outside, and where the officials in their zeal for departmental interests are apt to overlook the interests of the public and the fact that they are *public servants*, not servants of a department. (Italics in the original.)

The note goes on to give a number of concrete instances of the misdoings of the Government of India in *every* department of administration, and remarks:—

The cases illustrate the powerlessness of Local Governments and the extent to which administrative improvements may be blocked by narrow departmental views.

It will thus be seen that all that I have said in the previous chapters about the necessity of comparative independence from the harassing control of the India Office over the Government of India applies with even greater force to the control of the Provincial Governments by the Supreme Government. For in this case with highly-organised Secretariats of immense power within such convenient striking distance, the opportunities tempting to incessant meddling become irresistible: while in the back-ground there is also the distant India Office to meddle and muddle. The late Sir John Strachey has some very true remarks in his *India* (p. 290 2nd ed.) on the serious limitations under which the Head of a Local Government exercises his powers. He says :—

> **There is no branch of the administration in which he is not bound either by positive law, or by the Standing Orders of the Supreme Government, or by the system which has gradually grown up under his predecessor.**

The above sentiment was due to his experience both as the Head of a Provincial Government, the United Provinces, and as one of the most powerful ministers of the Supreme Government. It will be perceived that the net in which the Local Administrations are enmeshed is both fine and strong, and from it there is no escape. This, while limiting efficiently the power for evil, limits still more their power for good. Under such a system all initiative is effectually killed out and the spur to ambition, to do one better, is blunted and one dead level of mediocrity and conservatism secured. The late Sir George Campbell (Lieutenant-Governor of Bengal) who perceived this all-absorbing tendency of the central power so long as seventy years ago and strenuously fought a losing battle against it, demanded in his *Modern India* (p. 173) an *Administrative Code* which would clearly lay down the different spheres of work of the Provincial and the Imperial Governments and prevent encroachment by the stronger on the preserves of the weaker, and put an end to squabbles by the avoidance of overlapping and the definition of the spheres of control.

The Decentralisation Report while fully conscious of the wholly untenable state of affairs jibs when squarely faced with the only possible remedy—

Provincial Autonomy—and in the right orthodox well-trained manner docilely goes off towards the easy well-worn track with the platitude :—

> In India the Provincial Governments are, and *should remain*, subject to the general control of the Government of India in *all respects*, and their functions and powers should be variable by the *Central Government* or by the *Secretary of State* as circumstances require. (p. 24) (Italics mine.)

One expected a really statesmanlike, bold pronouncement from the Commission and not such a tame, inane mumbling. It was left to that great English statesman and diplomat, Lord Hardinge as Viceroy of India to point out with unfaltering fingers the true remedy—*Provincial Autonomy*—however unpalatable it might be to vested interests and to bureaucracy, in his famous Despatch of 25th August 1911.

But this autonomy would be a very dear purchase and a sad mistake, if it were only to result in the setting up of a number of Local autocracies in place of a distant Imperial one. *If it is to be fruitful of good instead of evil, it must be guided and controlled or stimulated into activity by enlightened Indian public opinion, able to make its voice effective through its control of the Executive and Legislative Councils.*

GOVERNORSHIPS.

The Decentralisation Commission has, however, luckily taken a long step in the direction of Provincial autonomy by advocating the raising of all the Provinces to Governorships, though they qualify it by saying :—

We recognise, however, that change in the existing system is not equally urgent in the case of all Provinces. (para. 446.)

The late General Sir George Chesney was, however, of a different opinion. He was for raising forthwith all of them to the higher dignity, and in his *Indian Polity* has outlined a definite scheme for ten Governorships, and has necessarily been led to advocate a readjustment of Provincial boundaries in connection with it.

The question of having Governors being settled, the question of their qualifications comes up at once. The Indian contention is that no European who has served his term in the country is fit for this high position, and so their demand is for a Governor who has a standing in the *public life* of Great Britain and has done good work in the House of Commons. The Decentralisation Report (p. 155) however tries to steer a middle course by saying :—

We do not think that a Governor need invariably be appointed from England. The Governorship of Bombay has occasionally been filled by a distinguished Indian Civilian, and men are from time to time found in that Service who could adequately fill such posts in other Provinces. It is, therefore, not desirable absolutely to close such appointments to the Indian Civil Service. The prospective loss to that service of some of the existing Lieutenant-Governorships would be made up, in considerable part, by the creation of new memberships of Council. (p. 155.)

When one remembers the *personnel* of the Commission, one understands at once the inevitable bias that led to the above statement. It was a psychological impossibility for the Commissioners—composed exclusively of I. C. S. men, even to its Secretaries—to arrive at a conclusion which would condemn their Service as incompetent for such work. Nor could vested interests be forgotten, as the words "prospective loss, etc" prove unmistakably. But for these two ultra-potent disturbing factors, one may shrewdly suspect the Commission would have reported wholly in favour of Governors straight from 'Home.' A few selections will clearly bring out the internal conflict.

> **A Lieutenant-Governor drawn from the same service as his colleagues, and possibly junior to one or more of them, would not ordinarily command their deference in a degree sufficient to obviate friction. (p. 440.)**

Could the feared friction be obviated by a mere juggling with names and calling the Indian Civilian Lieutenant-Governor, a Governor? One is afraid that an Indian Civilian, His Excellency, by the very fact of his more exalted position, will be forced to accentuate the social difference between himself and his Civilian colleagues more than would be the case if he were merely a His Honor and so of a lower grade of exaltation not much above his colleagues!

> **The introduction of a *fresh mind*, possessed by a Governor whose position and *antecedents* would command the deference and support of his colleagues. (p. 441, iii.)**

The words italicised above by me show that the conditions wanted cannot be met with in the I. C. S. And so, while conscious of the supreme importance of importing Governors directly from 'Home,' they naturally made some reservations by saying that the Governor need not *invariably* be appointed from England, and that it was not desirable to *absolutely* close such appointments to the I. C. S.

I may briefly put some more of the arguments which tell against an I. C. S. man as Governor.

Too long and too intimate a connection with the daily routine of Indian administration is bound to dull the *freshness* of view of an Indian Civilian, and lead to a lack of initiative—a condition of affairs which will be helped considerably by the fact that he is sure to be an elderly man and will be unwilling to face hard work and trouble as a younger man from England would do. Besides, a statesman from England will resist the deadening pressure of Indian environment and will not succumb helplessly to pressure like an administrator from India. He will have his reputation to maintain, if not to create, *unlike* the Anglo-Indian, who has nothing to look forward to after his time of service is over. The latter may be equally conscientious, but the spur of ambition will be totally wanting. An Anglo-Indian Governor would be wedded by long habit to a *system* and would be as a rule largely influenced by vested interests which would warp his insight and his actions. Even Sir George Chesney while vigorously advocating the appointment of Anglo-Indian Governors cannot help recognising the advantages which would accrue from the selection of English politicians for Indian Governorships. He says :—

> It brings Indian official life to that extent in touch with the English political world and creates a certain amount of interest in Indian affairs among persons who might otherwise be without it. Further the possession of personal experience is not always without disadvantage in one respect. It is scarcely possible that a man should be raised from the ranks of a Service in which his life has been passed without taking with him more or less of bias for

or against some of his old associates which may be displayed in the subsequent distribution of patronage. (page 95.)

The question of raising Bengal to a Governorship was pushed aside by the Executive Council of Lord Curzon in the interests of the Service, for while by splitting Bengal many more higher posts would be created, by keeping it one there was a danger of losing the Lieutenant-Governorship. So the argument for an Executive Council was strongly denounced in such terms :—

The two Councillors would be drawn from the same province as the Lieutenant-Governor and might be smarting under the sense of supersession themselves.

The obvious and conclusive rejoinder to this would be and which Lord Curzon and his Council, for reasons of their own, persistently refused to see—'*Change your system of Anglo-Indian Lieutenant-Governorship in favor of a Governor from England*'. The above-quoted opinion further distinctly and unequivocally shows that there will be no possibility of smooth working if an Indian Civilian is appointed a Governor. A man unconnected with the Service will have no prejudices for or against men or measures. The plea often put forward that the administration would be wrecked by an English politician as Governor, wanting in Indian experience, is much too interested an argument from the Civilian side to need serious notice. However, it may be pointed out that a Governor is not in the same plight as a Lieutenant-Governor or a Chief-Commissioner, who is always the "sole monarch" of all he surveys ; he is given expert advice in the shape of a well-selected Executive Council. Bagehot in the VIth Chapter of *The English Constitution* has pointed out with convincing logic how the English system of administration, combining, as it does the carrying on of the daily routine of office by a set of *permanent officials*, possessing a precise knowledge of the action of the administrative machinery, controlled by *political chiefs* who bring as their own quota to the work, a large and wide experience gained amidst different surroundings, makes for efficiency with its quickening impulse on the permanent staff which, however capable and zealous, is by the very nature of its work incapable of taking a comprehensive and statesmanlike view of situations, immersed, as it is in the ruts and grooves which it has cut out by generations of steady application to the work of merely *carrying* on the administration. All this applies with far greater force to India.

The salary of the Governor in India is simply extravagant and so also are his sumptuary allowances. There is absolutely no reason why these should not be on the very same scale as in the Colonies namely £5,000 per annum. Their sumptuary allowances and household should also be reduced to the level of that of a Lieutenant-Governor if not that of a Chief-Commissioner. For instance, the Military Secretary, and the large number of A. D. Cs are useless and costly superfluities and should be done away with.

SALARY-PRINCIPLE.

I may as well state here, as anywhere else, what

I regard to be the principle that should govern the fixing of salaries for the various public offices. The Indian as a rule should never be given the same salary as the Britisher; even if he has entered the Services through the English door. He should be given a higher salary than his brother Indian recruited in India itself, but only that much more which would cover the extra expense of an education in foreign lands. The Britisher recruited in England should receive the same salary as the Indian recruited in India for the same work *but* he should be given a sufficiently tempting *expatriation allowance* over and above the salary which would allow of India getting the pick of the British market for every one of its departments. The question of invidiousness, of color-bar can never arise if this principle is rigidly acted up to. A uniform and not too high a scale of salary fixed for each post; an expatriation allowance for a *foreigner* recruited in England for it; and for an *Indian* recruited in England, say between two hundred to four hundred rupees over and above the fixed scale. The demands put forward before the Islington Public Services Commission by the Europeans were ludicrously extravagant, and they were imitated in this by the Indians who should certainly have been less covetous and open-eyed to the poverty of the country; the short-sighted Commission blissfully ignoring the frightful economic burden thus sought to be imposed upon the long-suffering, poverty-stricken tax-payer of India coolly advocated a good many of those demands! In this respect not England, but France and the other European States should be our model, and above all Japan.

The *proportion* of the salaries of public servants in Japan is very well worthy of imitation in India. It is more 'humane' and takes much better account of human needs and necessities. In the first place it does not emphasise so acutely the difference between rich and poor, higher and lower, which is the cause of so much bitterness, jealousy, class-hatred and class-arrogance in the West, and finally is more in accord with the general poverty of this country.

PROVINCIAL BOUNDARIES.

Once the supreme importance of raising all the Provinces to the status of Governorships and of granting to them autonomy is conceded, there inevitably arises the question of Provincial boundaries. A re-arrangement of these—though not in the way which produced the stupendous muddle of the Partition of Bengal—is desired by all thoughtful Indians. Sir George Chesney as pointed out above would divide India into *ten* Provinces each under a Governor. Acute and serious differences arise, however, when concrete suggestions for boundary rectifications begin to be made. Lord Curzon was not very happy in his schemes of boundary rectifications. Bengal had to be reunited. His lopping off of Districts from Punjab to create the North-West-Frontier Province has been another lamentable failure and raised a storm of protest even from the Punjab Civil Service, some even going the length of resigning the service in protest. Mr. S. S. Thorburn in his *The*

Punjab in Peace and War has most outspokenly, for an Indian Civilian, criticised the policy of creating a border Chief-Commissionership. It has to be remembered that all his service-life was spent in Punjab where he worked up every rung of the official ladder till he reached his final post, that of Financial Commissioner which ranks next to that of the Lieutenant-Governor only. He says :—

If the literature on frontier affairs for the last twenty years be examined it will be seen that the Subordinate Government, when consulted, almost invariably gave advice, which, if followed, would have saved India from the misdirection of energy and waste of resources which culminated in the troubles and humiliations of 1897. (p. 344.)

The comparative success of frontier management by the Local and Supreme Governments may be gauged by the facts that up to 1887 the aggregate cost of roundly twenty blockades, and frontier expeditions—exclusive of Ambela (1863) which was directed by the Government of India, was less than half of that incurred after 1892, and that the tribes are to-day as little amenable to our friendly offices as at any former period—1897 excepted—in our long connection with them. (p. 344.)

He goes on further to remark :—

The Peshawar Agent will often be an ambitious man 'in a hurry,' in which case he will push the forward policy and amongst future Viceroys, Aucklands, Lyttons, Lansdownes, and Elgins will be more frequent than Lawrences and Curzons, and then we shall have complications, coat-trailings, warlike movements, perhaps even wars, as was the case through the nineties, extravagance trans-Indus, and crippling retrenchments, or tax enhancements Cis-Indus. (p. 348.) Looking back for twenty-five years, remembering the causes of the Afghan War of 1878-80, the straining of our relations with the Amir 1890-93, the subsequent thrusting of 'friendly relations' and a protectorate upon the independent tribes beyond our frontier, the enforced delimitations of some of their hinterlands, the futile consequential wars of 1897-98, unprejudiced minds must recognise that the tax paying masses of India have received scant consideration, and that some of the heads of Governments and subordinate officers answerable for the blunders and wastage of the different periods, should have been discredited instead of being rewarded. So long as the Government of India is practically an irresponsible despotism, and the Indian public merely a powerless mass of uninformed and inarticulate tax-payers, muddling, misrepresentation, and waste in the conduct of India's foreign affairs will not cease, and high-placed blunderers in authority will never be called to account. Until some force in India arises with the power, the will, and the ability necessary for securing a common-sense management of affairs, business-like prudence will not always be practised.

Present methods suit a bureaucracy: unless forced from the outside, reforms from inside are hopeless. Without the certainty that the truth will come out and be intelligently examined and judged, no Government will proclaim its mistakes or alter its ways. The fear of public opinion is the force which secures right mindedness in men in power in England, but in India there is no public opinion—at least published opinion except to some extent on domestic matters entering into the daily life of the people—*e.g.*, plague regulations—hence the Government of India in their foreign proceedings are irresponsible, and in pursuit of the chimeras of "high politics"—sometimes a mere mount for vaulting ambition—they plunge light-heartedly into adventures and wars which may benefit a few individually, but injure the people of India collectively. When things go wrong in India hardly a voice is raised against the wrong doers; officials may not speak, the press has little information, and if it had more, is timid, the line between treason and criticism being finely drawn, and as for the masses, their horizon is the evening meal and the next instalment of the revenue demand. Outside India nobody cares John Bull is ultimately responsible, but as he does not pay the bills, and his immediate concerns engross him, he is not exacting, and accepts without scrutiny whatever statements the Government of India may lay before him. Take instances: Lord Lytton in 1877 forces a war against Afghanistan; it costs twenty-five millions sterling; India bleeds silently. Again, from 1890 onwards push and pinpricks upon India's North-West frontier plunge her into many wars; the proceedings cost six or seven millions sterling; once more India bleeds silently. To particularise, an agent trails his coat in Chitral, a war follows, India pays, and the agent is knighted and promoted, and there the matter ends. Again some of the Trans-Indus Pathan tribes, mistaking our intentions are frightened into fighting for their independence; the Khyber Pass is abandoned, the events of August 23, 1897, take place, a serious war follows: once more India bleeds, this time happily, not quite silently. The Viceroy in Council calls the risings "fanatical outbreaks," no one objects until an official indiscreetly speaks the truth: eventually the blunderings are condoned, the blunderers rewarded, and the Secretary of State for India endorses —with hinted qualifications—the Viceregal fanaticism myth, and records in a Despatch to Lord Elgin his entire agreement "in regarding fanaticism as the principal motive," for the tribal risings, and on the part of Her Majesty's Government their high

approval of the manner in which your Excellency's Government has met an arduous crisis."

Is that the way in which Indian Foreign Affairs should be administered? Would not any private business, conducted on similar lines, be soon in liquidation? Is it unreasonable, then, to hold that there can be no remedy until some force comes into being outside what in Lord Lytton's time was irreverently called "the Simla Mutual Adulation Society", and does the work which public opinion and the press, working together, perform in England. (pp. 349 to 351.)

The above is rather a long quotation, but it was worth while making it, as in the process of criticising the Curzonian policy of the creation of a N. W. F. Province, incidentally a good deal of light is thrown on the bureaucratic methods of Government. The obvious remedy for all this mismanagement is Provincial Autonomy, coupled with Responsible Government.

To fully grasp the arguments and indictments of Mr. Thorburn it has to be remembered that there is a gradation of control by the Government of India over the different kinds of the Provincial Governments—though every one of them is being rigorously brought under a system of uniform control. The Chief Commissionerships are directly under the control of the Viceroy in the Foreign Department, which means in practice Secretariat Government at its worst—for in these cases the high authority of the Viceroy covers every act and there is little if any consultation or dissent in the Executive Council.

If an equally outspoken account of the other frontiers were available, a similar tale of woeful mismanagement, of fearful waste of life and money, and of reckless high-handedness would be unfolded.

Lord Curzon tried to play the same old trick with Tibet, but was foiled for some unknown reasons by his friend, Mr. Brodrick (now Lord Middleton) then Secretary of State for India, who while permitting the free-booting expedition hung back when the inevitable question of a Protectorate came up, and even went to the extent of incontinently revising the treaty arranged by Sir Francis Younghusband, thus destroying the prestige of the Government of India and further putting it to serious monetary loss by cutting down the amount of tribute levied on Tibet. The latest instance known to the outside public of a similar thrusting of "friendly relations" resulted in the Abor expedition on the borders of Assam. The late Lord Dufferin got a Marquisate for his successful annexation of Burma, though it took ten years of "resolute Government" afterwards to pacify the country. Bernard Houghton has lifted a corner of the veil from the whole sordid transaction (pp. 133-138) in his *Bureaucratic Government.*

We may now, after this somewhat long but very illuminating digression, come back to the subject in hand, namely a re-adjustment of the Provincial boundaries. To work out a detailed scheme which would at the same time be agreeable to the people requires a roving commission to collect evidence, and submit a Report, but some tentative suggestions may be made here. Many such suggestions have been made from time to time but no *principles* on which such were based have been put forth. The Government of India Despatch of 25th August 1911 makes an attempt by adumbrating some general principles on which such readjustments of boundaries may be made. According to the Despatch a settlement of boundaries should :—

(i) provide convenient administrative units ;

(ii) satisfy the legitimate aspirations of the people ; and

(iii) be clearly based upon broad grounds of political and administrative expendiency.

But the above three principles are so very general, that they are necessarily very vague and hence open to much misunderstanding according to the view-point of the interpreter.

As I understand them—

(i) means that the Provinces should not be either too large or too small. In a fixing of the area, the density of population must also be taken into account. If the population is sparse the area may be larger than the average ; if the population is dense, the area may be smaller than the average. An inevitable corollary to this is that the ideal of "One Province, one language" is an impossible one. (*a*) It must not be lost sight of either that people speaking the same language are not only divided into different British Provinces, but form parts of Native States as well.

A word here about the *non*-interdependence of ethnic and lingual affinities would not be amiss. It is not generally realised by persons who have not paid attention to the science of social anthropology that because certain people speak the same language they are not ethnically one; nor the converse, that because two languages are found to be spoken by certain people, therefore, they are necessarily ethnically different. Language has nothing to do with race, and everywhere are to be met with groups which are ethnically one, but speak different languages, as also seemingly homogeneous peoples who speak one language, but who really belong to different ethnic groups.

The area covered by the Hindi-speaking people and their numbers are much too large to "provide a convenient administrative unit" even for a Governor with a full complement of Executive Councillors. (*b*) Some of the Provinces would be so small, that they would not be able to pay for a highly-organised administration and develop properly all their economic, educational and political interests. Whether large or small the tax-paying ability of a Province will also have to be taken into serious consideration in settling its area.

From all these considerations it emerges, then, that roughly-speaking, each Province should comprise an area of about eighty-thousand square miles, about forty millions of inhabitants and an income of about three crores of rupees, sub-divided into about thirty Districts each.

The question of having a sea-board and a good harbour is of vital importance to every Province. Witness the perpetual wrangle between Bombay and Karachi; between Calcutta and Chittagong; between

Madras and Vizagapatam and so on. Trade jealousy always attempts to hamper the rise and growth of any port that threatens to be a rival. But for this sinister financial influence over the Government, the harbours of Baroda, Cochin, Travancore would have been developed long ago bringing wealth to the hinterland, as also many a British seaport, and coastal trade in Indian-made and Indian owned ships would have continued to flourish. With a developed *Indian* Mercantile Marine, there would inevitably be again brought into existence an Indian Navy manned by Indians, and Indian dockyards to build the Navy, and which but for the jalousy of the British Admiralty would have continued to exist to-day, and on a much larger scale too.

(ii) and (iii) may be taken together.

The question of "administrative expediency" mentioned in (iii) seems to be the same thing as (i) 'convenient administrative units"—and has been fully dealt with above.

Now remain "political expediency" and "legitimate aspirations". Both these are inter-dependent factors, for only that is political expediency which satisfies the legitimate aspirations of the people, and not that which thwarts them.

Sir George Chesney in his *Indian Polity* (page 113) grasped the situation very clearly as to how the present Provinces have grown to be what they are. He says :—

The present distribution of territory among the Provinces of India has come about in a more or less haphazard way, governed by the circumstances of the times, and in many cases *without* regard to distinctions of race and language.

One has only to remember that it was quite a common topic of conversation among the London East India circles in 1839 that the separate Province of Madras might be divided up between the Provinces of Bengal and of Bombay and the city of Bombay made the seat of the Government of India instead of Calcutta. It may all sound very ludicrous now, but it is not more so than the present-day arrangements to which only custom reconciles us. Anglo-Indian Bengal has not yet reconciled itself to the change of capital from Calcutta to Delhi—though absolutely necessary it was—nor to its originator Lord Hardinge—whom it still continues to abuse. A territorial readjustment, then, taking into account all such factors, would be hailed with delight by all the different units whom the present conditions affect more or less adversely. Some little overlapping is, however, inevitable, for there are no hard and fast, definite demarcating lines in nature, and it is beyond the wisdom of any administration to produce sharp, clear-cut divisions, where none exists. What it can do is to try for approximate results.

We may now make concrete suggestions towards the rearrangement of Provincial boundaries. It may be remarked in passing that the main reason given by Lord Hardinge and accepted by Lord Crewe for the transference of the capital from Calcutta to Delhi was that while *socially* and *politically* the Government of India overshadowed the Government of Bengal, *administratively* it was overshadowed by a subordinate Government by both being located in Calcutta which was in the administrative charge of the Local Government of Bengal. But a similar evil collocation exists at Simla, and Lord Curzon fully realising its drawbacks tried to shift the summer capital of the Punjab Government to Murree or Montgomery, and make of Simla a purely Viceregal *enclave*, but for some unpublished reasons the scheme fell through.

The *Nine* Provinces that I suggest are :—

(1) Madras and Ceylon (Coorg to be amalgamated with Madras, and not kept up as a separate Chief Commissionership under the Resident for Mysore. Its interests suffer a great deal by its political isolation.) The upper half of Ceylon is mostly peopled by Tamils and there is a steady and growing labour migration to the plantations from Madras. A railway too has been built connecting Ceylon with India. Geographically, ethnically, socially, linguistically, and finally theologically it is intimately connected with India. There is not a single good reason for keeping it apart as a Crown Colony. This arrangement will have the further advantage of combining the tea and coffee interests of India and Ceylon and prevent the usual trade jealousies between the English planters of the two British possessions. So everything points to the utility of having them both under the same administration. Nothing is gained by keeping them so very

far apart administratively. All the Uriya speaking tracts should be handed over to Orissa, right up to, if not inclusive of the Agency Tract of the Vizagapatam District; while South Canara should go to Bombay.

(2) Bombay and Berar. The Canarese-speaking people who at present are scattered between four Governments, namely that of Bombay, Madras, Mysore and Hyderabad, cannot, of course, be wholly reunited till the interests of the peoples become supreme and of dynasties subordinate. But there is nothing to prevent South Canara from being reunited to North Canara, under the control of the Bombay Government, as it was some years ago. The Marathi-speaking Districts of the Central Provinces should all be handed over to Bombay. All this will more than compensate for the shearing off of Sindh from it.

(3) Orissa. This to include the Uriya-speaking population of Madras and Bengal. Rather large rectifications may be necessary in this Province. The recently added Berar with some more of the Marathi-speaking tracts to go to Bombay; while many changes on the frontier where it touches the U. P. and Bengal will also be necessary. A bit of Madras may also be necessary to allow of a decent port. The present arrangement by which Orissa has been tacked on to Behar is altogether unsatisfactory. The only 'reason' for such an incongruous arrangement seems to be that Behar by itself would be a very small change. It will be seen that it is proposed

here to break up into its component parts that mass of inchoate, heterogeneous mass known as the Chief Commissionership of the Central Provinces by uniting the Marathi-speaking peoples with their brothers of Bombay; the Uriya-speaking with their brothers in Orissa; and the Hindustani-speaking with their brothers in the United Provinces. Up to the year 1861 the Saugar and Nerbudda Territories formed part of the present United Provinces. So also did Delhi Territory, up to the right bank of the Jumna tracts.

(4) Northern India may be re-distributed into Punjab and Beluchistan. Lord Curzon's North-West Frontier Provinces to be reunited to Punjab; as also Sindh. Sindh would develop much faster under Punjab, than it has done under jealous Bombay. Punjab too will develop much faster than it has been able to without a seaport under its own direct control. The Sindhi and the Western Punjabi are ethnically and linguisitically practically homogenous; while the Sindhi has nothing in common with the Maratha or Kanarese. There is also a strong sentimental reason for the disappearance of the Frontier Chief Commissioner. The higher dignity of the Provincial ruler will prove a more valuable asset in dealings with the Frontier tribes, who will certainly appreciate at its full worth the difference between His Excellency the Governor, and a mere Honourable the Chief Commissioner.

The solid reasons against a Frontier Chief Commissionership have been set forth at length above and so no re-statement of them so soon is necessary.

Before passing on, it would be useful to dwell on one objection that has been sometimes made. It is this : advanced tracts suffer by being tied down to backward ones and the administration is hampered by having to deal out the same civilised laws to both the advanced and the savage Border Communities. The objection would be a serious one, if the Government had no remedy. But it has the remedy, which it employs off and on. It is that while these troublesome districts form a part of the regular administrative agency, they should be kept separate with regard to the laws to be enforced there, as is freely done in the unsettled districts of Bengal (Santal Perganas), U. P. (Kumaun, Garhwal, Non-Regulation districts), Madras—all these possess what may be called agency tracts. If this were to be done quite freely, instead of the advanced being dragged backward, would be under a steady pull forward by the former.

Another thing. There should be no non-regulation Provinces. It is an anomaly that Oudh, the Punjab, the Central Provinces and others should continue to be non-regulation ones. There is no justification for such an arrangement. It only makes for personal, autocratic rule and the concentration in single hands of all sorts of incompatible and incongruous powers, as against the rule of law and division of powers according to civilised notions of Government.

We now come to what is a rather difficult work of demarcation namely the proper allocation of the country between the Punjab and Bengal.

(5) Western Hindustan; that is to say those Districts or portions of them on the Eastern boundary of Punjab, which are Hindi-speaking and have an affinity with the western districts of the United Provinces; the Hindi speaking Districts of the Central Provinces—about ten or twelve; all the western Districts of the United Provinces.

(6) Eastern Hindustan; that is to say all the remaining portions of Oudh, most, if not all of the Gorakhpur and Benares Divisions, Behar, Chota Nagpur and any non-Bengali-speaking Districts or portions of them that may have been recently left behind to Bengal on the separation of Behar from Bengal.

(7) Bengal, comprising all the Bengali speaking peoples.

(8) Assam, comprising the port of Chittagong and of course all its hinterland; this maritine district has no natural affinity with Bengal; all the borderland between it and Tibet and Bhutan; and a large slice of Burma, for instance, the land of the Kachins and possibly of the Shans as well. Burma which is one hundred and seventy thousand square miles and will be still larger under the proposal next to be made, might very well hand over to Assam sixty to seventy thousand square miles of territory. Chittagong should become the capital of Assam.

(9) Burma and the Federated Malay States.

These latter formed a part of the Indian Government, but were taken over by the Colonial Office in 1867 as the Government of India found it difficult to manage such distant island administrations. With the acquisition of Burma, that reason does not hold any more, and it is to the interest of both the administrations that they should be under one Governor.

The penal settlement of the Andamans should also be handed over to it.

Nothing has been said about Ajmere-Merwara, because "political expediency" requires that no change of administrative methods be inaugurated there. The toy Province of Delhi is a Viceregal *enclave*, and needs no dilating upon either,

It may be pointed out, that a Province may very well have more than one High Court and more than one University, and if this point is borne in mind both by the government and the people who like the Telugus demand a Province all to themselves, much of the point against large Provinces embracing more than one language within their territorial jurisdictions will be blunted. Bengal for instance is going to have a second University, at Dacca. Madras may very well have also a second University situated amongst the Telugu speaking people. It may have a second High Court as well, situated in the University town. Some such arrangement will amply meet all the needs of the situation without indulging in expenditure which the country can ill-afford but which would become inevitable if a large number of small Provinces were to be created. Very many small Provinces also have the disastrous effect of delaying, if not hindering the formation of a United India, by emphasising parochial interests.

The scheme outlined above of nine full-blown autonomous Provinces with a full complement of Ministers and large Legislative Councils is a very large and bold one, and lays its author open to many a vigorous onslaught, and even contempt from the wiseacres of the Anglo-Indian Press. But when these describe even such a document as that presented to Lord Chelmsford by nineteen of his non-official colleagues on the Legislative Council as "impertinence," their abuse will be only so much wasted labour.

EXECUTIVE COUNCILS.

The universal Indian demand for Council Government in place of one man rule having been fully endorsed by the Decentralisation Commission, no further discussion on that point is needed. But the Report while clearly pointing out the drawbacks incidental to the rule of a Lieutenant-Governor in para 439, says nothing about those of a Chief-Commissioner. But the very same arguments hold good against a Chief-Commissioner and even more strongly.

With regard to the functions and *personnel* of the Executive Councils all that has been urged in the previous chapter with regard to the Supreme Executive Council applies with even greater force to these Provincial Councils. For it is here that the real growth of

India will take place. It was the perception of this factor that made the Commission report in favour of not *less* than four members besides the Governor. But those three doughty champions of Bureaucracy, Lords Macdonnell, Sydenham and Curzon forced Lord Morley to withdraw all those sections of the Bill which he, in his far-sighted statesmanship, had inserted in the interests of Indian aspirations. Such an elastic section would have permitted the creation of additional Ministries from time to time as the need for them arose, without the necessity of appealing to Parliament and the party interests that reign supreme in it. Even at present there is enough work to demand the energies of at least six members.

Our concrete suggestious are —

(1) that the Governor should hold no portfolio, but be simply the directing, controlling, co-ordinating head of all the Ministries. This is enough work to absorb all his energies;

(2) that while there must be individual Ministerial responsibility, Members must work as a *body*, must not feel and act as if they were absolved from responsibility in subjects outside their own particular department;

(3) that not *less* than half the Ministers shall be Indians and not *more* than half may be Englishmen;

(4) that none of them shall be taken from the I.C.S.;

(5) that their emoluments shall not be more than those of the High Court Judges, namely Rs. 4,000 per month.

It is further necessary that the Provincial Political Departments should be totally abolished, and all their work concentrated in the hands of the Government of India. The condition of affairs by which Indian States continue to be attached to the Provincial Governments is a relic of those days long since past, when these Local Governments used to make war and peace on their own account and the Central Government, very different from what it has been since the assumption of the Government of the country by the British Crown, sixty years ago. There were neither Railways nor Telegraph then. When the status of independence of the Provincial Governments was changed to one of subordination to a central Government, their control over the Semi-Sovereign Princes of India ought at the same time to have been handed over to the Supreme Government, but somehow it was overlooked at the time. Now with Provincial administration coming under popular control, this change cannot safely be delayed any longer.

The six Ministries might be :—

(1) Ministry of the Interior.

This will allow of the reduction of the posts of the Inspector-General of Police and the Inspector-General of Prisons.

(2) Ministry of Education and Sanitation.

This will allow of the reduction of the posts of the Director of Public Instruction, the Inspector-General of Civil Hospitals, the Sanitary Commissioner, etc.

(3) Ministry of Finance and Revenue.

It is the practice in this country to couple Revenue with Agriculture, but it is not good for the interests of Agriculture, which are always sacrificed to the overwhelming claims of Revenue. The Provincial Inspectors-General of Registration, Stamps, Excise, etc., will have become useless posts and should be brought under reduction.

Excise must be under the control of that Ministry which would be overwhelmingly interested in *diminishing* crime, poverty, and drunkenness without the least consideration for the revenue side of its administration.

(4) Ministry of Agriculture.

This will comprise the Departments of the Director of Land Records ; Forests, Fisheries, Irrigation, etc. This last is generally under the control of the P.W.D., but such an arrangement has been proved time and again to be against the best interests of the cultivator. The P. W. D. should deal only with the repair of old canals and the construction of new ones, but should have no voice in the fixing of rates and little in the aligning of the canal ways. This will allow of the reduction of the post of the Chief Conservators of Forests, of the Directors of Land Records, and other such very highly-paid, superfluous, *separate*, supervising, agencies.

(5) Ministry of Public Works.

This will deal in the usual way with roads, railways, bridges, culverts, public buildings, canals, etc. It will, besides absorbing the post of the Chief

Engineer, do away with the necessity of Divisional or Supervising Engineers as well.

On this Department the Report observes (*para* 452) :—

> The fact will, however, remain, that in the Public Works Department, the Chief Engineers are also Secretaries to Provincial Governments. Seeing that this Department deals with matters involving large expenditure of money, and requiring an intimate knowledge of the country and the general knowledge of administration, we think it undesirable that an over-burdened Lieutenant-Governor should have to control it with the advice only of departmental officers, and we think it equally inadvisable that the Public Works portfolio should, as is now usually the case in Madras and Bombay, be similarly left in the hands of the Governors. Our proposals for the general institution of Council Governments with enlarged Executive Councils, will, however, enable the portfolio to be entrusted to one of the Ordinary Members of Council, as it is in the Government of India ; and so long as it is so, we think it an advantage that the Secretaryship should be in the hands of an officer of technical knowledge and experience.

The case for a separate Ministry is much too strong to permit of mere make-shift arrangements especially when the abolition of the P. W. D. of the Central Government is strongly urged.

(6) Ministry of Commerce and Industry.

There may not be much work for the Minister in the beginning in some of the Provinces ; but those are the very Provinces which need a special Minister to *create* work and justify his office by the strenuous enlarging of the Industries and Trade of the Province.

The Judicial Department should be handed over to the High Court ; this coupled with the separation of the Judicial and Executive functions will help to purify justice and re-establish the faith of the people in it. But if it be thought impracticable to hand over wholly the Judicial Department to the control of the High Court, then the Department may be split up in two, one dealing with those matters which ought to be under the control of the High Court, but which unfortunately are not at present, and another dealing with those matters which may be in charge of the Ministry of the Interior. This will absorb the office of the Legal Remembrancer, and will be the Department in charge of Law-making. The present state of affairs in which the Legal Remembrancers and the Registrars of the High Courts are not Vakils and Barristers, but non-expert laymen from the I.C.S. is very undesirable and needs immediate change.

By what I have said above about the reduction or abolition of the many Provincial supervising agencies, I mean that these officers—Inspector-General, Deputy-Inspector-General, Directors, Deputy-Directors, etc., etc.,—should be merged in the Secretariat. In the Punjab for instance, the Director of Public Instruction is also the Education Secretary to the Government, instead of the United Provinces arrangement where a junior Civilian bosses it over the veteran D.P.I. Worse still, this Civilian is a constantly shifting quantity; as the exigencies of *his* Service require he is tossed about from post to post, and seldom acquires an intimate acquaintance with the needs of the Department or of the people. What I therefore mean is that the Civilian Secretary should be replaced by these *experts*, who will combine in their own persons, their present supervising duties with the Secretarial as is the case in the United Provinces; also with regard to some of the technical departments, for instance, the Engineering. This sort of arrangement will lead to a great deal of saving, besides removing the useless, when not mischievous intermediaryship of non-expert Civilian Secretaries between the Ministers and these expert officers, now kept at arm's length.

It will be beneficial to have Advisory Boards, consisting of not more than eight and not less than six members, attached to each of these Ministries as have been suggested above for the various Ministries of the Government of India also. They are in no way to interfere with the details of the Administration, the Ministers being solely responsible for the efficient working of their respective departments. The function of the Boards to be purely consultative and advisory. They will offer their opinions on any point laid before them by the particular Minister concerned or give him advice unsolicited, but he remains free to accept or reject all such advice. The Board is to meet at least once a month. Its *personnel* to consist of members half of whom should be elected by the non-official members of the Legislative Council either from amongst themselves, or from outside experts: the other half to be appointed by the Government either from amongst its own servants or outsiders. The members to be appointed for four years, but open to re-appointment. To keep up the continuity of the Board, half the members to go out every two years by ballot.

With a Council Government the post of Chief Secretary is an anomaly ; all the Secretaries should be on the same level.

SECRETARIATS.

The Secretariats are the real strongholds of the bureaucracy. It is thence that all the strings are pulled that set the District marionettes dancing. It is, therefore, absolutely necessary that their self-created complete isolation should be broken down at once, and they should be brought into the fullest touch possible with the daily and hourly needs and aspirations of the *people.* With the Secretariats manned as they are, wholly by imported agency, alien in colour, in speech, in religion, in education, in sympathies, in customs, in manners, how is it possible for them to " get into the skins " of the ruled ?

There are two ways in which this difficulty can be remedied.

One is by the removal of the colour bar, and of vested interests. The Secretariat should not be a preserve of the I.C.S. It should be thrown open to members of the other foreign-recruited services also, like the educational, to give an instance. It should freely take into its ranks Indians, thus bringing an Indian atmosphere into the alien environment. Not less than one-third of the Secretaries of *every grade* must be Indians. It might, perhaps, be helpful if the principal Secretary of an Indian Minister were an Englishman and of an English Minister, an Indian.

It may be pointed out that no Head of a Local Government, be he Governor, Lieutenant-Governor or Chief Commissioner, has ever had an Indian even as Assistant Private Secretary. Why should not every Provincial Head make it a point to have an Indian as a full, Deputy, or Assistant Private Secretary? He would be saved many a social mistake and thus escape a good deal of easily avoidable and unnecessary unpopularity.

Vested interests and colour bar thus removed there remains the *second* remedy to be mentioned. It is the abolition of hill capitals.

HILL CAPITALS.

It is absurd that very highly paid, young and energetic secretaries should find it indispensable that their work should be done in these Elysian abodes where dance and jollity and every frivolity is the order of the day, remote from the heat and dust of everyday life. There is no end to specious pleas in favour of Hill Capitals, but Lord Carmichael, late Governor of Bengal, has so far been the only high official who has had the courage and the honesty to publicly expose the hollowness of all those official arguments. Let there be no misrepresenting of our meaning. It is not the Hill *Station* that we are so strongly opposed to; it is the making of these into Hill *Capitals* that is so strenuously denounced. The leave rules are very liberal and there is nothing to prevent any official who feels low and jaded to run up to a Hill Station or go down to a quiet sea-coast town for a few weeks to recruit his health. But to have the whole machinery of government from the Governor downwards carted over to remote Hill stations for more than half the year, and all at public expense, is very reprehensible. If the health of those high functionaries is so delicately poised that they can "work" only on these cool heights, resorts of fun and frolic, safely screened from the gaze of the profane, then such people have no business to play at government. Let them take pensions and go. The sooner the better. We do not want Moses on the mountain top. We want him in our midst.

Mr. Bernard Houghton has devoted two whole chapters of his essay on *Bureaucratic Government* to a delineation of the bureaucratic mind and its methods and of its apotheosis of the Secretariat, but as the book is an easily available one and besides deserves to be studied from cover to cover, I give no quotations from it.

BOARDS OF REVENUE.

The question of the Boards of Revenue was carefully gone into by the Commission, and the Report unhesitatingly condemns them, in favour of *enlarged* Executive Councils. It is in favour of "complete absorption of the Board into a Governor-in-Council system." It also suggests that its present appellate judicial work should be made over to Judges and Commissioners. But as in our scheme there is to be no Commissioner either, all its judicial work should simply be made over to the Civil Courts. This will be merely reverting to the good old practice which prevailed up to almost the third quarter of the last century, and was done away with in a moment that was evil for the owners and tillers of the soil.

The only thing to do now is to keep up a persistent demand for the abolition of these Boards, and of the Financial Commissioners, where these take the place of the Boards of Revenue.

DIVISIONAL COMMISSIONERS.

The Divisional Commissioners are a set of officers with very undefined duties. Their work seems to be chiefly to serve as transmitting media between the District Administration and the Provincial Government. They are nowhere doing any such substantial work as could not be *better* done by already existing other agencies. A good deal of the work also seems to be very superfluous, almost seeming to have been created to give some employment to these highly-paid officers who, over and above their already very high salary, have now been supplied with a motor-car each with upkeep also free at public expense. To an outsider they give an impression of being rather an irresponsible sort of officials acting as a *wedge* between the District and Provincial Administration and preventing that thorough understanding between those who carry on the actual day-to-day business of ruling a District, and those who constitute the supervising and directing machinery of the Provincial Government, which understanding is absolutely essential to smooth, sympathetic and quick administration. The official evidence tendered by the Madras Government strenuously resisted the suggestion of introducing into the Presidency any such obstructive media, which would only tend to make friction and be more of a hindrance than a help to the quick and efficient despatch of business. The Hon. Mr. Gokhale also, in his evidence, spoke against the costly waste of Commissionerships. So far back as 1830 when barely a few years had elapsed since their creation, this question was being agitated. It was even then felt that the office was an anomaly, costly and obstructive, making for red-tape instead of quick and responsible despatch of business. Two such well-informed Civil Servants as the Hon. Frederick John Shore (son of Lord Teignmouth, Governor-General of India) and Henry St. George Tucker, both of whom rose to be Commissioners themselves—the latter becoming later a Director of the East India Company—advocate in no uncertain terms the abolition of the post which they themselves had held and whose uselessness and even mischief they had found out by personal experience. Anyone interested can study their remarks in *Notes on Indian Affairs*, of the former and *Memoirs of Indian Government* of the latter. This playing at a sort of Sub-Governorship is scarcely needed in a modern, well-knit administration. For most of us such a complete unanimity of opinion between the official and therefore expert evidence of the Madras Government and the well-informed but lay public opinion voiced by Mr. Gokhale, and which presumably is based on a fairly full trial of the system in its highly developed condition in Bombay, seems to be proof positive that no such officer is necessary.

The Decentralisation Report, however, has pronounced in favour of Commissionerships, and has even gone the length of recommending its introduction in the Madras Presidency, in the face of all the official and non-official opposition. Only general, vague affirmations are indulged in, and plenty of details about the work that should be given them. But no solid arguments in favour of Commissionerships have been advanced. Paragraph (472) cl. (1) distinctly points out the *advantage* that has accrued to Madras District Administration by the *absence* of this worse than useless fifth wheel in the administration:—

> District decentralisation has proceeded farther in Madras than in any other Province, and the Collector there occupies a position of higher authority than he does elsewhere. While this may be partly due to the large size of the Districts, it may also be fairly ascribed to the absence of territorial Commissioners.

This puts the whole case against Commissioners in a nut-shell. If there are intervening officers like Commissioners between the British unit of administration, the District and the Provincial Governments —they will inevitably affect for the worse the powers and the prestige of the District Officer. The Report is wholly wrong when it mentions as one of the causes of the higher position of the Collector in Madras, the large size of the Districts. Burma has the largest Districts of any Indian Province; Bengal too has Districts, like Mymensingh with four millions of inhabitants, richer and more densely populated than any in Madras; but the Collector or Deputy Commissioner remains dwarfed and stunted, simply because of the dense overshadowing by the Commissioner. With really representative Legislative Councils—as they emphatically are not at present—and enlarged and democratised Executive Councils there should be no intermediary between the District Officer and the Provincial Government. It was urged before the Commission that the Commissioners do a lot of useful work, and the Report would have more work thrown on them. Now it is our contention that all this work is neither all necessary nor is it necessary that it should all be done through the present agency only.

The system of territorial Commissionerships of Bombay is the most highly developed of all, but even that is full of very serious defects as the Report itself points out (p. 166.):—

"(i) There is reduplication of work in the various Commissioners' offices.

"(ii) There is absence of co-ordination and guidance, etc."

The Commission, however, failed to grasp the situation firmly and though one of the remedies suggested is an "expansion of the Executive Council," they being misled by their faith in the other remedy, suggested by them, namely, more

> **full and frequent opportunities of consultation between the Divisional Commissioners and the Commissioner of Separate Revenue,**

stopped short of the only real remedy, namely a *very fully-manned* Executive Council. An Executive

Council made up of seven to eight members including the Governor which would absorb all these Commissioners, and make them *publicly responsible* for the advice they might give is what is required.

The Report has similarly blundered in the case of Madras, as said above, by suggesting that Territorial Commissionerships be created there. If this wrong policy were to be carried out, it would only mean much heavier expense for administration and a thick veil between the Government and the District administration! The only proper remedy here also, is the *full* expansion of the Executive Council to comprise seven or eight members including the Governor.

The North-West Frontier Province, and Beluchistan like Madras, have also no territorial Commissioners.

The evidence of Mr. G. S. Curtis, I.C.S. (vol. VIII, p. 106) contains one of the fullest, most well-reasoned, and convincing arguments against territorial commissionerships, but it is too long to be reproduced here. Unfortunately, since the pronouncement of the Decentralisation Commission in favour of Commissionerships, there has been a steady tendency to increase their power and prestige, and gradually make them into a sort of Sub-Governorships, the result of which would inevitably be, in the words of Mr. Jackson, another Bombay witness, that they would "become a barrier between Government and the Collectors"—a result which he strongly deprecated.

To sum up. The work of administration is of two distinct kinds, namely (1) that which lays down the policy, guides and controls, and inspects to make sure that the policy is being carried out, and (2) that which executes. The former work is done by the Executive and Legislative Councils. The latter is done, or ought to be done, by the District Officer, whether known as Collector, Magistrate or Deputy Commissioner, and the staff subordinate to him. Between the two, no intermediaries, no curtains, no barriers are wanted. The Provincial Government and the District Administration should be left face to face.

DISTRICT (ADVISORY) COUNCILS.

I must begin by pointing out that it is a mistaken view that honorary non-official Chairmen of District Boards would ever be as successful as, to say nothing of their being more so than, paid official Chairmen, that is to say, the District Officers. The size of the Districts is too large (an average of 4,000 sq. miles) for any unpaid Chairman who will generally have more than enough private work of his own, to be able to even know all the requirements of his charge, much less be able to see them fulfilled. He is bound to be a failure, so neither the politicians should clamour for such appointments, nor should the Government yield to such shortsighted demands. But even with an official Chairman, the size of the Districts will have to be reduced. Districts going up much beyond 4,000 sq. miles must be divided up. On an average a radius of 30 miles from the Head quarters seems to be, taking every thing into consideration, a sufficient size for a District.

At present, there are Districts as large as 17,000 to 18,000 sq., miles, and a great many ranging between 6,000 to 8,000 sq. miles. Now it needs no pointing out that District Boards, as at present composed, can never carry out *efficiently* the duties laid upon them by the various District Board Acts. They can only be bodies for registering the decrees of their President, the District Officer. Local Self-Government to be real and effective must confine itself to smaller areas. Sub-Divisional (Sub-District) Boards, known as Local Boards, or *Taluka* Boards and Village Unions, are the only really workable units. Assam is the only Province in the lucky position of not being saddled with District Boards; while in the United Provinces affairs have been so ill-arranged that there are neither Sub-Divisional Boards, nor Village Unions. Madras is provided with all the three grades of Boards—District, Sub-District, and Village Union. Briefly, I suggest that District Boards of the present type should be abolished, and in every District, every revenue unit under a Tahsildar, or Mamlatdar should have an elected Tahsīl Board with the Sub-Divisional Officer as *ex officio* President for the present, and non-official honorary Vice-Presidents and Secretaries. Below these should be a number of Village Unions, (Pargana Boards) wholly elected and appointing their own office-bearers.

We may now go on to deal with the District Boards or District Councils of the kind that are being advocated by large numbers of thoughtful Indians, and even by officials, for instance, the late Mr. Jackson of Bombay and many others. But the scheme I advocate is rather different from the late Mr. Gokhale's scheme. It is this. The District Officer, for whom I propose the name of Commissioner, should of course have his authority left wholly unimpaired. The Council should be a purely advisory and consultative body and in no way *administrative* ; but, (and here comes in the difference of my scheme) it should be composed half and half of *ex officio* and elected members. The District Officer (Commissioner) to be its President, the Superintendent of Police, the Government Pleader, the Public Prosecutor, the District Engineer, the District (civil) Surgeon, the Inspector of Schools, and all the sub-divisional officers (who, by the way, must reside in their charges as is the excellent Madras, Behar and Bengal practice, and not at the Head Quarters of the District as is the undesirable United Provinces and Bombay practice); and the Chairman and the Executive officer of Municipal Boards should also be *ex-officio* members. There should be at least an equal number of elected members. Every school, teaching up to the Entrance Examination, every college, (whether 1st Grade or 2nd Grade), every Municipality, every Tahsil Board, every Village Union to elect at least one member each. If the District has other organised and registered bodies, whether confined to single castes, or devoted to political, social or other recognised purposes, these too should elect a member each for the Council. The Council must meet at least once a month. It would take me too far afield to minutely enter into the work that may well be handed over to these Councils, but as a general rule it may be said, that a good deal of work that the territorial commissioners do, for instance, the passing of Municipal Budgets, may all be safely delegated to the *Commissioner-in-Council*, as also a good deal of work of a similar kind that goes up to Boards of Revenue, for instance, Excise, or to the Secretariats, or to the many Directors and Deputy Directors, Inspectors-General, and Deputy-Inspectors-General. In short this arrangement of a (District) Commissioner-in-Council, will allow of a large amount of decentralisation, without the fear of turning every District Officer into a local tyrant. On this whole question the admirable evidence of the late Mr. Gokhale in the Decentralisation Commission Report Vol. VIII, deserves careful study.

One official argument is advanced against such (Advisory) Councils, namely that consultations do take place and advice is generally, if not freely, sought even at present, and for such a purpose merely these bodies would be useless encumbrances. Such official arguments may well be left to be answered by an official. Major General Sir John Malcolm who rose to be Governor of Bombay in 1821 wrote *Notes of Instructions* for the guidance of his English assistants. These are printed in his work, *Central India*, Vol II, pps. 447-448. He writes :—

> The next *important* point to be observed in official intercourse with the natives is "Publicity". . . . He should avoid, as much as he possibly can, *private* conferences, with those in his employ or others. These will be eagerly sought for; they give the individual thus admitted the appearance of favour and influence; and

there is no science in which the more artful among the natives are greater adepts, than that of turning to account the real or supposed confidence of their superiors. I know no mode of preventing the mischief. . . . but *habitual publicity* in transacting business. (Italics mine.)

Every word of the above is as true to-day as it was nearly a 100 years ago, when it was first written. I would only add as a qualification that the "artful natives" only mostly frequent the official circle, the genuine ones keeping at a distance for want of encouragement. I need not enter into the psychological reasons, which give rise to another seriously disturbing factor in the matter of private and irresponsible advice as compared to public and responsible advice. Every one knows that one and the same person giving advice under these different conditions gives very different counsels! I may make a suggestion here about the best way of utilising the experience and responsibility of the heads of the various Departments under the control or supervision of the District Officer. In addition to what I have suggested above, regarding their inclusion as *ex-officio* members of the District Council, I would suggest that the official subordinates of theirs should form a sort of Executive Council or Cabinet for him, and instead of being consulted privately and individually as is the usual practice, they should be consulted *collectively*.

I have already said that the delegation of much greater powers to the District Officer, which has been universally demanded by the I. C. S., would lead to the great evils of irresponsible autocracy and popular discontent. Such delegation would be not only harmless but very useful, nay, is necessary, but only when safe-guarded by such Councils.

EDUCATION.

The essential minimum of education for national and individual purposes is—that girls should become fit for motherhood, and mentally and technically fit for managing a household; and boys fit for fatherhood, and mentally and technically fit to earn a living wage for a *family*. Can anybody dare to say that such a standard holds true of even 5 p. c. of the more than 315 millions of India? What a contrast is Japan with its 95 p. c. of the population trained to citizenship! Even the Filippinos who were so downtrodden by the Spanish barely 20 years ago, have made tremendous advances under the truly altruistic administration of the U. S. A. The principle of free and compulsory primary education is now pretty widely accepted even by the official hierarchy which so strenuously resisted the late Mr. Gokhale's very mild Bill on the subject. It is only to be hoped now that the newly born goodwill will speedily materialise into action and within the next five years every boy and every girl begin to receive some instruction.

This question of universal instruction raises one very vital issue, namely that of script. This has a double bearing,

(1) On the illiteracy of the masses, and

(2) On the efficient administration of the country.

(1) The burden of numerous complicated scripts is ruinous to the country, both economically and educa-

tionally. These scripts take a very long time to master thoroughly, and so the expenditure necessary to keep the children for the time required for the instruction would be so increased that the financial burden on the State for maintaining a staff twice or thrice as numerous as would be necessary with a single and a simple alphabet, might very well be taken to be prohibitive. Then again the cost in buildings too would be correspondingly doubled or trebled. For instead of, say, ten millions of students at a time, twenty or thirty millions would have to be kept in these lowest classes, simply because of the difficulty of the alphabet. The poor students too will be sufferers in another way. All this time that is wasted in mastering the difficulties of the alphabet would otherwise be saved for much more valuable instruction. Many complicated scripts are further anti-national forces. They make for divisions where there need be none. If for instance, Marathi, Gujerati Hindi, Urdu, Maithili, Bengali, Uriya, were all to be printed and written in one script, how very much easier it would become for people to understand each other and read each other's literature; for the languages are not so very different from each other as to require more than two or three months' training in each to make one fairly at home in them.

(2) For efficient administration it is essential that every official should be able to read some at least of the Indian languages with *fluency*. Now this cannot be said of any foreign official, and even the native Indian official finds the task a difficult one. There are very few

Indian officials who are thoroughly at home in Urdu Shikast, in Nagari Ghaseet, in Kaithi and in Mahajani in the United Provinces for instance; similar is the plight of the Indian officials in the Madras Presidency with its eight different and difficult scripts. When educated Indians find the task so hopeless, is it any wonder that the European finds it even more so.

Personally I am whole-heartedly in favour of the immediate adoption of some simple phonetic form of the Roman alphabet (as I am for a simplified English spelling, if English is to be much more widely spread than it is at present) for all *government purposes* and for primary instruction. The type-writer would then become as universal in India as it is in U. S. A. with its clean and quick work, and accuracy and ease of duplications of the original. What this means in the saving of time and temper needs no harping upon. Mr. J. Knowles has been the most persistent advocate of alphabet reform in India, and it is to be fervently hoped that his labour of love may soon be crowned with success. I cannot do better than wind up this discussion with one sentence of his. He says:—

> The mental and material [and I may add moral and religious] progress of India depend largely on the answer which will be given to the question; Is India for ever to have the biggest Babel on Earth, or is a beginning to be made of national unity by the factor of a common alphabet for Indian vernaculars?

Will our leaders move in the matter and ask Government to help them to evolve a cosmos out of the present chaos; or will they allow themselves to betray the true interests of the Nation for fear of the clamour of pseudo-patriots, and thus gain a cheap popularity?

It may be necessary to guard against a misunderstanding which might arise in the mind of a hasty reader that it is proposed to *abolish* altogether the vernacular scripts. Nothing of the kind; these will continue to be necessary for special purposes, and they will continue to be learnt by the persons who devote themselves to these special purposes, or leisured people with a love for such studies.

Coming now to secondary education; it is absurd to regard it as a species of advanced book-learning. It is nothing of the sort. As the function of primary education is *preparatory*, so the function of secondary education is to produce mental development, to teach a child to *realise her or his personality in its relation to the world.* Is this possible with the present curricula prescribed for the High Schools, and with the very inefficient staff which mans them? Then the number of these schools is so few compared to the need for them.

The situation can only be met by drastic reforms all round. (a) The curricula must be recast and made so elastic that they will adapt themselves to every local need; these inevitable variations should not be forced into one shape through an official cast-iron mould. (b) The numbers of these High Schools should be so multiplied that every Sub-Division (there are as a rule not less than two or more than five in every District) will have at least one such fully equipped school. Besides these, there will of course be a number of such schools in every Municipality. (c) The *personnel* has to be considerably improved the present pay and prospects of the teachers are miserably poor and the profession does not attract the best men, but mostly only those who can find no better paid employment for their energies. Not European headmasters (who are failures everywhere) but European-lady teachers are the real need not only for girls, but even more so for boys' schools. Every headmaster, however, may well have had some European training and have a few assistants also similarly trained.

To come finally to collegiate or University education. Here again the three defects pointed out above with regard to secondary education exist even more glaringly. (a) The curricula are much too literary in their trend and the examinations are devised to lay an over-great strain on memory as against thought, culture and mental development. Even where science is attempted, it is mostly theoretical, all in the air so to say. Even in the Roorkee Engineering College, which is a professedly professional institution meant to turn out *practical* engineers and supposed to give the best training in India, the complaint is that the training while very thorough in its theoretical portion, lacks very much on its practical side. Similar is the complaint with regard to Medical, Agricultural and Commercial Colleges. To give instances, while every student is supposed to learn to deal with the eyes and teeth, how many of them are ever given the training to become practical oculists and dentists ? The Pusa Agricultural Institute, the Tata Institute, the Cawnpore

Agricultural College are all huge shams; for the amount of money spent on them they do next to no good to the country. We badly need an immensely larger amount of teaching of Applied Science.

Then there are serious defects needing immediate modification in the University Acts and Regulations. Why should not there be *separate* pass and honors courses for every degree examination? Why should not pass degrees be permitted to be taken by 'examination in compartments'? Why should not the Regulations about attendance at lectures be relaxed in certain cases? Does attendance at these blessed lectures have such a saving grace that a judicial officer or a practising pleader must not be permitted to appear at the law examinations, however otherwise fully qualified, if he is wanting in the 'open sesame' of a certain percentage of attendance at some law college? Will Assistant Surgeons and Engineers, who are daily employed in the practice of their respective professions gain anything by being required to attend professional lectures for higher degrees? Is it just, is it fair that while on the one hand the *numbers* of students that can be admitted to any class is rigidly limited, on the other hand it should be insisted on that even failures will not be permitted to appear at subsequent examinations without such attendence? Why should not free migration from College to College and from University to University be permitted, as is the case for instance, in the German Universities? If I begin pointing out every one of the endless vexatious restrictions on the good of the students imposed by unsympathetic and unenlightened government pressure, this section would grow into a big chapter. I will finish, therefore, by making just one suggestion about the staff. It will be economically impossible to get the very best Englishmen out as professors in sufficient numbers for the work, so the only sensible way is to send large numbers of Indians who are already doing teaching work, and have proved their capacity for such work, at public expense for a course of post-graduate studies in Europe and America. For these people it would not be necessary to pay at the enormous rate demanded by the foreign agency.

POLICE.

The Indian Police Commission presided over by Sir Andrew Fraser, whose Report was published in 1905 condemned in scathing terms the Indian *personnel* of the Police force, while it exonerated from all blame the European Cadre. I am afraid, however, that in this respect for some mysterious but yet guessable reason the Report has gone wide of the actual facts of the situation. If the supervising European cadre were what it should be, things would be very different from what they are universally admitted to be. To import young boys of eighteen with next to no education, and sometimes at least the ne'er-do-wells of good families, recruited in England, and environ them in India with a Police force whom the Report has condemned in no uncertain terms, and then to affect that these young uneducated British lads thrown at their most impressionable age amidst such demoralising surroundings have blossomed out into model officers is to deliberately put the telescope to the blind eye. Public opinion, on the contrary, believes that the District Superintendent of Police is often the canker, working at the roots of Criminal Justice. He listens to all the tales his native subordinates bring him, and as he has the ears of the District Officer, he generally inoculates him with all his prejudices against persons and cases, and these get reflected in the action of the Subordinate Magistracy. Reform must commence with him if the Police is to be made what it is in England. To begin with, it is a misnomer to call the department by the name of Police. It is more or less organised on the lines of the Royal Irish Constabulary—a sort of semi-military organisation, discipline and training—as an auxiliary to the military proper, for keeping the peace of the country and checking turbulence, and not so much for purposes of watch and ward, or detection of crimes, civil and political, which is now the work of the C.I.D. Then again to satisfy popular clamour the government has clearly drawn a red herring across the trail, by the creation of that mongrel cadre: the native Deputy Superintendent of Police. If the situation is to be honestly faced, the *system* which is responsible for all this muddle must be changed root and branch. Not babies but adults must be recruited. My suggestion is that the persons best suited for these higher grades of the Police Service are officers of the Army—Indian and European. Some may also be taken from those next in order of marks after those selected for the I. C. S. by examination. The Assistant Superintendentships of Police should be divided up *half and half* between Indian and European officers.

Further these higher officers of Police should also live close to the populous quarters of the towns in their charge. Is it not absurd that the highest Police Officer of the District should reside miles away in suburban villas along with other European officials in a close colony, where access to him is not very easy?

COW-SACRIFICE RIOTS.

In connection with the above subject it is very necessary to say something about this perennial source of trouble and anxiety, and the attitude proper for all concerned—Hindus, Mussalmans and the Executive.

Not till drastic measures are adopted, will this serious blot on the administration be effaced. If the 'man on the spot' about whose merits we are being constantly regaled with such eulogistic rhapsody is worthy of his salt, there should never occur any such sect riots. These occur only at particular festivals whose date is known months in advance, and ample precautions can always be taken to prevent them. To stimulate the officials to do their duty properly, my well-considered and long-meditated suggestions are :—that the District Officer and the Superintendent of Police, in whose District the riot takes place, should be *permanently degraded* and not merely temporarily superseded or in the case of the District Officer he should be shunted over to a judgeship. Further, the Inspector of Police and the Tahsildar or Deputy Collector within whose immediate jurisdiction the rioting occurs, should be forthwith dismissed from the service.

The punishment suggested is mildness itself, compared to the terrible effects on scores, sometimes hundreds and even thousands of families of such outbreaks of fanaticism. I am certain that there would be no such riots if such a Damocles' sword were to be kept hanging over the necks of the Executive. It would be some help to the administration to be told publicly what the popular belief about the origin of such riots is. It is widely believed that the Police in the majority of cases act as *Agents Provocateurs* and instead of strenuously attempting to prevent a breach of the peace, for sinister reasons, produce conditions making for fanatical lawlessness. Whether there is any truth in such rumours, which float about in the air after every such outbreak, or whether they are pure figments of disordered fancy, it is impossible to assert positively for, they have never been brought home to the officials thus maligned. But widely and lastingly held popular beliefs are seldom without some foundation.

The attitude proper to Hindus and to Mussalmans over this question needs must be frankly stated here also.

Both these must understand once for all that they have got to live together as members of a joint-family where each member has to be helpful to every other member and tolerant of the peculiarities of every other member. Constant pinpricks, intolerant bigotry, can only lead to perpetual strife and unending grief. As the

Gita says :—*through thwarted desire arises hatred and anger, these blunt the conscienee and produce confusion in the sense which discriminates what is right and what is wrong, whence proceed all unrighteousness and evil.* This national joint-family fortunately or unfortunately is of such intricate structure that there can never be a partitioning and separation as in the case of individual joint-families. Realising this we must so shape our behaviour towards each other that neither of the two partners will ever give cause to the other for the rousing of theological bitterness and strife. For weal or for woe we Hindus and Mussalmans have got to live together for eternity and it behoves us, therefore, as reasonable beings, that we shall determine forthwith that our conjoint life shall be not only as little unpleasant as possible, but as fully pleasant as mutual good-will and charity can make it.

If the religion of the Prophet of Arabia lays down that a cow and a cow alone is the sacrifice acceptable to God, then I appeal to all my Hindu brethren to tune their religious emotions so that they will not feel outraged by this act of his brother, which he firmly holds will wipe out all his sins and secure him his heaven; but if such is not the obligatory commandment of his Prophet, then it behoves the Mussalmans not to outrage the religious emotions of his brother by such unobligatory but highly irritating sacrifices. Are there no other animals which will bring him equal if not greater grace? Cannot a buffalo, which is larger and at the same time cheaper than a cow be an equally accept ablesacrifice? or goats? or camels; even if more expensive—for is not the goodwill of our neighbours and brethren very well worth-purchasing for even much greater price than that of camels? It is absolutely no use going into reasons in such a matter of the religious beliefs of the masses. They are arbitary on either side. The only point to consider is "Does the Quran make the sacrifice of the cow compulsory?" This is obviously not difficult to decide! Let it be decided by the *Shams-ul-ulamas* publishing clear passages from that sacred Book. If *it is* compulsory, then let the Hindus tolerate it whatever their scriptures say. But if it *is not,* then let the Mussalmans refrain from it, whatever the added money-cost or other inconvenience.

Coming now to music, another source of Hindu-Muslim strife, it must be admitted that the Muslim contention is the right one. Music is taboo to Islam though modern Mussalmans have taken kindly to it. The reason, apparently, is that in the early days, music could attract Bedouin marauders: while, later on, with the growth and firm establishment of Saracen power, the terror disappeared. But this does not justify the Hindus in taking processions with music so that they have to pass Islamic processions or have to traverse the roads over which mosques abut, whenever there is any chance of hurting Mussalman feeling on the point. Surely the Hindu can very well and indeed stop all music under these conditions. His religion does not require that music must be played uninterruptedly; when it nears a Mussalman religious procession or has to pass under a mosque at prayer time, it must cease.

PUNITIVE POLICE.

Few people have an imagination strong enough to realise the true nature of this utterly un-English, indeed barbarous, method of terrorising and coercing large numbers of His Majesty's Indian subjects. To bring home to my readers the distress that is inflicted by this cat o' nine tails in the hands of the Executive, I have only to mention that it is little better than the quartering of troops drunk with the lust of power on the inhabitants of a conquered town, under martial law. This despotic tyrannous method of punishing vast numbers of the innocent even more than the guilty and from which there is no appeal to any Court of Law nor any other means of escape, deserves the utmost condemnation possible. We can only charitably suppose that the Head of any Local Government when sanctioning such methods of barbarism under the persuasion of the 'man on the spot' has not imagination enough to realise the horrors to which he has condemned a whole tract of the country. The system of Punitive Police must be at once made illegal by the legislature, and a stop be put to this uncivilised device of panicky administrators.

THE C. I. D.

The Crimes Inventions Department, as the initials C. I. D. are interpreted by the people at large who have to suffer much and gain nothing through its mischievous and ubiquitous activity, is another engine of oppression. It was designed with very good motives namely that of detecting civil crime, like thefts, robberies, murders, etc., on the one hand, and on the other for giving timely information to the Executive of anarchist plots which had been imported into the country from the West. But it has been a woeful failure in respect of both its duties. The detection of civic crime is no better than what it was when in the hands of the regular police, nor is the detection of political crime any better. The C. I. D. is ever engaged like the notorious witches of Africa in smelling out sedition, and if none exists then to justify its existence and the enormous expenditure of the poor taxpayer's money upon its upkeep, it sets its inventiveness in motion to manufacture plots and treasons. This Department is mainly the legacy of the last Police Commission. Can nothing be done to put a stop to its activities and direct them into those helpful channels for which it was created ?

JUDICIAL AND EXECUTIVE FUNCTIONS.

The late Professor Sidgwick in his balanced, dispassionate way has shown the psychological necessity of the dissociation of such conflicting functions. He says :—

> It is evident that these two businesses require to a great extent different intellectual faculties and habits for their efficient conduct; the former needs a thorough and exact knowledge of the rules of civic duty that Government has to enforce, and impartiality and expertness in applying them to particular cases ; the latter demands skill in organising and combining the labour of a number of subordinates—policemen, prison officials, etc.—with appropriate materials, for the attainment of particular definitely prescribed

results. We have, therefore, *prima facie* reason to allot these functions to separately constituted organs....(*Elements of Politics* p. 333.)

The executive temper is active, bustling, motor, militant, swift to see and swifter to act, impatient of legal formalities, despises them, regards the pleader and the Evidence Act as arch-enemies, believes in Jedwood justice—hanging first, trial afterwards— is hustling, headlong, commandeering; the judicial temperament is passive, critical, doubting, minutely conscientious, regards the pleader and the Evidence Act as friends who save it from pitfalls, is philosophic, balanced, not swayed by passing moods or *ex-parte* and uncorroborated statements, lacks initiative. It will be seen from the above how incompatible the two are. If a man is a good revenue-gatherer, thief-catcher and riot-queller, it is impossible for him to also possess side by side with these abilities the immobility and quiescence of the judge and play the mill for grinding out judgments. The executive officer is the keeper of the King's peace and his treasurer; while the judge is the keeper of his conscience. Chaplain and policeman rolled into one is a most undesirable and dangerous combination from every point of view.

Unfortunately every time the question of the vesting of these two functions in two *separate* individuals *independent* of each other is pressed, the Civil Service with one accord raises the ery of Government in danger in which it is joined by the planting community and the Anglo-Foreign Press. We have only to turn to the pages of Henry St. George Tucker and of Frederick John Shore to see how thoroughly these conscientious and able administrators of nearly a century ago realised the evils of such a combination and spoke out straight in the good old way, untrammelled by modern-born official squeamishness. Tucker says :—

> Upon principle, I consider the reunion of the revenue and judicial authorities in India to be unsafe and inexpedient. The combination of such powers in the same hand is liable always to generate abuse—it is difficult to control the exercise of them by any wholesome and efficient check. These powers, so combined, were at a former period, *notoriously absurd.* (Italics mine.) (*Memorials of Indian Government.* p. 74.)

The above was called forth by Lord Bentinck's retrograde policy of *recombining* these two antagonistic functions in the same person, which policy had been condemned after a long and fair trial so far back as 1793.

Even more strong is the condemnation pronounced by Shore. In speaking of the necessity of an entire separation of the Collectorate department from the Magisterial he says :—

> The objection to the union of the two offices are, that the Collector is thereby constituted a judge of his own actions; that he is relieved from control and responsibility; and that there can be little protection to the people against extortions in realizing the Government revenue, where the same person as Magistrate, will decide a complaint against his own acts as Collector.

It may be pointed out that the strictures of Shore given above and those following apply not merely to the I. C. S. Collector, but equally strongly to the Indian agency—the Deputy Collector, the Tahsildar who both exercise magisterial power and a horde of other such subordinate officials.

This is undoubtedly a strong objection, and theoretically, quite sufficient to condemn the system at once. But unfortunately, the Collector is empowered, under color of law, to commit so much extortion, oppression and injustice, in order to realize the Government revenue,

[The writer might have here added with equal truth the words 'and also to enhance it to almost breaking point when acting as Settlement Officer.']

that, *in practice*, (italics writer's) the Magistrate is prevented from exercising any check or control over the officers employed in the collection of revenue. Provided these have a little tact, they may oppress and extort to any extent that the people can or will bear; and even should they go a little beyond their already ample legal powers, a Magistrate who should venture to punish them would soon feel the effects of the displeasure of the Government, from the representations of the Collector that he had been thwarted in his laudable endeavours to fulfil the main end and object of his appointment—namely, to realize the utmost possible revenue for the British Indian Government. Of course Government would not openly express such sentiments; it would as usual, be profuse in liberal professions, and declarations of its anxiety to put a stop to any abuse of power. . . . . . (*Notes on Indian Affairs.* vol. I. p. 68).

The words of the above quotation deserve to be pondered over carefully, for they are almost as true to-day when Lord Chelmsford is our Governor-General as they were when the above was published, during the Governor-Generalship of Lord Bentinck, ninety years ago.

Incidentally, the above quotation brings out in clear relief the truth of another Indian contention, that as all appeals in revenue matters are really appeals against the actions of a subordinate official to a higher official both acting under instructions and both equally interested in squeezing out the highest possible revenue, strict justice is more often thwarted than satisfied. In rent cases also there is a little bias present.

Would it not, therefore, be best that all rent and revenue cases went before the Civil tribunals, as is the good practice in Bengal? The quotation also proves yet another Indian contention that if the fount of Justice is to be kept free of even the suspicion of being tainted, no judicial officers should be in subordination to any executive officer. Whether he be a Magistrate or a Judge, he must look to the High Court for orders, for praise or blame, rewards or punishments. The bogey of loss of prestige is trotted out, and if it fails to frighten, then the financial nightmare of enormous increase of expenditure necessitating heavy additional taxation is produced, which dumbfounders all but those who are the true well-wishers of both the rulers and the ruled, and who refuse to be frightened out of their impregnable position by these bugbears.

What is the *prestige* of which so much is made in this country? Is it not a legacy from the vicious days of old, of that subtle power to inspire fear in and extort obeisance from the ruled towards the ruler? To what is due this power to inspire fear? Is it not the possibility, due solely to this combination of judicial and executive functions, of being injured and oppressed, and his life made one long agony, according to the enormity of his contumacy to the powers that be, and all without any redress, that is the root cause of this fear? It is because this unholy combination of powers makes of every lower Criminal and Revenue Court in India, in the memorable words of the late Professor Maitland with regard to the notorious Star Chamber, *a Court of politicians enforcing a policy, not a Court of judges administering the law*" (*Constitutional History of England.* p. 263), that it produces effects similar to if not worse than, those so strongly animadverted upon by Mr. Maitland.

Do the advocates of the argument of 'loss of prestige' realise what it means? Should people believe that because Commissioners, Governors, Members of Council, etc., have no judicial powers, therefore they are less respected than the district and deputy magistrates? This combination keeps up 'prestige' by giving to the executive officer the power to interfere in a non-judicial way in affairs, and make his will respected by means of the fear in the minds of the people of his ability to take unfair advantage of his judicial powers to get into trouble any recalcitrant person. Whether the apprehension of the people is justified by facts within their cognisance or not, is a different question and rather hard to prove or to rebut. But that this fear of an *unjudicial* interference with judicial matters is very widespread and causes resentment is certain. A question naturally arises as to which leads to greater and nobler prestige: a latent distrust of official integrity and impartiality due to the afore-mentioned fear of his confusing his two separate functions and bringing to bear the power of *both* in dealing with his separate executive and judicial duties; or the convincing of the people that any disastrous mixture of these two incongruent functions was absolutely impossible, by actual separation of them and so that officials might be absolutely trusted to deal impartially with all questions arising within their respective spheres? I firmly believe that *the loss of prestige* that the Government has been suffering from, latterly, is very largely due to this combination of the two functions, and they would recover it the day such separation was brought about and the people realised that they need no more be doubtful of the utter impartiality of the officials. The present feeling of fear and distrust will be replaced by the old one of confidence and affection and on a higher plane, because of the greater spread of knowledge now-a-days of adminstrative questions.

The argument of financial insolvency is less easy to deal with. It requires a mass of details and statistics. The well-meaning but unfortunately short-sighted gentlemen who are oppressed with the terrible fear of danger to the stability of the British Empire in the country is if such a dreadful thing as the separation of the two functions is effected, have like their Protestant Irish brothers, worked themselves into a fit of Ulsteria. If they were to calmly consider the matter they would see that *any arrangement, however admirable, if it breeds loss of trust and thence of respect and finally of good will towards constituted authority should be modified at all costs*; that no cost is too great to win the trust, the respect and the good will of the people. Politicial danger, if there be any, lies not in separation, but in keeping together in unholy wedlock two antagonistic things, which are by their inherent nature precluded from running harmoniously together in harness.

The sting of the situation lies not so much in the trial of cases by the District Magistrate himself—for it is well-known that he tries very few cases, and even these he could very well give up without imposing a burden which would break the financial back of the Government—but in the fact that while he is the head of the police, he is also the head of the magistracy, and he can make things very unpleasant, if he so chooses, for the 'native' magistrate—be he Honorary Magistrate, Deputy Collector or Tahsildar. Rightly or wrongly all the *bazaar* says that the European Superintendent of Police has his ears and the Kotwal, the S. P.'s. The Indian magistrates have to be therefore very circumspect. All this may be mere slander, but there can be no doubt of its being the current belief; and no possible ground should be given for it, whatever the cost.

But the "expense" argument too has not much leg to stand on. Complete statistics are not available, at any rate to the outsider. But it may be pointed out roughly that the money difficulty cannot be so very serious as is sought to be made out by the opponents of the schemes. If the bulk of the criminal work of the country is disposed of by Indian magistrates, could not a device be found which would, while separating the two functions, add next to nothing to the expenses of the reform ? I believe the solution is simple. *One is*, by concentrating all revenue work in the hands of a few Deputy Collectors and relieving them wholly of magisterial work. This will leave a large number of Deputy Collectors free to concentrate on criminal work. Similarly the criminal work of the Tahsildars should also be dealt with. In short the total judicial, and executive work that is done in a District, say by twenty officers, mixed and combined, should be divided up into the two classes and be done seperately by ten each out of those same twenty officers. In Madras this is largely so. There is a class of sub-magistrates who do all the criminal work while the Tahsildar does all the executive. This bifurcation works very well. It may safely be asserted that such separation cannot lead to extra expense. Mere *division* of work does not mean increase in the *cadre.* The *second* is by adding very largely to the number of honorary magistrates and thus doubling and even quadrupling the number of *benches.* Instead of, as at present, only *one* honorary court in a town, create 3 or 4 separate courts situated at reasonable distances from one another, and even in Tahsils. These benches already exercise 2nd class powers and if their numbers are increased it is to be hoped that they will be able to dispose of the bulk of the criminal cases.

I may in passing make a few remarks on this question of Honorary Magistrates. These gentlemen are now appointed simply because for some reason or other, the District Officer has taken kindly to them—an educational qualification is not an indispensable element for the nomination. There are cases where the magistrate is so unlearned that he is unable even to sign his name at the time of his appointment. The District Magistrate does not interest himself any further in the gentleman, after he has once appointed him. Now this is clearly not right. His training should be as much a matter of moment as that of a police or revenue official. If the honorary magistrate is to rise to the newer situation, his selection should be less haphazard. Even in England they found that the appointment of justices of the peace could not be left absolutely in the hands of the Lord-Lieutenants of the Counties, and an advisory committee was brought into existence a few years ago to help them to choose the right men. The District Councils, when they come into existence, would be able to give similar help. But as a beginning I would strongly urge that the gentlemen chosen for the honor —for it is an honor and people count it so, and are prepared to make some sacrifice for it—should, before being gazetted, pass an examination showing an elementary knowledge of the Penal Code, the Criminal Procedure Code, the Evidence Act, and Jail, Police, Municipal and District Board Manuals, and before they begin work they should be given a month's training in judicial work and another month in police work at some police station. I may also observe here that the Madras arrangement by which honorary magistrates have as colleagues stipendiary magistrates is a scandalous waste of time and money.

As I have suggested above that the proper designation for the Collector is *Commissioner*, so to keep with it my suggestion here is that the adjective 'Deputy' be dropped out and the Deputy-Collector should in future be known as *Collector*.

M. Chailley in his *Problems of British India* has

dealt with sympathy and intelligence with this problem of the separation of the two functions, as also with another burning topic—Europeans and the *Indian Courts*—but has in dealing with this latter subject where color-prejudice and race-passions are so easily and violently roused, most judiciously withheld all expressions of his own opinion.

While about this subject, a few remarks about the methods of Criminal Courts within Cantonment limits and on the *personnel* of these courts would not be amiss. These courts are presided over by a junior military officer who knows little of law and even less of Procedure; the result is, that not judicial but martial law is dealt out right and left. Worse still, cases arising *beyond* Cantonment limits are also sent to him for trial. All this requires remodelling. It is not at all necessary that the magistrate should invariably be a European military officer. He is not engaged in trying Europeans but Indians. Then again is it necessary that he must be a military officer? When the *executive temperament* unfits a person for holding a judicial post, much more then does the *martial temperament* unfit a man for such work requiring a nice balancing of evidence. As Tennyson says :—"Theirs' not to reason why, theirs' but to do and die." As these courts administer the ordinary everyday Criminal Law of the land and not Military Law, in the interests of tens of thousands of Indians a reformation of these courts is essential. The magistrate must be a fairly elderly man with a *sound* knowledge of the spoken language of the district as also of Criminal Law—especially of the Evidence Act and of the Criminal Procedure Code.

After all that has gone above it needs no pointing out that the present method of recruiting for the judgeships from the I. C. S. cadre is radically wrong, and should be given up. All judicial officers should be recruited from the legal profession, as is done at both ends of the line. The subordinate judiciary is appointed from among the practicing lawyers of the country, and two-thirds of the High Court Judges from among Barristers and Vakils. The District Judges may well be recruited half and half from the Indian and the English bar. With regard to pay, the gentlemen recruited in India whether from the bar or by promotion should be given a fixed salary of Rs. 1,200 per month; while those recruited in England over and above this fixed sum, an *expatriation* allowance of Rs. 1,200 per month or say a total of £ 2,000 per annum.

CONFIDENTIAL REPORTS.

It would be well to recognise that the I. C. S. officers are also made of flesh and blood, even though they be European, and are not above limitations. The widespread irritation against the system of confidential reports is not due to any absurd and unreasoning touchiness on the part of the subordinate Indian officials, on being reported on by supervising officers, but because of the present arrangements according to which they are kept confidential—and quite consistently too—not only from the public and the service but also *from the official reported on.* It is this police method of spying and tale-bearing behind one's back, that is the root-cause of all this irritation. The secrecy allows of full play to the prejudices of the reporting officer, the officer reported against becomes aware of the existence of black marks against him only by inference, when he finds that he is being constantly moved on from district to district, never gets good districts, is condemned to pass the larger portion of his service in unhealthy districts and is constantly passed over for promotion; while superannuated members of the service who are in the good graces of the powers that be are getting liberal extensions of service and thus blocking all promotions. The system requires a drastic change if genuine dissatisfaction is to be allayed. All reports favourable or otherwise should invariably be communicated to the official concerned, and in cases of adverse reports, the official concerned should be given every opportunity to vindicate himself against the charges made. At present it brings more black marks if the poor officer has the temerity to submit an application for the consideration of his case and asks for information about adverse reports against him. It may even lead to his being degraded. As reported in the papers at the time, one Burmese witness before the Royal Public Service Commission went so far as to say that the Civilian head was not always above the human infirmity of abusing his position by introducing malicious and vindictive remarks against his subordinates. This may or may not be true, for I have no first hand knowledge on the point, but I will unhesitatingly assert that equity demands a *judicial* and not an *executive* attitude in this matter. It affects the *morale* of the P. C. S. as a whole. The procedure is so characteristically un-British in its disregard of fair-play and of justice that one wonders that this method of stabbing in the dark has not been thoroughly discredited long ago. Fairness imperatively demands that all such reports should be communicated to the official concerned, and he should be asked for an explanation. Simply because a subordinate official has not been able to please his superior by playing up to his whims and crotchets, he should not carry permanently a black mark in the service, which he could very often easily explain away if only informed about it.

In this connection I would also like to say something about the "character books" of the non-official visitors and other prominent people of the district kept by the I. C. S. Collector. It is generally an innocuous thing, containing facetious, humorous, or sensible notes on the characteristics of the visitors according to the idiosyncracies of the note-writer, and handed on as an heirloom to each successor to be his guide. But sometimes an unfortunate individual has the misfortune to tread on the corns of some officer, and then woe betide the unlucky offender. It becomes a case of the Police *badmashi* Register, in a milder form! Each successive official looks askance at him and makes his life a burden, full of pinpricks, if not of much more serious trouble. I have known of such cases. Now all such people should invariably be given the chance of re-establishing themselves in the good graces of the Government. It is a very serious matter to be libelled in the dark by such powerful agencies and be without the means of rebutting the charges. Another thing. It is the offensive way in which this 'character book' is used by some officials. He keeps it before him, when a visitor is ushered into his presence, and coolly turns over its pages, to refresh his memory! I have known of such cases also.

FATAL DRAIN.

As many of the above sections have dealt with the different departments of the public service, I may now refer to the fatal drain of knowledge and experience caused by the present system of practically reserving all the high posts for Europeans.

European publicists and even a number of responsible officials who ought to know better, and most unfortunately even some Indians, regard this persistent agitation, this continuous demand, these strenuous efforts to secure a foothold in the higher adminstrative posts and especially the Secretariat, where all policies are hatched, as nothing more than a sordid and selfish hankering after the sweets of higher offices and their enormously larger emoluments. It is nothing of the kind. India feels that it is steadily losing its self-respect by being kept down to subordinate positions only. This hurts the pride of a people who were great and civilised when the Englishman was yet a naked savage in the jungles covering himself with skins and painting himself with woad. Further and still more serious injury is done to the future of the country by this system of keeping Indians out of the higher appointments. It is making them lose more and more the craft of administration and of statesmanship. The Indian has been realising that while he is employed only as a semi-skilled labourer to mind the machine, he is not given the opportunity to learn to run the machine himself. He is not being trained to be even a foreman, much less the directing head. He feels that the men at the head of affairs are all foreigners and have neither domicile nor interest in the country. So soon as their term of service is over, they carry with them to their distant oversea homes all their talent, their hard-won knowledge, their life-long experience acquired in India and at our expense, which gets lost to us totally. We, therefore, are naturally crying out in season and out of season that the children of the soil be also allowed in ever-increasing numbers to acquire the art of Government by being given the necessary training and thus of steadily building up for future generations a well-formed tradition of administration. The advocates—whether English merchants or English officials—of the policy of total exclusion of the 'natives' from the higher appointments are too late with their nostrums. The Dutch policy of keeping the 'natives' practically enslaved and ignorant of European languages and services, engaged in producing goods for the benefit of their masters as is being done in Java, South Africa and other places, cannot be carried out with safety in India with its very different past and present conditions of historical evolution, civilisation and education.

SOCIAL INTERCOURSE.

A few words on the subject of good manners and of social intercourse between Europeans and Indians would not be amiss. It is not by the herding together of hundreds of Indians with the Europeans of the station at stray garden-parties for an hour or so that real social intimacy and sympathetic understanding of each other's attitude is possible. At most of these parties there are two distinct, marked off 'pens'—Indian and European—in which gather the gentlemen, each in his own pen, and the exceptions are very rare indeed where an Indian ventures to stroll into the European crowd, or a European wanders into the Indian, unless it be the official host. Such big crowds are naturally unmanageable for all social purposes, and the only result of the time and money wasted is a sense of emptiness and dissatisfaction. It would be far better to have many more and much smaller parties of not more than 10 to 15 persons. These would allow of less formality, greater freedom and opportunities of sensible, connected conversation, instead of the snappy, frivolous nothings of big crowds. The club life of the European is also responsible to a fairly large extent for his narrowness, his ignorance and misunderstanding of Indian life; for no Indians—with very rare exceptions—may be made members. The atmosphere is also very deadening to all intellectual life, it is mostly bridge and whist and Poker. There are many minor social amenities also to be considered which, though minor, are none the less of far-reaching consequences, for instance, the question of rising to receive a visitor, of shaking hands with him, ringing for his carriage, seeing that a properly furnished room with the convenience of fans, etc., in the hot weather and a portico for use in wet weather, is set apart for visitors. The visitor should not be made to feel that he has come to worship at the temple of a god and must behave humbly. No English official ever calls on an Indian or returns his visit. The plea often put forward, that Indian homes are so arranged that it would be a burden and a bother if a European called, is not a good plea. Do not English missionaries freely call on Indian gentlemen and are gladly received and treated with all honour and politeness? Do not European travelling agents of firms call equally freely? Does the civil surgeon who is as much a gentleman as the Civilian, find it derogatory or find respect for him diminished, because he freely goes into Indian homes? The European official need not fear that he would make himself 'cheap' by such visits. He would learn a great deal more of the country and its people than he does now, wrapped up in his insularity. This bad custom of not calling on Indians has got such a firm root that even the College professors do not get into closer touch with their pupils, but stand apart like beings from a different world. The drawing room is always *taboo* to the 'native.'

In this connection it should be pointed out that some fault lies at the door of the Government also. Two little examples will make my point clear. All P. C. S. officers are addressed as Lala, Babu, Pandit or Maulvi, etc., but no sooner do they get promoted to one of the listed posts, than they begin to figure as Mr.; similarly Indians who are Barristers or hold European degrees are addressed as Mr., while the stay-at-home is given the Indian forms of address. Such a differentiation carries invidiously the suggestion that Babu, etc., are lower than Mr. Again there is the marked differentiation between English and Indian titles. An Indian does get, though sparingly, the English knighthood or baronetcy; though no Indian has yet got a peerage; but an Englishman is *never* given an Indian title. This definitely gives it a lower status. The Moghul Emperors were wiser, they made no such racial and credal difference in their awards. Hindus were made Mirzas, Nawabs, etc., Mussalmans, whether pure-bred foreigners or Indian born, were made Rajas. Why should not the so far solitary example of a Raja Brooke of Borneo be extended and Europeans in India be also made Rajas and Nawabs, Rais and Khans, Diwans and Sirdars, Shams-ul-Ulamas and Mahamahopadhyayas? Such a procedure would raise the value of these in the people's eye, and by putting both the Indian and the European in the same titular 'pen' make for better social intercourse.

I will close with a word about the suggestion worked out in detail by Sir Theodore Morison, in all good faith, we believe, but full of danger, all the same. Sir T. Morison has failed to realise the full bearings of the solution he has suggested and as to how it strikes an Indian.

In one of his books—*Imperial Rule in India*—written many years ago and presumably with a thorough and sympathetic understanding of all the conflicting factors governing the ruling of this great dependency by Britain, he has advanced the startling proposition that some *un*-important Province be *wholly* made over to "Native" agency and that the cadre composing its various services from the Head downwards should be made up wholly of Indians, without any European intermixture. The writer is discreetly silent as to the *personnel* of its military side.

We are wholly opposed to any such administrative juggling. On the first blush the suggestion made looks reasonable and very tempting; but a little closer inspection displays the cloven foot beneath the gorgeous exterior. We do not want a Republic of Liberia planted on the shores of Africa, made up of liberated serfs by the 'generosity' of America, to be set up in our midst. What we demand is the right to stand shoulder to shoulder with our European fellow-subjects of the King-Emperor and not isolation in water-tight compartments. We will not be denied our birthright to work for our country and the Empire alongside of our English co-equal fellow-subjects, in every part of it. We can afford to wait for the day when we have won by strenuous work the right to be regarded as brothers and equals and when even the most captious critic will be silenced before the irrefutable logic of facts. We in India who are in touch with the actualities governing the situation here cannot but see through this fair outer covering to the core, which is nothing else than the dominant race-prejudice which wrecked the good and humane principles of the sagacious Government of Lord Ripon and so loosened the reins of even official discipline, that Sir Rivers Thompson, the L. G. of Bengal, went out of his way to excite a "white–mutiny" against the large-hearted Viceroy, and raised up a tremendous outcry over what came to be known as the Ilbert Bill—the embers of which controversy are not quite cooled even by now. (See the whole story in Sir Henry Cotton's *Indian and Home Memories.*) In fact, it was owing to the same feeling that the Local Self-Government Scheme of Lord Ripon came to naught; year by year Administrative Circulars played havoc with the projects of the truly religious and God-fearing statesman till only a mere shadow of the original was left us, the substance having never been allowed to come into actual existence. It is the ever-present feeling of racial superiority which will not brook taking *orders* from a person of the *inferior* race or allow a "mere Native" to be in a position of authority over a European, however well-qualified he may be. The question of color is so tremendously strong, that *color-blindness* is not easy to produce. It is because of this overwhelming color-sentiment that the hands of the Government have been so tied, whenever the question of the promotion of a "Native" Civilian comes up. Not till this feeling has utterly died down will a satisfactory and lasting system for both Civil and Military arrangements be evolved; when European and Indian will work side by side and the criterion governing each case will not be race and color prejudice, but sheer, downright ability to do the work in hand. Only when this comes about will come the real heart-felt loyalty and the permanence of the British overrule in India be secured. It was only when the Mussalman rulers of India fully accepted this principle, even to the extent of intermarrying freely in the country, that their rule came to be regarded as indigenous and not alien. The Hindu was no whit behind his Mussalman fellow-subject in rendering obeisance and whole-hearted fealty to the Muslim Emperor; for was not the latter *his* Emperor as well, and were not some of them not only not ethnically different but even kith and kin, being sons of Hindu queens? By a repetition of the same process, will the Indian people receive a further increase of strength and expansion of nationality, and to the Hindus, Parsis, Mussalmans and Indian Christians, including Eurasians or Anglo-Indians being added English, Scotch, Welsh and Irish and even other

Europeans—all equally interested in the welfare and uplift of India and in the preservation of the connection with Great Britain, to the benefit of both.

SUMMARY.

1. Nine Provinces, each with a Governor and an Executive Council of six Ministers exclusive of the Governor, who will be his own Prime Minister, but without a portfolio. Their salaries and sumptuary allowances to be reduced.

2. Not less than half of the Ministers to Indians and not more than half to be Europeans. A these to be appointed by the Governor himself within three months of his taking office, and to go out within three months of his resigning the Governorship.

3. Boards of Revenue; Financial, Settlement, Excise, Territorial, etc., Commissioners all to be abolished. Their appellate work to be handed over to the Civil Courts and their administrative work to the various Ministers and to the District Officer, who should be given his correct designation namely that of *Commissioner*.

4. The other higher supervising agencies, known as Director, Deputy-Director, Inspector-General, Deputy-Inspector-General etc., etc., should be drafted into the Secretariat replacing the present Secretaries.

5. The Provincial Governments to possess full powers of *initiative* in *all* matters, subject only to the

veto of the Supreme Government, but with the right of appeal to the Secretary of State.

6. The Executive Council should meet at least once a week.

7. If a vote of want of confidence is passed by an overwhelming majority in the Legislative Council against any Minister, he must resign.

8. No less than one-third of the higher grades of the Secretariat of each Department should be filled by Indians.

9. Advisory Boards whose *personnel* should be selected from the Legislature, to be attached to each Ministry.

10. Hill *capitals* to be abolished.

11. The High Courts to be in complete *administrative* charge also of all the judicial officials.

12. Chief-Justiceships should not be a preserve of the British bar, but should be freely thrown open to *Indian* Barristers and Vakils also.

13. Not more than half the High Court Judges should be Europeans. Nor should the Registrars etc., be taken from outside the legal profession as at present.

14. Territorial limitations of the Provincial Universities to be abolished. Educational facilities to be immensely increased—especially in *applied* Science, Medicine and Engineering in all its departments—*Electrical, Mechanical, Military, Naval, Civil, Sanitary etc.*,

15. District Advisory Councils are an urgen need.

16. The Punitive Police system should be abolished totally.

17. In case of religious riots, the local officials must be punished departmentally, as a rule, without enquiry.

18. Separate the Executive and the Judicial functions and send Rent and Revenue appeals to the Civil Courts.

19. Confidential Reports against persons should invariably be communicated to them.

20. There should be fixed a reasonable salary for each post, on the basis of the Indian market. But for those services which continue to be recruited in England, over and above this, *expatriation allowances* should be given, which would be sufficiently tempting to attract the best type of men for the purpose. If an Indian has undertaken the economic burden of a higher qualification by going to Europe or Amrica he should be indemnified by an *economic allowance* of Rs. 200 to Rs. 600 per mensem according to the expenditure incurred by him.

CHAPTER V.

THE LEGISLATIVE COUNCILS.

When in the autumn of 1907 the Government of Lord Minto sent round the circular letter inviting the opinions of the Provincial Governments and of the public about the best means of so remodelling the Imperial and the Local Councils that the people of the country may be associated with the governing of their country in a much larger measure than they had been heretofore, hopes ran high that the long years of weary waiting were now to end, and our standing grievance that the people who were to be governed were allowed no voice in the matter which concerned them so vitally was going to be redressed.

But alas! for human hopes. The just and generous intentions of the two noble lords—Morley and Minto—were most effectively perverted to very different ends by the bureaucracy rampant in the Secretariats of Simla and the India Office. Lord Morley's reforming Bill, which ultimately became the Indian Councils Act 1909, and which narrowly escaped becoming a total wreck over the rocks and shoals in the shape of the Tory Lords, Curzon and Macdonnell, by the throwing overboard of some of its most important frieght, became a most mischievous law through the power it gave to the Government of India to make Regulations under it for the purpose of enlarging the Legislative Councils and arranging the machinery and method for its composition and work. The Bill, as it was originally drafted, was in itself more or less a measure of compromise, as it did not embody all the recommendations put forward by the Royal Decentralisation Commission; for instance, one of the recommendations was that not *less* than four members were to constitute the Provincial Executive Councils, the Bill had, not *more* than, this change of one word making a world of difference; and it was further shorn in the House of Lords.

Coming back to the Regulations laying down the rules governing the *personnel* of the Councils and their rules of business, we find that, hatched as they were, in the secrecy of the Home Department of the Government of India, under purely official influences, they became the source of endless strife and mischief, producing exceeding communal bitterness and ill-feeling. If only Lord Morley had remembered the words of one of his predecessors in the office, Sir Charles Wood, much unnecessary heart-burning would have been avoided, and the Hindu and the Muslim not set by the ears as they have been most lamentably for many years now, by the ill-considered action of the Indian Government. Sir Charles Wood, during the course of his speech in the House of Commons, while introducing the East India Council Bill, said:—

> I have seen a measure which I myself introduced in 1853, with one view, changed by the mode in which it was carried into execution so as to give it an operation totally different from that which I intended. The mischiefs resulting from that change have been great; and I am therefore anxious, in any

measure which I may propose, to avoid the likelihood of misconstruction or misapplication by the Government of India. (p. 175, *Indian Constitutional Documents.*)

Every one of the above words, instead of being spoken in 1861, may well have been uttered in 1909 for denouncing the Council Regulations.

Luckily for the life of the budding Indian nationality, the trend of events in Turkey, in Egypt, in South Africa, in Persia, in short, not only in Europe, Africa and Asia, but even Australasia, in the United States of America and Canada, proved to the hilt, if any further proofs were wanted, that unless India composed its benumbing creedal squabbles in matters political, her case for a self-respecting manhood asserting its rights of equality of treatment within the British Empire and of international status without it, would be lost for ever. After many tribulations and heart-searchings, the desired consummation has come and in the memorable Christmas week of 1916, the Hindu and Muslim leaders met together in Lucknow and reached the haven of a working compromise.

REPRESENTATION BY RELIGIONS.

What is the proper constitution for a Representative Assembly, which would show its true function, is easiest understood by an analogy.

As a map is which reproduces on a smaller scale all the important features of the country surveyed, and shows their inter-relations as well, not showing them as mere isolated, unrelated, or even inimical features as a superficial observer might conceivably mistake them to be, but as an inter-dependent organic whole, such should be a Representative Assembly. It should reproduce all the main interests going to the composition of a people under one administration in their proper juxta-position and their proper proportion.

Most unfortunately the scheme promulgated by the Indian Government put the Hindus in a most invidious and humiliating position of inferiority *due to their religion*, and the Muslims on a pedestal *because* of their being Muslims. The favoured creed-treatment was not extended to the Hindus in those Provinces where they were in a numerical inferiority, it being reserved for the Muslims alone.

All this roused great resentment throughout the Hindu community, with its inevitable psychological reaction in the Mussalman community, breaking down, luckily only for a time, the bridge of amity and of brotherliness of the days of the great Akbar that was being slowly rebuilt between the two.

The separatist policy which under official inspiration was in the ascendant for the last three decades has now been found out by our Muslim fellow-citizens to be a very perilous one. They have begun to realise that every community in India is necessary for the well being of the other, and none may be condemned and antagonised without peril to the whole. But it will take long before the evils of the past die, and Mussalmans realise that *separate* electorates do not make for *united* nation. The demand for a representation of all the main religions should be continued to be satisfied as long as such demand exists in its present intensity, *but,* let us hope and pray that the good sense and patriotism of our co-citizens will convince them of the disservice that an insistence on a creedal electorate register does to the cause of United India. Lord Morley, out of his great sympathy with our political aspirations and his keen insight into the ways and means of promoting racial and creedal amity and brotherliness among divergent peoples, acquired in the difficult school of the administration of Ireland, suggested a very helpful scheme, but which at the time, most unfortunately, met with a curt reception.

His scheme was to create an Electoral College in which both Hindus and Muslims would be represented in the proportion in which they existed in a Province, and this Electoral College was to elect so many Hindus and so many Muslims, each member having only one vote. He laid stress on this point of a single vote, because he realised what the Government of India would not see, having determined to shut their eyes for reasons best known to themselves, that the scheme proposed by the Indian Government while it would give Muslims plural voting, and that too on a register best calculated to fan into flame the religious animosities and fanaticism, bringing to the top creedal bigotries, it would shut Hindus out from any part in the election of Muslim candidates. He points out that after being given special electorates, the Muslims should be prevented from voting in territorial electorates, for "if that were not done, they would evidently have a double vote, and this would probably be resented by other classes of the population." The Government of India in spite of the definite and unequivocal disclaimer of the Muslims against being given a double vote in their Memorial to the Viceroy in 1909 (of the All-India Moslem League) and the warning of Lord Morley still gave them this strife-breeding privilege!

To come back to the scheme, he wrote :—

> In this way it is evident that it would be in the power of each section of the population to return a member in the proportion corresponding to its own proportion to the total population.

Now mark his reasons for advocating single voting in mixed electorates:

> The political ideas at the bottom of that recommendation which has found so little favour was that such composite action would bring the two great communities more closely together, and this idea of promoting harmony was held by men of very high Indian authority and experience who were among my advisers at the India Office.

All Lord Morley's good intentions came to nothing. He was successfully 'bluffed' by the Indian Government into dropping his wise and equitable plans in favour of its own. Everybody knows that no organism, howsoever feeble it may be, ever willingly parts with any attribute or power it may have. What, then, about such a mighty bureaucracy which holds India in its grip? No blame to it that it will not allow any of its powers and privileges to be diminished. Do we not see this fight for power going on every night on the floor of the House of Commons? No quarter is given or asked. Party supremacy is above all the laws of Ethics. The Indian Government, past masters in the art of what on a famous occasion

Disraeli described as "dishing the Whigs," practised this art of "dishing" by so manipulating the electorate that instead of the threatened bridge being built between the two communities the chasm was made wider, and for the time being the danger was averted and the power remained where it had been for so long.

However, all this has become 'ancient history' now, and a *via media* has been found by the two communities. It would, however, not be equitable to the other smaller communities now, not to extend to them this same principle of being represented by men of their own faith and in a larger proportion than they bear to the population at large the Sikh, the Parsee, the Indian Christian, (these would, of course, include the "domiciled community", the Eurasian, Anglo-Indian, etc)., as also to the Hindus in those areas where they are in a numerical inferiority. The question of Jains and Buddhists does not arise, for the former are for all practical purposes as much an integral part of the ocean of Hinduism as the numberless other sects; while the Buddhists are all concentrated in Burma, and Ceylon, which last is still unfortunately kept politically separate from India and of which it ought to be made an integral part, the sooner the better. Sikhism is on the border line, and it is best to give it the benefit of the doubt. It will be to the lasting good of the country to help to make this 'protestant' movement in Hinduism, a prepotent one and not allow its force to be dissipated.

In winding up all this discussion over separate

creedal electorate registers and representation by members of their own pursuasion, I cannot do better than quote the memorable words of Sir Edward (now Viscount) Grey when speaking in the House of Commons in 1912 on the Home Rule Bill for Ireland. We have only to substitute Muslim for Ulster and Indian Congress for Irish Nationalist for every word of that wise exhortation to apply to the conditions of India. Referring to the animosity of Ulster and the opposition of the Conservatives which was based on that animosity he said :—

From what does the real opposition to the Bill proceed? It is not the question of the Constabulary, of Customs and Excise, whether there is to be a Senate, whether nominated or not. Those are not the real causes which inspire the opposition. There are two things which inspire the opposition. One is the vehement opposition of Ulster to the Bill and the support which it receives. It is exceedingly difficult, I admit, for us to deal with the question of Ulster. We are told that it is they who will suffer and not we; that they know and we do not know, that we have no means of mitigating their animosity. They must let us state our point of view. We have here a great problem to solve, and it cannot be solved by strong feeling or the use of strong language. (*Cheers.*) One thing we cannot do for Ulster, and it is to sacrifice the House of Commons or the Central Imperial Government to Ulster feelling. (*Cheers.*) If Ulster defeated the solution we propose, or succeeded in making it impossible, we cannot afford to continue the present state of affairs. Some other solution will have to be found through this House to put the control of Irish affairs in Irish hands. That has to be done : It is necessary for the House of Commons, it is necessary for the Cabinet. You cannot in the long rnn have a Cabinet to manage all the important external and imperial affairs, and at the same time undertake the task of being responsible for the Executive in Ireland when that Executive may not have the good will of the people behind it. (*Hear, hear.*) On this point the Nationalist members are equally convinced of the importance of Ulster in the good working of Home Rule. (*Cheers.*) I will come in a moment to the difference of national feeling between the British and Irish peoples, and I admit that there is some difference. But it is not a difference which means that political resistance is not going to yield to moderation, toleration, and circumspection, to that sense of obligation which is in every civilized community. (*Cheers*). When Ireland is responsible for the Government of Irish affairs, I am quite certain the last thing an Irish Executive or an Irish Parliament will do will be to provoke a strong minority in Ulster to resistance based upon the moral wrong and unreasonable treatment. (*Cheers.*) Though members from Ulster may not believe that, I believe that nothing can resist the working of those forces, and that the animosity which may exist between different parts of Ireland to-day is no measure whatever and no guide to what the feeling will be when the different parts of Ireland have for the first time a sense of joint responsibility. (*Hear hear.*) Once put them in a condition in which they know that the welfare of both depends on the good will of each that will work. It will be effective in Nationalist circles and it will be effective with the Ulster minority. (*Hear, hear.*) Nothing I believe can resist that. They have never had in Ireland that sense of responsibility. Neither party has had it. On the contrary, they have been free to let their animosity and differences of view reach whatever point they like between them, feeling that all the time it is the business of a British Government here to protect either of them or both of them from the consequences. Therefore, the feeling which exists under present conditions is no measure or guide whatever to what it may and, I believe, will be, under other conditions (*Cheers*).

FUNCTION OF THE LEGISLATURES.

Every such assembly, if it is to do its proper work, must not be confined to the work of assenting to the laws proposed to be enacted by the Executive as the Indian Legislatures largely are. The very nature of its being demands that it should be the 'grand inquest' of the Nation. It must not be fettered if it is to fulfil its mission. It follows from this that all rules and regulations for disallowing questions ; of restricting the rights about supplementary questions ; of moving resolutions ; of 'dividing the House'; of initiating legislative measures; of control over the Budget, are so many fetters hampering it in its proper work. Why should there be in the Executive the power to disallow questions, when it has the power of not answering such as are against the public weal ? Why should the power of asking supplementary questions be restricted to the person who has asked the question on which it arises? There is no good reason why every member of the legislature should not have the power of putting such questions irrespective of whether he or some brother-legislator was responsible for the original question. Why should there be any restrictions on the power of elected members to introduce Bills? We shall suppose for argument's sake that there is a large non-official majority in the Council. Is not the Government assumption on which such restrictions are based, tantamount to saying that the whole body of these elected members are either so corrupt or so dishonest or such noodles that one and all will easily lend themselves to a few designing anti-Government and anti-people miscreants? It is a very untenable position. The stability of the administration is in no way endangered, even taking for granted the monstrous proposition that neither the brains nor the characters of the 'Honorable Members' is to be trusted, for has not the Administration the full mastery of the situation by a regular hierarchy in an ascending scale of the power of veto? Even where the Executive is wholly under the control of the people, 'the power of the purse' is specially jealously guarded against all encroachments of the Executive and even of an Upper Chamber. What shall we then say about its essentialness in countries where the Executive is the master of the situation. If extravagance and wild-cat schemes involving huge waste in the selfish interests of the Services and of favoured adventurers are to be prevented and the people saved from grinding taxation and economic ruin, then it is the barest justice that their representatives should have control over taxation and expenditure.

The question of 'freedom of speech' does not seem to be very clearly settled. There is no mention of the subject in the Act nor does there seem to be any in the Regulations. As it is a matter of very serious import, it ought to be specifically included in the Act itself, as it has been in the cases of the Acts granting Constitutions to the Dominions.

SESSIONS.

Further, as the sessions of the Councils are discontinuous, and solely dependent upon the will of the Executive, which is not under its control, it is essential that a minimum period be fixed by the Act, (not by Regulations) for the number of times that meetings must take place, and the time that may elapse between a previous meeting and the next. The power of prolonging it or holding extraordinary meetings should be left to the legislatures as also to the Executive.

More than three months should not be permitted to intervene between one meeting and the next of the Imperial Council and more than one month of the Provincial Councils. It will probably be found that a minimum of forty working days for the Imperial Legislature and of sixty such days for the Provincial would be none too much.

The despatch on the reform of the Legislative Councils of the Government of Lord Minto to Lord

Morley among other matters specifically pointed out two drawbacks to the proper utilisation of the Councils as they then existed, namely,

(*a*) "their meetings are too infrequent to offer the means of confidential and intimate consultation between the Government and its subjects," and

(*b*) "the strict procedure by which they are restrained naturally tends to formality."

With regard to both these drawbacks so definitely pointed out by the Government, the question naturally arises whether it is not the Government itself which is to be held to blame in the matter. There are various ways by which the rigidity of the procedure could be softened and the cast-iron forms made sufficiently malleable when circumstances so required, without destroying the necessity of formality in everyday matters, to allow of free and easy or "confidential and intimate consultation" if the Government were so minded. The procedure of the House of Commons will suggest many such ways.

With regard to the charge of *infrequency of meetings*, the attitude of the Government is very peculiar. The Government of Lord Minto complains of infrequency of meetings, and a decade later we find the Government of Lord Chelmsford resisting and out voting the motion of Pandit Madan Mohan Malaviya for *less erratic* and *less* infrequent meetings! To a psychologist seeing the motives below the surface, inspiring the apparently opposed attitudes, the explanation is clear. The *head* of the bureaucracy recognises the necessity of frequency of meetings, but its *heart* rebels against it. A Council of Representatives in *permanent session* before which the Executive has to be incessantly justifying its 'omissions and commissions' is a nuisance, besides being so degrading to its *prestige*; so let us have as little of it as decency and the necessities of the situation will permit!

On this point the views of John Dickinson criticising the bureaucratic attitude of mind which sternly repudiates the doctrine of *Government of the people, for the people, by the people,* in favour of the other, namely, Government of the people, by self-appointed Governors and only so far in the interests of the people as these do not clash with the interests of the Governors, deserves quotation in full. The whole pamphlet, published in 1853, deserves even to-day careful study, especially two of its eight chapters, namely, the Ryotwar System, and Finance and Public Works. He says:—

> But now see the cruel injustice we are doing to India! We do not find it too much for ourselves to have a Parliament sitting for months every year, to correct and extend our legislation and suit it to our social changes; to have besides, the most perfect representation of all our complaints and desires in the press which it is possible to conceive; and with all this to watch vigilantly the responsibility of every depositary of power amongst us, as our only security against official tyranny, neglect, incompetency, and plunder; and, after all, we probe many serious greivances, and the reader of the public journals for the last year alone is familiar with much deserved blame of every department of our Administration, of the Foreign Office, the Colonial Office, the Horse Guards, the Admiralty, the Customs, etc. Can we then affect to believe that a sham enquiry once in 20 years, with almost total neglect in the interval, is sufficient to redress the grievances of India? Can we pretend to think that the despotic administration of 150 millions of men, conducted at a distance of many thousand miles away from us, by a few hundred foreigners, having little intercourse with the

natives and no permanent stake in their country, and directed by irresponsible Home Authorities, who betray the utmost anxiety to conceal the truth from the public, can we pretend to think that such an Administration has done or is doing justice to the people of India, without being checked by a particle of anything like political representation ? Would not any man who had studied history or human nature, divine all the injury and injustice to the natives which I have described, from merely knowing the conditions of our irresponsible Indian Government ? Let the reader conceive any one English question, parliamentary reform legal reform, free trade, any one of them, being turned over to the Ministry of the day and their successors for 20 years, to give or withhold at their pleasure, without hearing one word of explanation, or remonstrance, or information of our interest in the matter, and our sufferings for want of a legislative remedy. Would not this seem monstrous in our own case ? Why then do we unscrupulously apply it to India ? Why do we treat, not one, but all, of her vital questions and dearest interests in a manner which seems monstrous when applied to ourselves ? Oh, my countrymen ! do not continue this inhuman system. Do not consign India to an irresponsible Government for another 20 years, and coldly tell her "abi in pace," as the Inquisition used to say in sending its victims back to the torture, when you know it must lead to cruel neglect and mal-administration. (*India : Its Government Under a Bureaucracy.* pp, 193 to 195.)

PLACE OF MEETINGS.

Lord Hardinge, with shortsightedness that was strange in a statesman so alert and so sympathetic, would not listen to the protests of Mr. Gokhale against the making of the Legislative Council chambers an *annexe* of gubernatorial palaces. The Indian statesman with truer insight into the future, rightly insisted that the future Parliaments required buildings standing in their own grounds, wholly dedicated to their work and under their complete control. Even though the meeting place of the Imperial Council in new Delhi has been built as a wing of the Viceregal palace, bricks and mortar cannot make it a "settled fact." The demand for a separate building must be insistently kept up till such time as not only new Delhi, but every provincial capita also has its own separate housing arrangements for its Parliament. Plans of the 'Parliament' buildings of the Continent, of the Dominions, of the United States of America, should be obtained and with their help a fitting plan devised to suit our conditions, for the Imperial Legislative Council (the Senate) and the Provincial Legislative Councils (the House of Representatives.)

It should be clearly understood that no Council meetings should ever take place up in the Hills. Government from the safe playground of hills has been the bane of Indian Administration. Not only we but also the non-official Europeans have been crying themselves hoarse over this playing with such awful responsibilities as those of governing a vast and varied country. There should be no such mischievous things as Hill *Capitals*. So far there has been only one single voice, namely, that of Lord Carmichael, which has been blunt enough and honest enough to confess that hill stations are not the ideal places for real hard work as they have been made out to be by those whose interest it is to enjoy life there at the expense of the poor Indian taxpayer.

ELECTION DATE.

It is a good arrangement by which the dissolution of all the Provincial Legislatures takes place almost simultaneously. It would be immensely better to so arrange affairs that the life of the Legislatures should correspond with the tenure of office of the Governors. Those rare cases, where a Governor has died in office, or has resigned, or been recalled might be supposed to create a situation which would make such squaring of the gubernatorial tenure of office with the fixed quinquennial Council period impossible. It is only a seeming difficulty. As the five year term of office of the Governors is only a matter of convention and not fixed by statute, it can be easily arranged that when a term comes to an untimely end, the successor's tenure of office might be either shortened, if the predecessor had been in office for a very short period only; or lengthened if he had been in office for the major portion of his tenure. Thus will be reproduced here the condition of affairs in Great Britain and the Dominions, where a new Prime Minister with his new Cabinet meets a new Legislature. In those countries this is brought about by the dissolution of the Lower Houses; here it will be brought about much more simply and much more economically by a manipulation of the term of office of the Governor. To fully understand the bearing of the above argument it has to be remembered, that the Governor-General and the Provincial Heads are their own Prime Ministers.

CONTROL OVER THE SERVICES.

One constantly hears in India the phrase 'rulers and ruled'; the universally-accepted connotation of which is that the I. C. S. is the ruler and the Indian the ruled. Courtesy bred of modern circumstances is, however, making the Britisher mildly deprecate the phrase when used publicly and give some such inane explanation as that we are all fellow-subjects of the King, etc. But the actualities of the position will unfortunately not allow of such a cheap cove ring up of the reality.

Mr. Fisher (now a member of the British Ministry, in charge of the Education Department) one of the Commissioners on the Royal Public Service Commission on India and so one who cannot be flippantly dismissed as the globe-trotting Pagett M. P. of Anglo-Foreign papers, says of the English Civil Service :—

It is brought into continual contact with Parliamentary life and Parliamentary criticism by the questions addressed to Ministers in Parliament, and, lastly, it works under the direction of Parliamentary chiefs. The Civil Service of Great Britain is never permitted to forget that it is in a true and literal sense a body of servants whose work is liable at any moment to be brought under the master's eye. That it has escaped or can entirely escape the characteristic vice of all bureacracies cannot, perhaps, be confidently affirmed, but if it is comparatively free from that senseless surplusage of reglementation which is common in autocratic countries, the cause is to be found in the last two of the four safe-guards which have been mentioned, the Parliamentary critic in the House, and the Parliamentary chief in the office. In other words, administrative questions cannot be considered in a purely dry light; they must be viewed in a political light. And it is an essential part of the skill of an experienced civil servant to feel how a measure will represent itself to the vision of Parliament, and with what modifications it may be made acceptable. The machine is continually up against the living forces of opinion, which, despite all party discipline, make themselves felt in the House of Commons, and since the members of the Civil Service are obliged to furnish answers to parliamentary questions and apologies for departmental actions to their parliamentary chiefs, they acquire a wide kind of political education, tending perhaps towards a certain spirit of caution or even timidity, but based upon a close apprehension of the views, prejudices, and aspirations of the country.

In the Crown Colonies, and more particularly in India, the spirit of the Administration is widely different. Here the Administration is the Government, and nothing else particularly matters. Questions, indeed, may be asked in London about Indian affairs, but nobody is particularly interested in them, and the Indian Budget night is notoriously regarded as one of the least interesting occasions of the session. . . . In reality the last word lies with Indian Official opinion in the sense that a measure would not be forced upon India against the united opposition of the Indian bureaucracy. . . . . The work of administering India is not done in London. It is done in India itself. It is for this reason that the organisation of the Public Services of India is a matter of such great importance. . . . The Indian Civil Service is the Government. . . . Cabinet Councils, Government majorities, diplomatic agencies in the Native States, administrative agencies in British India—all are provided by the Indian Civil Service, which is expected to turn out Judges, revenue officers, heads of administrative departments, pro-consuls, legislatures, political officers or diplomatists, and under the new regime, parliamentarians as well.

The supremacy of the Indian Civil Service among the Public Services of India is one of the leading facts which every student of Indian administration has to take into account. The Civil Service is the political, the governing service of the country. . In the Table of Precedence an Indian Civilian will always rank above a member of any other Indian Service. . . the other services are excrescences. . . however distinguished an officer of these services may be, he is always subordinate to the head of the district who is a civilian.

This pre-eminence enjoyed by the Indian Civil Service in India is, perhaps, most clearly illustrated by the position of the Secretariat. In view of the fact that parliamentary government does not exist in India it might have been expected that the Governor or Lieutenant-Governor of an Indian Province would rule with the assistance of a Cabinet composed of the administrative heads of the different departments, that the Education Service would supply him with a Minister of Education, the Public Works Department with a Minister of Public Works, the Forest or Agriculture department with a Minister of Agriculture. This, however, is not the case. These departments indeed do possess official heads, but they are not part of the Provincial Government. Their work comes up in the first place before a Secretary to Government, who is always a member of the Indian Civil Service, and no large proposal can be carried into effect without the imprimatur of the premier service. Some day, with the growth of specialisation and complexity, this hegemony may be broken down . . . There is a wide demand that the Indian Civil Servant shall no longer rise to the Judical Posts of District, Sessions and High Court Judge or exercise magisterial functions, and that the Indian judiciary should be filled by a separate form of recruitment. . . In India the Civil Servant is, as has been said, the most highly paid agent of the Government. In Nigeria the Civil Engineer commands a higher rate than the head of the District. If an administrative system had to be created for India for the first time to-day, it is very unlikely that it would assume the shape which a long train of historical circumstances has given to the present system. There would be a single Civil Service of India, divided into a number of branches, executive, judicial, medical, agricultural and the like, each recruited at the rate at which work of the type required can be supplied. There would be no one service so prominent among the other services as is the Indian Civil Service, or so exclusively entrusted with the central functions of advice at the head quarters of Government. The executive head of the Government would have a wider choice of secretaries and advisers. There would be more eqality in pay and prospects between the different branches of the public service, more interchangeability, a less rigid system of administrative caste. (*The Empire and the Future*, pp. 51, 57).

The above rather lengthy extracts from the lecture on *Imperial Administration*, included in the above-named work may seem like a digression ; they are not really so. It was necessary to fully bring out the super-eminent position of the I. C. S. before their restiveness under criticism could be properly realised. For, persons not intimately acquainted with the situation are apt to be misled by the name Indian Civil *Service* into regarding it in the light of their English experience as an organisation of glorified clerks, of subordinates, and not as an oligarchy of masters.

It will be seen that out of the four safeguards against the misuse of its powers by a bureaucracy mentioned by Mr. Fisher, two of the most important ones do not exist in India, while a fifth, which is no less serious, and which does not occur in the statements quoted above is, that this bureaucracy is wholly alien—differing in religion, in colour, in race, in language, in traditions, in temperament, in almost everything but a nominally common humanity. This makes the factor of its complete isolation from the social life of the people, and with its almost total independence of their wishes, the problem becomes much harder in India.

It is for putting a curb on this omnipotence, that we so strenuously demand a powerful Legislature. It is for enlightening this omniscience that we so insistently demand a representative Legislature. It is because the Indian Civil Service despises light and hates a curb, that it so zealously resists the demand for a wide franchise, for non-plural voting, for direct elections, for larger councils, for non-official majorities, for permanent sessions, and finally for non-official Presidents of the Legislatures appointed by themselves. As Legislatures are, according to its conception of its work in India, evils, though unfortunately unavoidable ones, it has made them as inert and as innoccuous, as bureaucratic ingenuity could make them, though in its attempt to utilise them as weapons against the budding national consciousness, thanks to imperative circumstances, it has not been wholly successful.

MISNOMER.

I may, in passing, point out that the name *Legislative Council* is a misnomer. It would be correct enough if its function was merely to grind out Acts, but as it even in its present manacled condition is something more than that, it should be renamed fittingly. There is a good deal in a name as every psychologist knows. A well-selected designation is a powerful factor towards the realisation of the purpose for which the name was bestowed. The House, Assembly, or Council of *Representatives* seems to be a proper designation. It has the high authority of the late Prof. Sidgwick to recommend it, and still better its adoption by the United States of America and the British Dominions and Crown Colonies. The Supreme Council should be named the *Senate.*

NUMBER OF MEMBERS.

The joint scheme of the National Congress and the Muslim League asks for a membership of 150 for the Imperial Council with four-fifths elected and one-fifth nominated, and for the Provincial Councils a like proportion between elected and nominated but a smaller number, namely, 125 for the major Provinces and 50 to 75 for the minor ones.

This is rather an arbitrary way for fixing the number of representatives. A much better way, and which has universal practice to support it, is the fixing of the number of such representatives on a *population basis*, as bearing a definite relation to the population to be represented, and rising or falling automatically after each census. I would suggest for the present one representative for every half-million of the population for the House of Representatives (Provincial Council) and one Senator for every three million of the population for the Senate (The Imperial Council). This comes near enough to the numbers demanded in the Congress-League scheme. If the demand put forward by the scheme were to be fully granted, it will mean that twelve-hundred legislators will have to be forthcoming. I am afraid, however, that for sometime to come we will not be in a position to meet such a large demand, satisfactorily. The scheme suggested here would require only a little more than half that number.

The Congress-League scheme has unfortunately erred also in neglecting to take account of Indian India, and has thereby left out seventy millions of the population of the country. If I may make bold to offer some suggestions on this point I would suggest that the 'Native States' of India should not be left out. It is a very short-sighted policy which would keep *British* India and *Indian* India in watertight compartments. Indians at least should not be guilty of such a blunder. Mr. H. A. L. Fisher, M. P., son-in-law of Sir C. P. Ilbert, after his tour through India as a member of the Islington Royal Public Service Commission, realised the *vital* nature of the action and re-action of Native States and British India. In his lecture on *Imperial Administration*, reprinted in *The Empire and the Future* he says :—

> If ever India is removed from the category of dependencies into the category of dominions, the constitutional pattern of the new state must be a federation in which hereditary monarchies and principalities are included as constituent parts. (pp. 66, 67).

We need not stop to squabble over the portentous "if ever" which may mean *never*, nor over his other suggestion that Great Britain should create many more Native States in British India, (he is wisely reticent as to whether they are to be of a Monarchical or Republican pattern) and which Mr. Fisher candidly admits will meet with no support from the Indian leaders of political thought. Mr. Fisher cannot but be ignorant of the woeful conditions of affairs in many of the Indian States, for his two winters in India were fully taken up with his work on the Public Service Commission, and he could scarce have had enough time to devote to a deep study of 'Native' India. An open-eyed tour through some of the Hindu as well as Mussalman States after a course of studies of the secret archives of the Foreign department containing the annual Reports of the Residents, would have opened his eyes to the true state of affairs. But when men of great Indian experience like Sir Walter Lawrence, or Sir Thomas Holdich (see his latest book *Boundaries and Frontier-Making*, where his rabid color prejudice stalks abroad unabashed) advocate the creation of a congeries of Native States out of British India, one cannot help suspecting their motives, and rubbing his eyes and asking:—Can it be that they wish the *Native* to stew in his own juice?

But, as here we are only concerned with the ways and means making for the much desired *rapprochement*, it is not worthwhile going further into that matter. One of the most helpful ways is by giving a representation to the Indian States in the Imperial Legislative Council. I have already outlined in my chapter on *The Indian States* a scheme for marshalling these States in five groups and how each *group* is to be represented in the Council of Princes. This group system would come in very handy for sending representatives to the Supreme Council. Each group should elect for the period of five years five representatives, thus making a total of twenty-five. This is a very right proportion also, seeing that while the States cover a third of India, their inhabitants number only a fourth of the total population. One limitation about who may not be elected is very necessary, namely, no ruling Prince should be eligible; these should sit only with their peers in the Council of Princes. Beyond this there need be no further restrictions. The question of the electorate for these will have to be settled in consultation with the States, and need not detain us here. Whether these should have representation in the Provincial Councils also, in those cases where their territories are mixed up with British India, is a question worth serious consideration.

With regard to the question of the one-fifth *nominated* members, while expediency requires that there should be a number of members under the direct control of the administration, no case seems to have been made out for these being non-officials or 'experts.' Instead of the discredited system of nominations, the plan of having one-fifth *ex-officio* members has far more to recommend it. The Viceroy, his Ministers, the principal Secretaries and other high officers of his Government would thus be automatically members of the Supreme Council (the Senate), while the provincial Heads, with their official entourage would be equally automatically members of their respective Provincial Councils (the House of Representatives). Marshal MacMahon understood how much odium nominations brought to the nominator and was very careful in not being made the scapegoat for the sins of his nominees. J. E. C. Bodley in his *France*

(p. 275) says: "He foresaw that the President, if he accepted the right of nomination, would be identified with the performances of his nominees" and so refused to accept the dubious privilege. The position of the nominated non-official member is a very invidious and thankless one. He cannot sit on the fence. Come down he must to the arena, and get flattened out between the upper official and the nether popular mill-stone. The affectation of free and independent discussion and vote is a pitiable farce unworthy of such solemn occasions. It deceives no one but only makes the administration an object of ridicule.

With regard to "Experts" how can the Government be helped in the matters in which it keeps the right of appointing one or at most two specialists. Their votes would not be enough to turn the scales in case of an adverse attitude of the Council. These could be fully and properly utilised by so modifying the procedure that the whole Council could sit as a committee, as is done in the House of Commons, and hear and question the expert on the points which the administration thought it necessary to get expounded by a specialist to the members.

OFFICIAL MAJORITIES.

Lord Minto was for permitting non-official majorities in every Council. Lord Morley, hovewer, vetoed the proposal as regards the Imperial Council, while in the Provincial Councils, though the doctrine of non-official majorities has been accepted, this has been done with such stringent limitations, that it is as good as non-existent. It is because of this ever-present prejudice against non-official majorities in the minds of our rulers that an expansion of the membership of the Councils presents such formidable difficulties. There is always present the necessity of having a very large number of Government officers to take part in the deliberations, which would mean enormous cost and great dislocation of work. I would ask here, is it necessary to increase very much the numbers of these highly paid official members, and take them away from their own legitimate work for the sole purpose of watching the Viceroy's face and saying ditto to His Excellency? When nobody even dreams of questioning the power of veto exercised first by the Governor-General in Council and finally by the Governor-General individually and then again by the Secretary of State, where is the danger, with such *triple* barred gates, of the power of the Government being defied and set at naught? The presence of the official members in the Council is a make-believe which deceives no one. They are there not for a free and independent discussion of the subjects presented to that body but only for voting with the Government. Why should Government with its triple veto make elaborate arrangements to keep up this farce of an independent discussion and voting? It straightforwardly declares that "if two men are not able to wield one sceptre, it is idle to dissemble that fact in constructing political machinery."

The question, then, as to "what number of official

members of requisite standing and experience can, without detriment to the public service, be spared from their regular duties for attendance in Legislative Councils" in my humble opinion does not arise at all. I have not the least hesitation in asserting that for this purpose alone not *one* official can be spared without detriment to the public service. All the officials that the Government proposes to bring into the Legislative Council might, with great advantage, be left to do their own legitimate work; while the power of the veto when necessary might be exercised a little more directly than as at present through the mouth of nominated members, and so avoid adding to the already heavy financial burden of the country in the shape of the pay and travelling allowances of these official members. This safeguard is *quintupled* in the case of the Provincial Councils; for there two more authorities—the Governor and the Governor-in-Council—intervene. Once this fact is realised, that however large the number of non-official members a legislature may possess, it exercises its *powers* under very stringent safeguards, and so can never become mischievous; (if one may permit oneself to make use of such an expression in regard to such responsible bodies composed of the elect of the Indian nation) the official opposition to large numbers would get considerably modified. The opposition to elective majorities would be still further weakened, when it is borne in mind that the Defensive and the Political Departments will be virtually independent of the Legislature for some time to come.

ELECTORATE.

The detailed scheme for the franchise can only be properly worked out by a select committee of all the Legislatures but some of the principles on which such a scheme should be based may be briefly enumerated here.

(*a*) It should be territorial. This does not imply that artificial single member constituencies are to be created. Single member constituencies invariably result in the practical disfranchisement of very substantial minorities.

(*b*) It should not permit of plural voting. At present there are cases where so many as seven votes are permitted to one individual!

(*c*) It should not, by prescribing rigid rules of domicile or by limiting the choice as for instance of landlords to a landlord, or high property qualifications, make it difficult to return a worthy representative. Lord Bryce in *The American Commonwealth* has very clearly pointed out the evils of such restrictions. He says:—

> Inferior men are returned because there are many parts of the country which do not grow statesmen; . . . . men of marked ability and zeal . . . are produced chiefly in the great cities of the older states.

And, as

> there is not room enough there for nearly all of them

and as

> no other doors to Congress are

open to them

> the nation is deprived of the benefit of their services.

Such limitations have the further demerit of interrupting careers which might have proved of great service to the country:—

A promising politician may lose his seat in his own district. . . . (and) since he cannot find a seat elsewhere, as would happen in England, he is stranded.

(*d.*) It should be on as broad and as direct a basis as is possible in this country at present.

How very irritating and undesirable the present franchise is, is best brought out by the fact that the representative of the University of Madras is a gentleman who is professionally pledged to denounce as false every Asiatic religion except that of Christ, and whose ideas of what is a proper education for Indians are all dominated by his belief that only such education should be given to them as will bring them to the feet of his Saviour! Incidentally this throws a lurid light on the composition of our University Senates and Syndicates, and shows how little they are in touch with the interests of the people.

The Congress-League scheme rather vaguely lays down that the franchise should be widened as far as possible on the lines of the electorates for Mussalmans for the Provincial Councils. But the qualifications vary so widely not only from Province to Province but even within a Province, as for instance, in Bengal, that no real lead is given by the scheme. For instance, Bombay and the United Provinces allow graduates of any University of the British Empire to exercise the franchise while other Provinces restrict this reasonable right very much in varying degrees. The payment of land-revenue of Rs. 100 is enough qualification in the Presidency of Bombay, it is as high as Rs. 3,000 in the United Provinces; similarly the Income-Tax qualificatians vary from incomes of Rs. 1,000 to Rs. 3,000. The receipt of pension is no qualification in Bombay, while Madras allows votes to persons in the receipt of even up to Rs. 15 per mensem. There are many such variations and the only right course would be to lay down a nearly uniform standard of qualifications for all the Provinces. As affairs are at present, the legislators feel no responsibility to the electors, nor do the voters realise their duty of exercising a wise choice. There are so many intervening bodies between the elected and the elector that the close personal tie, which only can be mutually educative and beneficial is wholly non-existent. The official mind which elaborated this travesty of an electoral system evidently never really cared to give a system which would not be a sham but a reality.

(*e*) The "intellectuals,"—the lawyer, the teacher, (the two classes whom the Government of India's despatch anathematises,) the physician, the engineer, *etc. etc.*, should be very largely represented. Special arrangements may be necessary to get in large numbers of the last three professions, as the lawyer is very well able to take care of himself. It may be necessary to fix a certain definite proportion, as in the case of Mussalmans and Landlords, in which they should be present in the Councils.

(*f*) No one should be simultaneously a member of both the Legislatures.

(*g*) The adult members of the Hindu Joint Family must not be neglected, as they are present, whether as electors or as candidates.

(*k*) Some method should be deviced which would make it possible for an appreciable number of the sixty millions of the untouchable castes to come on the Voters' Register. This would serve as a powerful lever in the raising of their social and economic position, much to their benefit as well as that of the Nation as a whole.

With regard to the Supreme Legislature, it is doubtful whether direct elections would be the best. The electorate would be so vast that it would not have much chance of knowing the candidate nor would these be able to canvass on such an enormous scale. On the whole the Provincial Legislatures seem to be the best electoral media for it. The expiring Provincial Councils in the last month of their existence should meet to elect members for the Supreme Council. This procedure has many points in its favour. It will allow of Provincial Councillors offering themselves along with others as candidates; and all those who are not returned to the Supreme Council will have a chance of trying for the new Provincial Council.

As regards Zemindar, European, Mussalman or any other special community or interest to be represented on this Council, it is not possible to reconcile oneself to separate electorates on a communal or professional basis. The reasons that Lord Morley gave against such a register are so wise, so sympathetic, so genuinely inspired by the wish to develop the budding Indian Nationality, that nothing could add to their cogency. While all the different elements should and indeed must be represented on the Imperial Council, their selection should not be left to small coteries. Such electorates can only have a divisive effect, making for mutual distrust and sharp antagonisms. They are the favourite breeding grounds of fanaticism and extremism of every kind. But if the Provincial Legislative Councils *as a whole* take part in the election of *every* interest, then practicality, compromise, reasonableness, commonsense will come to the fore, and vested interests thrust in the back-ground. The need for convassing will lead to a good deal of social intercourse and consequent mutual understanding of each other's view-points, and of the psychology of clashing interests. In short not a creedo-professional register of *electors* but of *candidates* is the real solution of the problem, so unwisely discarded by the Government of India under the baneful influence of the then Home Member, Sir H. H. Risley.

With regard to the electorate for the Provincial Legislatures (the House of Representatives) a good deal of spade-work has yet to be done before any reasonably final solution can be arrived at. The present system of double, triple and quadruple distillation cannot produce the wished-for result. Just one instance to show the drawbacks of the present method. In the United Provinces the members of the District and Municipal Boards elect Legislators. But they themselves are elected on very varied qualifications, the qualifications of electors as well as of candidates being diverse for the various Municipalities, while in the case of District Boards, they are the acme of chaos. And how could it be otherwise, seeing that the electors are the nominees of the local officials, and personal idiosyncracies, in the absence of well-defined rules, naturally find full vent?

There will also be definite interests that must be represented on the local legislature, and the organised bodies representing them will have to be the primary electorates, for instance, the Universities, and the Chambers of Commerce. With regard to the Universities, I would suggest that they should send not one Representative elected by the Senate but ten, two for each of the Faculties of Science, Arts, Medicine, Engineering and Law elected by the graduates from amongst themselves.

As regards qualifications of the candidates, there should be an age limit, but lower than for the Senate. Thirty and over would be reasonable. The educational qualification of a sound knowledge of English is as indispensable for the Representative as for the Senator. If property-qualification be required it should be the very minimum possible. There is no need to have it higher than that now required from members of Municipal and District Boards.

POLYANGULAR CONTESTS.

One very important matter, not properly dealt with by the Regulations determining the mode of election is this of polyangular contests in the constituencies. With no definite party organisations each running its own candidate as in England, the contest in India often becomes a scramble for votes. It has happened not once or twice but many times, that irresponsible persons have come into the field, out of sheer spite against some particular candidate, either self-invited or egged on by wire-pullers, just to prevent the election of that particular candidate by the scattering of votes. The result is that not the person, whom the community would have been only too glad to have as its representative, gets in, but some person, who has by sheer chance secured a majority of votes. To prevent such flagrant abuse of electioneering methods, it is imperative that a scheme be devised which would prevent the return of any but the candidate really wanted by the majority of electors. There are many methods in vogue, but perhaps the system of vote by *elimination* may be the least irksome and the most helpful. The method is quite simple. *All* the candidates are voted for in the first instance. The candidate getting the least vote is eliminated. A second balloting takes place in which *all* the voters including those who have voted for the eliminated candidate divide their vote among the remaining candidates. This process continues to be repeated till only one candidate remains. Under such a system the nuisance of being 'represented' by one whom the majority of the people do not want would be got rid of, and a general sense of comfort and of trust diffused through the community.

PROPORTIONAL REPRESENTATION.

A good deal is being heard these days about proportional representation, as the one panacea for the manifold recognised disadvantages of the systems in vogue in Great Britain and her oversea Dominions. The procedure is simplicity itself. To begin with, the constituencies should return more than three members but not an even number of members. For in a three-membered constituency, there would still be left unrepresented a very large minority, for only a minority amounting to a full-third of the electorate can secure representation. And in an even-membered constituency, a simple balance of votes might stultify the actual predominance of one set of opinions. An ideal constituency, then, would be a five-membered one. With five seats there may be any number of candidates. Each elector, then, will have a voting paper on which he can give his one vote to any one candidate in the event of his first choice (1) having more than the quota required; or (2) being out of the running altogether. It is asserted that under such a system, the whole political life of the country would occupy an ever-increasing higher and higher level. A politically better educated electorate will elect better representatives, and better representatives will educate the electorate better; so acting and reacting both, will go on improving steadily. (See the Right Hon. J. M. Robertson's article on the subject in *The Edinburgh Review* for July 1917 for an illuminating discussion of the subject).

PAYMENT OF MEMBERS.

The Congress-League scheme is silent about the remuneration of the elected legislators. In the earlier days the members of the Imperial Council were paid ten thousand rupees each annually; but since the new Act has come into force, this has been replaced by the system of travelling and halting allowances.

Such a system of payment is radically wrong and unfair; putting as it does a premium on mere wealth, and making it impossible for the poor but otherwise eminently fit person to represent his people. A legislator is as much a 'public servant' as any one of the thousands of officials, from the Governor, and Judge, down to the village Chowkidar, carrying on the daily work of administration. In every civilised State he is paid a fixed salary just like his colleagues, the Judicial and Executive officers. India cannot afford such high salaries as the United States of America (£1,000), France (£600), Australia (£600,) or England (£400) pay. But as things are in modern India a salary of £400 *per annum* (Rs. 500 per month) would be fair rumenaration for work in the Supreme Council; while for the Provincial Councillars half this sum, namely £200 *per annum* (Rs. 250 per month) would amply meet the needs of the situation. This would make it possible for men of the Gokhale stamp to dedicate their lives to public work. I well remember his telling me once that but for the salary paid for his work on the Council by the Government, poor as he was, it would have made his work in Calcutta almost impossible.

TENURE OF MEMBERSHIP.

Our demand for a longer term than the then existing short two years, which, as Lowell points out in his *Government and Parties in Continental Europe*, exists nowhere, has been met in a very unsatisfactory fashion by the Government. The prolongation of the term to three years is not enough. It is strange that while for their still-born Advisory Imperial and Provincial Councils of Notables, they suggested a term of five years' membership, they should have whittled it down to three years for the Legislative Councils. Bryce in his *American Commonwealth* points out very clearly the evils of a short tenure. He says :—

> There are few walks of life in which experience counts for more than it does in parliamentary politics.

If the

> members are too much harassed by the trouble of procuring their re-election they will not have time or motive for the serious study of political problems.

Sidgwick also in his *Elements of Politics* advances some very cogent arguments in favour of a duration of tenure for five, six or even seven years. He says :—

> If a body of electors is normally called upon to express a practically decisive opinion on the conduct of their representative, only at intervals of some years, the more intelligent electors will probably be able to judge of at least important parts of his conduct after events have unmistakeably shown their wisdom or unwisdom. This consideration, I hold, shows us the grounds on which the proper duration of Parliaments should be determined: While they should not be so long as to weaken the sense of responsibility in the person elected, they should be long enough to give an honest and intelligent elector a fair opportunity of taking the measure of the intellectual and moral qualifications of his representatives. It is, of course, impossible to deduce from general considerations the exact number which fulfils best these two conditions; but I may perhaps say that a period of five, six or even seven years, appears to me to fulfil them very fairly. A period of this length gives the electors fair opportunities of judging, with regard to members of Parliament who offer themselves for re-election, whether they have consistently carried out the principles and pursued the aims avowed by them at the time of their election, and how far their

forecast of consequences has been confirmed by events; while, on the other hand, the period is not long enough to lead either side to forget the promises and predictions made at the beginning of the period, or the account which will have to be rendered at its close. (pp. 556, 557.)

After these weighty reasons little remains to be said in favour of the demand for a five years' tenure. Indeed I am not certain whether it would not be advisable, especially for the membership of the Imperial Council, to extend the tenure to even seven years. For the Supreme Council may be taken to be our "Upper House" and most States and Colonies find it helpful to give its members a longer tenure than to those of the "Lower House."

Even in such a thoroughly democratic State as that of Australia, the Upper House (the Senate) is elected for six years. In South Africa, it is elected for ten years. The drawbacks of a short tenure are these: (*a*) It lessens the responsibility of the electors. They feel that if an inferior person gets in, it does not matter so very much, for at the next election, he will get displaced by some other. This is demoralising to the electors. A fairly long, but not too long, term would force them to awaken to their responsibilities and vote for the best man available. The present unedifying scramble, with its 'first come first served' would cease very largely. (*b*) The representative too is demoralised by the necessity of (i) having to show some immediate work; he dare not take time. (ii) He has generally a feeling that it will be a case of turn and turn about. He has had his fling, and he should retire giving place to the latest popular favourite. All this cannot but react upon his work. He becomes irresponsible, taking his duties light-heartedly, may be, even frivolously.

PRESIDENT.

Many political thinkers in the country are against the Heads of the Imperial and Provincial Governments even being members of the Legislative Councils, on the analogy of the self-governing British Colonies. There is also another potent but unexpressed reason behind this demand. It is felt that their position is so commanding that it becomes very difficult to speak out fully and frankly in their presence, or resist their requests for withdrawing motions, etc. I do not agree with the demand, for here the Heads actually govern, they are not merely pageant kings, they are their own Prime Ministers; and I think it is a good thing that they are so. But the question of the President and Vice-President-ship of the Councils is on a different footing. Here the demand is perfectly just and reasonable, that these high officials shall not be *ex-officio* Presidents, or the Vice-Presidents their nominees. The evils of such a system every elected member of the Councils realises only too well. The duties of the President are those of an *umpire*, and it is impossible for a *partisan* to hold the balance even. If such is the case with the rank and file of an administration, how irresistible will be the bias in the case of their Heads. The Speaker of the House of Commons is the one person who never makes a speech, can this be possible to gubernatorial Presidents, or their nominees, the official Vice-Presidents ? The Councils should have the right of electing their Presidents and Vice-Presidents, but perhaps, during the transition stage, it may be that, while Vice-Presidents may be chosen by the Councils, the Presidents may for the first and last time, be appointed on the *nomination of the Speaker of the House of Commons* for a period of five or seven years, from amongst the members of the House of Commons on adequate salaries, say Rs. 60,000 a year for the Supreme Council and Rs. 48,000 a year for the Provincial, half of these sums being regarded as the salary proper and the other half as expatriation allowance—for when Indians come to be appointed to the office, surely they should not be paid on this high scale.

A further duty that should be laid on the Presidents would be the headship of a department of independent audit for which Indian public opinion led by the late Mr. Gokhale has been all along asking. Ex-Presidents and ex-Vice-presidents might very well also be made *ex-officio* members of the Councils over which they have presided.

TIES.

It is the universal practice to resolve ties by the casting vote of the President. But is it not throwing a most onerous responsibility on a single individual, besides opening the door to much mud-flinging ? I would suggest that the final decision should be due to the action of the representatives themselves and not of the unfortunate gentleman who happens to be in the unenviable position of finding that his and his vote alone, means life or death to a measure. This decision can be secured if the President is allowed no initial vote, nor on the first tie. Whenever such occurs, the meeting should be adjourned for a few hours or even for a day, and a second vote taken; it will be found that by then fluctuations have been brought about, removing the deadlock; but if there be a tie even after this, then a casting vote may be permitted to the President.

BUDGET HEADS.

The schedule proscribes the discussion of certain heads of revenue and of expenditure. One can understand the reasons for keeping the budgetary provisions concerning the Army, Marine and Military Works out of the control of the Councils, though these might well be discussed, to allow of the Executive learning the mind of the country through the Council. But when Stamps, Customs, and Assessed Taxes on the revenue side, and Assignments and Compensations, Interest on Debt, Ecclesiastical, Territorial and Political Pensions, State Railways, and Major Works on the expenditure side are put out of the control of the Legislature, one fails to see the reasonableness of the arrangement. These heads do not affect the stability of the British Dominion in India, and there is no reason why these heads should not also be freely thrown open to the control of the Council like the other heads. All financial proposals should, therefore, be embodied in Bills and all such Bills and the Budget as a whole should be submitted for the sanction of the Councils, excepting, of course, all items concerning the Defence of the Country, and its Foreign and Political relations.

Incidentally I may mention here that two rich sources of Revenue have not been opened up yet. They are a graduated Income-Tax on the incomes of legal practitioners rising up to fully fifty per cent. in case of incomes of a lakh and over; and a graduated Inheritance Tax (known as Death Duties in England) on all landed properties. It is preposterous that Zemindaris yielding a rent roll of anything between 15 lakhs (one million sterling) to 60 lakhs (4 millions sterling) should go so lightly taxed. An Inheritance Tax modelled on the English Act, would yield a very large revenue. The proposer of these two taxes would incur a great deal of odium and even the enmity of the two powerful classes concerned, and it would be an extremely difficult matter to secure the sanction of the Legislature to such taxation, seeing that both these classes are so overwhelmingly strongly represented in it. But the interests of the people, as a whole, require that neither the fear of odium, nor the more serious risk of incurring enmity ought to prevent a well-wisher of his country from doing his duty by it.

BUDGET.

Every civilised country has provided itself with some machinery by which the national income and expenditure are controlled more or less fully. A Cobden Club publication on Budget Control gives full details how different countries of Europe have, by somewhat different but substantially similar methods, established some sort of a check on expenditure and taxation. Considering the conditions, however, under which India is governed, I would suggest that for the present the annual Budget be roughly divided into two portions, one portion, for instance, that dealing with the army might be discussed and passed as at present, the Council not having power to amend it or ask for a division, but, of course, exercising as at present the power of criticising and suggesting improvements. But the other portions of the Budget, for instance, the portions dealing with education, irrigation, railways, sanitation, agriculture, should be submitted to a full and *free* discussion with power to *amend.* The official members, too, should be released from leading strings and *invited* to give their votes *independently.*

The procedure of the House of Commons that prevents its voting money for purposes which in its opinion are necessary, unless and until the Ministry becomes of the same mind and itself demands such expenditure, is not justifiable under Indian conditions, nor is its necessary corollary that no proposals for the levy of a new tax or the enhancement of an existing one (the power to lower it is there) must come from the House. As the Indian Government is wholly independent of the Legislatures, owning no responsibility to the *people,* nor likely to become dependent on the legislatures in the near future, it is necessary, therefore, for their representatives to possess these two powers

Both in the Financial and Legislative spheres, as Sidgwick acutely points out:—

> an assembly chosen for a limited period, by the people at large, is held likely to know what the people at large want, better than any Council or assembly otherwise appointed, and to be more concerned to provide it. (p. 372).

It is because a properly-constituted Legislative Council is in touch with the people, which the alien British Indian Government can never be, and so will be "more concerned to provide" for their wants than the Executive, that it is necessary, that this power should not be withheld from it. The French practice is in accord with the above suggestion, the French Parliament having full powers to modify the Budget in any way it chooses, irrespective of the wishes of the Ministry and this freely modified Budget being accepted by the Ministry and not leading to its resignation as it would in England (*vide* President Poincare's *How France is Governed*). Similar is the American practice (*vide* Lord Bryce's *The American Commonwealth*).

A second suggestion is that a Committee of Scrutiny be appointed for a term of three years, composed of non-official members with the Finance Minister as its President, and this Committee of seven should make a detailed report on the Budget a fortnight after the Budget has been presented to the Council, which report should be printed and circulated, and the discussion in the Council should take place only after this report has been in the hands of the members for at least one week. The discussion should last through at least six sittings to allow of a full and fair deliberation on all the points raised.

A third suggestion is that, as for instance in Austria, and even in England, the Government should, every year, before presenting the new Budget, lay before the Council " an exact account of the preceding year touching the *management* and *disposal* of the sums allowed by the Budget legally voted within the limits thereby granted." This account should then be referred to the Committee of Scrutiny to be as carefully looked into as the Budget, and, on their submitting a full report, should be again brought before the Council for the expression of its approval or disapproval. The *whole* of the expenditure, including that for the army even, ought to be submitted to this searching scrutiny, and final discussion in the full Council.

The late Mr. Gokhale made a lifelong fight for an independent audit, and though he met with much official sympathy, it was all confined to words, and remains yet to be transformed into action. Since his days matters have improved and the Councillors are permitted greater latitude in their dealings with the Budget. But all this show of freedom barely touches the fringe of the question, and all real control over any portion of taxation or of expenditure is still in the hands of the administration. The voice of the representatives of the people is still a voice in the wilderness. How much longer are they to continue to " cry in the forest" unconsoled ?

The Budget is the linch-pin of every administrative chariot; but how many are the Indian legislators, who take the trouble to qualify themselves to understand in all its bearings its inner meaning, its deeper significance, and fit themselves, by years of patient labour over repelling figures, as Mr. Gokhale had done, to offer helpful criticism—destructive and constructive? It might safely be asserted that since his days—and it has to be remembered that the restraint on such discussions was much greater in those days—nobody has arisen to take his place, as the unsparing critic of Government proposals, and as well informed, as, if not better than, the originators and defenders of its policy themselves.

As this question of Financial control is of such supreme importance, a quotation from Sidgwick would not be amiss. It would by the way interest Indians to know that he was intimately related to the conservative governing class of England, his wife being a sister of the Right Hon. A. J. Balfour. This might make the I. C. S. if possible, attach greater weight to his reasoned conclusions, due to his world-wide recognised position as a philosopher-politician.

In his *Elements of Politics* he shows how very necessary it is that this power of taxation and expenditure should not be left to the Executive, if the people are to be reasonably secure against the arbitrary exercise of the power to take away their property and spend it at its own sweet will, even when such expenditure may not be to their benefit and may even be injurious. He says:—

> The proportion of the national income required for Governmental expenditure cannot be fixed once for all . . . . private members of the community must submit to the degree of insecurity involved in an indefinite right of Government to take their property. It seems, therefore, important, in order to minimise this insecurity and render the exercise of this power of taxation as little formidable as possible, that the taxes to be levied should not be determined by the officials who will have to spend the proceeds, or other officials under their influence; it is important that the "Budget" of the State should receive the assent of a separate and independent body, specially qualified to watch, in the interest of the taxpayers, the collection and expenditure of the taxes, and to prevent, as far as possible, any oppressiveness in the former or excess in the latter. It is, accordingly, an accepted principle in the construction of a modern Government that the ultimate control of Governmental finance should be in the hands of such a body. (pp. 335, 336.)

On this point, the otherwise enlightened and progressive British Government of India, wallows in mediæval darkness and refuses to be bound by the "accepted principle," at the same time setting its face against another equally "accepted principle, in the construction of a modern Government," . . . "that this money-granting body should be *elected by the citizens at large*." (f. n. to p. 336. Italics mine.)

FREEDOM OF VOTING.

One of the suggestions made above, namely, that official members should not be tied in the matter of their votes, but left free to follow their independent judgment, opens up a rather wide question. It involves also the position of the non-official nominees to the Councils. For these also—especially almost all the Indian ones—do not hesitate to cast in their lot with the official side. The latter are *supposed* to be free. But as far as the *theory* of Representative Government is concerned, every one, official and non-official alike is free to vote according to the light that is in him. But here we are concerned with the actual practice. Two factors—an ostensibly higher, and so avowable, another definitely lower, and so unconfessable—enter into the considerations, of the voting nominee, official and even non-official voting. The first is that the nominated member, being a repository of the trust put in him by the Government, so far betrays that trust if he votes against the wishes of the Government, and so becomes morally blameworthy, by embarrassing it. The second reason is 'expectations of favours to come'—honors, titles, re-nominations, appointments to non-competitive posts, for self, relatives, dependents, promotions if already in service, and so on, making it incumbent on those who are prepared to sell their conscience for these earthly goods to keep the powers that be in gracious mood by an attitude of deferential agreement with their beliefs, prejudices and interests. These subtle forms of bribery are well-known all the world over, and no number of Corrupt Practices Acts can ever completely put a stop to them, for the very good reason that no legislative mesh is fine enough to catch these. It might look perilously like a libellous statement to include members of the Indian Civil Service also in the above analysis and to suggest that they too are subject to these human weaknesses and allow themselves to be swayed by these lower motives; but there is very high official authority in support of this view. I need only name one. General Sir George

Chesney, K.C.B., M.P., Military Member of the Government of India, in his *Indian Polity*, with a strange amalgam of military bluntness, official cautiousness, and the natural feeling not to give his friends and colleagues away, asserts unhesitatingly that such is the case, and that there are people who are so swayed, and so, in the interests of a pure administration, members of the Executive Councils should not be eligible to Provincial Headships under Viceregal patronage.

As said above, actions done under the second motive cannot be prevented by Acts and Regulations. It is a question of conscience and of character.

The first factor, however, can be and should be eliminated through a proper regulation. It needs no painting out that the administration of the country is a "benevolent despotism" and not a Parliamentary one, to be shaken down by every gust of popular disfavour. There can then be no question of party loyalty, of stringent party discipline, and so on. The ever to be remembered words that Burke addressed to his constituents of Bristol, in 1774, should be laid to heart by every individual nominated member of the Councils, be he official or non-official. To fully understand his words, it should be noted that his colleague was a gentleman of an accommodating nature and had expressed his willingness to carry out any instructions which he might receive from his constituents. Burke said :—

Certainly, gentlemen, it ought to be the happiness and glory of a representative to live in the strictest union, the closest correspondence, and the most unreserved communication with his constituents. Their wishes ought to have great weight with him; their opinion high respect; their business unremitted attention. It is his duty to sacrifice his repose, his pleasures, his satisfactions, to theirs; and above all, ever, and in all cases, to prefer their interest to his own. But, his unbiassed opinion, his mature judgment, his enlightened conscience, he ought not to sacrifice to you, to any man, or to any set of men living. These he does not derive from your pleasure; no, nor from the law and the constitution. They are a trust from Providence, for the abuse of which he is deeply answerable. Your representative owes you, not his industry only, but his judgment; and he betrays, instead of serving you, if he sacrifices it to your opinion.

My worthy colleague says his will ought to be subservient to yours. If that be all, the thing is innocent: if Government were a matter of will upon any side, yours, without question, ought to be superior. But Government and legislation are matters of reason and judgment, and not of inclination; and what sort of reason is that, in which the determination precedes the discussion; in which one set of men deliberate, and another decide; and where those who form the conclusion are, perhaps, three hundred miles distant from those who hear the arguments?

To deliver an opinion, is the right of all men; that of constituents is a weighty and respectable opinion, which a representative ought always to rejoice to hear; and which he ought always most seriously to consider. But authoritative instructions, mandates issued, which the member is bound blindly and implicitly to obey, to vote and to argue for, though contrary to the clearest conviction of his judgment and conscience,—these are things utterly unknown to the laws of the land, and which arise from a fundamental mistake of the whole order and tenor of our constitution.

Parliament is not a Congress of ambassadors from different and hostile interests; which interests each must maintain, as an agent, and advocate, against other agents and advocates; but Parliament is a deliberative assembly of one nation, with one interest, that of the whole; where not local purposes, not local prejudices ought to guide, but the general good, resulting from the general reason of the whole. You choose a member indeed: but when you have chosen him, he is not a member of Bristol but he is a member of Parliament.

The above is the completest statement that I know of, of the case for the independence of the legislator. It applies no less fully to the Government members. Everybody concedes that a sane adult ought not to be interfered with in his choice of a physician. But his sanity would be much doubted, if he proceeded to dictate to the physician of his choice how he ought to treat him, beyond pointing out his special ailment and the measures that have disagreed. Similarly if a Board of, say, seven or nine physicians sits to diagnose some disease and formulate a method of treatment, with the prior condition that everyone of the members of the Board was bound to agree to whatever the President dictated, the position is so absurd that it needs only to be stated so nakedly to be laughed out of court. While the *action* to be taken should be that of the majority, the *opinions* of none should be trammelled by the supposed needs of a united front. If the purpose of any set of members is merely to act as a sounding board to swell the volume of the single vote—then it might be unhesitatingly asserted that no more mischievous performance is possible. The idea, referred to before, that the nominated members are *morally* bound by considerations of *loyalty* to vote with the Government, *i.e.*, the Head thereof who is their nominator—is rank fallacy. Unless there has been a previous pact between them (which would be illegal) the governing principle in the case is that the nominator has just trust in the *judgment*, and not in the *blind obedience* of the nominees.

MINISTERIAL TENURE.

As the various Indian 'Cabinets,' (including in this term the Head of the administration, Provincial and Supreme, and his Executive Councillors) are what Sidgwick calls Periodic, *i.e.*, immovable for a fixed term of five years, and not Parliamentary *i.e.*, dismissible at the pleasure of the Legislature; the present method of appointing these Councillors (Ministers) needs a complete change. The present method is for the newly-appointed Head, the Governor or Governor-General (Prime Minister), to take on all the old Ministers and try to work through them, and as the term of appointment of these expire, to go on appointing to each post as it falls vacant. This cannot but make for a great deal of friction hampering the machinery, about which, of course, the outside world hears nothing, it being kept a profound secret from the profane. Sir William Wedderburn and Sir K. G. Gupta have in their note published in *India* (Oct. 1915), suggested an exceedingly good way out of this difficulty. It is this: *Every Minister to be appointed by the incoming ruler and to lay down office along with him.* Somehow this very important suggestion has escaped notice, and has got crowded out among the lot of other, perhaps more insistent, suggestions. It deserves, however, to become as prominent as the others.

TREATY-MAKING POWERS.

The joint reform scheme put forward by the Congress-League expressly repudiates all wish to control the power of the Government of India in the matter of entering into treaties. We know that even the Government of India has no control over the treaty-making power, which resides completely in the Secretary of State for India, and that he too exercises that power, largely as a delegate of the British Cabinet, and as a member of that Cabinet, and not as an independent authority. This is not a desirable state of affairs. The Dominions have successfully asserted their right to be given a prominent voice in all treaty negotiations, and have even extorted the right to enter into independent treaty relations with other States even to the extent of such trade conditions as are prejudicial to the Mother-Country, as for instance, Canada.

I would suggest that treaties should be divided into two categories, namely, Political and Commercial. This would permit of allowing the Government of India and the Indian Legislature some substantial voice in their making. (*a*) I would say, then, that in all treaties of a political nature, but which *directly* affect India, the Government of India should be consulted *long before the time of ratification*, for at that last stage no modifications of conditions would be possible. (*b*) But such treaties or such portions of them as directly affect our trade and commerce must not be entered into without the matters being brought up before the Indian Legislature and its consent obtained. (*c*) I would also suggest that the Indian Government be allowed freedom similar to that permitted to the Dominions to enter into commercial negotiations with other States on its own account and through its own agents. Finally, (*d*) I would suggest that the Government of India also be given a representation on the Advisory Committee of the Board of Trade in England on the same principle on which the Dominions have been allowed representation, the representative being an Indian. As no treaties with Commercial clauses are entered into by England without consulting this Committee *betimes*, Indian interests would not then go overboard for want of an advocating voice, as they do now.

BICAMERAL LEGISLATURE.

So far I have said nothing about double legislative bodies, either for the Provinces, or for the Government of India. It is to be hoped that the scheme of having an Imperial Advisory Council and Provincial Advisory Councils of Notables, published by the Government of Lord Minto, has been given its final quietus, and that no such bodies bodeful only of mischief will ever be advocated again for India. The analogy of England, with its House of Lords and its House of Commons is totally inapplicable to India. The British Dominions have all copied it, but the results have been very different from what the imitators of the British institution fondly imagined would result. One has only to look into the pages of A. B. Keith's *Responsible Government in the British Dominions*, 3 vols. to see the sordid squabbles between the Upper and the Lower Chambers, and the utter helplessness of the former. These second chambers representing different interests and recruited on a different franchise, and demanding different qualifications from its members, are a device to serve as breakwaters against the headlong rush of first chambers in more or less democratically-governed countries. But nowhere have they been a success, not even in England. India has not the slightest need for them.

The landed interest all the world over is an intensely conservative, reactionary, and selfish interest. What it means in a caste-ridden and priest-ridden country like ours needs no enlarging upon. The faith of the Government of the country in the representative value of the owners of broad acres is so charmingly naive, that it almost disarms criticism! If they represent anything or anybody, it is themselves only. They emphatically do not represent the "dumb millions" of India. One has only to call to mind the furious fights in every Legislative Council in the country put up by the landed interest, whenever the Government has attempted to right the wrongs of the peasantry against the oppression of the landlords. Every Tenancy Act is a standing witness that the Government has never been wholly successful in its attempts to improve the status and economic condition of the actual cultivators of the soil. (In passing I may point out that the land-laws whether Rent or Revenue require drastic change, and that the Government as landlord is no better, when not worse than the 'native' Zemindar. But see on this very thorny subject General Brigg's *Land Tax in India* and John Dickinson's *India: Under a Bureaucratic Government*, where the evils of the land legislation are fully exposed.)

Sheldon Amos has most truly observed that:—

> It is pure legislative loss — without any compensating gain —to have one class of interests or views represented at one discussion of a measure and another class at another discussion, instead of having both represented simultaneously to the great gain of debate and the saving of time, expense and labor. (*Scienc of Politics*, p. 239.)

All that is expected from Provincial Upper Chambers in India apart from the gratification of mere personal vanity to which membership of an *Upper* Chamber from which less favoured mortals are excluded, may minister, will be far more efficiently performed by the Imperial Legislative Council. This is the real nucleus of the future Bundesrath of India in which the British Provinces and the Indian States will, in the no very distant future, meet to carry on the government of the country under the hegemony of Great Britain. It is obvious that no separate *Lower* Imperial Legislative Council is needed. I do not forget the Council of Princes, but as yet the body is in a very nebulous state, and he would be a bold prophet who would say definitely what shape it will take. Time only will show what place in the future government of the Greater India can be assigned to it.

PRIVILEGES OF MEMBERS.

Freedom of speech must be guaranteed by Statute. No member should be liable to any action or proceeding in any court, or to any penalty by an order of the Executive, by reason of his speech or vote in such Council. Nor should the printing of such speech by an authorised agency or its sale by any one bring the person or persons within the clutches of the law or the Executive.

DISQUALIFICATIONS.

Besides the two disqualifications above mentioned, namely, want of a sound knowledge of English and of being under thirty for a Representative and under thirty-five for a Senator, there are certain obvious ones. For instance, pauperism, bankruptcy (whether the person be a *discharged* or undischarged insolvent, or *certificated* or uncertificated bankrupt), disgraceful conduct, and crimes involving moral turpitude should be valid reasons for exclusion from candidature. The holding of any office of profit under the Government (Crown) excepting the cases of *ex-officio* members or of those in receipt of a pension, should also be a bar. That persons (*a*) dismissed from Government service, (*b*) debarred from practising as legal practitioners, (*c*) imprisoned for a term exceeding six months, (*d*) bound down to be of good behaviour, and, finally, (*e*) those declared ineligible by the Government under the plea that their reputation and antecedents are such that their candidature would be contrary to the public interest—that all these above-mentioned persons should be disfranchised, is rather a debatable point. Many believe for good reasons, that all these barriers should be removed.

QUORUM.

Seeing what the *personnel* of the Government of the country will be for a long time to come, *i.e.*, a judicious mixture of the British and the Indian elements in its composition, the question of preventing scratch majorities is of vital importance for the proper working of the Councils. It is not the difference of race, religion, or speech that so much matters, as the *difference of domicile.* The discordances arising out of the racial, creedal, or linguistic antagonisms, do get harmonised, when people have got to live side by side. Their angles and asperities must be rubbed smooth, if they are not to exterminate each other. But difference of domicile proves an effective bar to the straightening of the 'Angle of Vision.' Even when own brothers scatter into different portions of the world, their interests and outlook inevitably become dissimilar, if not actually opposed. Much more so is bound to be the case in the circumstances when a race differing so widely, and dominant, has its home six thousand miles away from the scene of its actions, and to which home it is most deeply, most passionately, attached. The clash of outlook and of interests is bound to be perpetual. Much good humour, much good feeling, and a very high sense of duty on both sides are essential, if they are to co-operate harmoniously for the good of the country. So we shall not be very wrong, in advocating a high quorum, and decidedly large majorities.

OUR CRITICS.

Two serious drawbacks to our fitness for real representative Government as against the shell of it, with which we have been so far cajoled by an all too paternal Government, are universally urged against us by our foreign critics and find some echo from a few Indian politicians as well. They are (*a*) our "unlimited capacity for futile negative criticism," and (*b*) our "innumerable divisions of creeds and sects, and castes and sub-castes making it impossible for us to have what may be termed national ideals, or a national will."

With regard to our faculty for criticising anything or everything, in season or out of season, I freely admit that there is a grain of truth in the charge, but no more than a grain. All over the world, whether in the East or the West, this factor does exist, and has to be taken account of by every Government, be it autocratic, oligarchic, or democratic. We have only to see what is happening in England, in France, in Russia, even while engaged in a death-struggle with German militarism. Is there not enough and to spare of this, from the official point of view, very undesirable commodity in all those countries. Permanent officials governing a country, by the very nature of their position, tend to become hyper-sensitive and intolerant of all criticism. They love to be surrounded by the subdued rosy light of adulation or at least acquiescence. But when an anglo-foreign daily like the Calcutta *Statesman*, while defending the administration of the Defence of India Act in Bengal, goes the length of saying :—

> It is true that all Governments, including the Bengal Government, are capable in certain circumstances of unjust and vindictive action, (April 7, 1916.)

does it lie in the mouth of our critics to say that we are ever criticising, for mere criticism's sake?

Taking it for granted for argument's sake that no constructive criticism is ever offered by the non-official members of the Legislative Councils, on whom does the blame for such an attitude of mind lie? Are not they eternally "His Majesty's Opposition?" Trust begets trust; responsibility begets responsibility. With the notion firmly implanted in their minds that they are unable to influence against its will even so much as by a hair's breadth, the Executive, and that all their interpellations and speeches are mere cloistered, academic performances, is it any wonder that that sobering effect, which is the outcome of the feeling that they too may become "the Government" some day and be confronted with their sayings, is naturally in abeyance in their verbal conduct? Give them something more substantial to do and they will not "criticise" so much. As Sir Pherozeshah Mehta said once, "We have nothing else left to do." Even officials recognise the demoralising effects of the situation. Sir Reginald Craddock, as strong and unbending a bureaucrat as ever ruled the Home Department, and now the Lieutenant-Governor of Burma, wrote when Chief Commissioner of the Central Provinces in his note annexed to Mr. Slocock's letter of the 18th June 1908 :—

> When a man knows that nothing that he says is likely to be put into effect, he lets his tongue or pen run away with him, but the risk that what he urges might have serious consequences is apt to check a reckless flow and to induce more sober expression.

The "intellectual" element in India has to be provided with legitimate opportunities and occupation.

The evil effects of permanent official majorities on the tone and temper of the Indian Legislatures were so clearly recognised by Lord Morley that he could not help making mention of them even while defending the system in his speech in the House of Lords. He said :—

There is one point of extreme importance which, no doubt, though it may not be over-diplomatic for me to say so at this stage, will create some controversy. I mean the matter of the official majority. . . . . anybody can see how directly, how palpably, how injuriously, an arrangement of this kind tends to weaken and I think I may even say to deaden the sense both of trust and responsibility in the non-official members of these Councils. Anybody can see how the system tends to throw the non-official member into an attitude of peevish, sulky, permanent opposition, and therefore has an injurious effect on the minds and characters of members of these Legislative Councils.

There could not be pronounced by any outside critic a stronger condemnation of the system than was done by its sponsor himself. But by some strange fatality, this wise and experienced statesman ultimately accepted the course whose wrongness he has himself described so incisively! How utterly mischievous is the method of standing official majorities is, he shows by pointing out, in that very speech, that the power was abused by a Provincial Government, and the Governor-General had to exercise his powers of veto to prevent the mischief. That this abuse of power was far from being an isolated case, a rare phenomenon, is known to us all too bitterly. Replying to the objections against non-official majorities, he observed :—

I know it will be said—I will not weary the House by arguing it, but I desire to meet at once the objection that will be taken—that these Councils will, if you take away the safeguard of the official majorities, pass any number of wild-cat Bills. The answer to that is that the head of the Government can veto the wild-cat Bills. The Governor-General can withhold his assent and the withholding of the assent of the Governor-General is no defunct power. Only the other day, since I have been at the India Office, the Governor-General disallowed a Bill passed by a Local Government which I need not name, with the most advantageous effect. I am quite convinced that if the Local Government had had an un-official majority, the Bill would never have been passed, and the Governor-General would not have had to refuse his assent. But so he did, and so he would if these

gentlemen, whose numbers we propose to increase and whose powers we propose to widen chose to pass wild-cat Bills. (*Indian Constitutional Documents*, p. 287.)

Lord Morley while permitting non-official majorities in the Provincial Legislatures, majorities by the way have not come into existence, steadily set his face against them for the Governor-General's Council, even though the Government of Lord Minto was quite prepared to concede the point, "and to rely on the public spirit of non-official members to enable us (them) to carry on the ordinary work of legislation."

Another point which should be carefully borne in mind by our critics is that the methods and technique of civilised political life have, to begin with, to be learnt and copied by Indian politicians from the English ways—the older indigenous methods and technique of constitutional monarchy, responsible government, and even downright republics having long been extinct. (See Mr. K. P. Jayaswal's admirable papers in the *Modern Review* for 1912, as also Rhys Davids's *Buddhist India* on these matters of *Gana-rajya* and *Sangha-rajya*, and the coronation oath and the king's responsibility and liability to be changed, and the ways of *varana* or election and of voting by *shalâkû* and deciding by *bahutara*, *i.e.*, majority, and securing the *gana-purti* or quorum, etc). An essential item in these days is Press-criticism. The Indian Press might well be excused if it imitated the ways of the English Press, in the circumstances. And yet, the tone and language of the Indian Press has, so far, been far more mild and moderate, and far less outspoken, than that of the British is. So, the language of the non-official Indian legislators has been far more courteous and subdued than that of British Parliamentarians in the Opposition is.

To mistake strong language in such cases for sedition is the greatest of mistakes. It is only the sign of the legitimate wish to change what has been subtly growing *in*-equal subjection all this while, into "*co*-equal subjection," in the phrase of Lord Morley. Also courtesy will breed courtesy. If the anglo-foreign Press—which makes up our critics mostly, being the understood organ of the official body—will change its tone of perpetual belittlement of and contempt for the Indians, and recognise Indians as brothers—even though younger in material science and power—the Indian Press could not possibly fail to respond.

Worse even than the prevention of non-official majorities is the fact that the non-official legislator owes his seat more or less to the grace of the Government. If he is in any way obnoxious to the Government, which, in such cases, generally means some one or more officials, he can be kept out of the Councils, for the Regulations have been so framed, that this can always be done. Nor is there any statutory provision safeguarding his personal liberty and giving him a privileged position for his actions and speeches as a legislator, such as is secured to every member of the House of Commons.

A couple of quotations from two well-known writers on the condition of Parliamentary Government in Germany will help to bring more clearly home to our rulers, the fact that when a defective constitution produces these evils of irresponsibility in such a highly instructed and homogeneous nation as the German, it is not to be wondered at that those evils should be great in a country like ours, so uninstructed in modern political ways, where united public life and public spirit of the new political (as distinguished from the old religious kind), are only things of yesterday, and where the rulers and the ruled are not of one nation, but the one is ever "dominant" and the other ever "subject" (*i.e.*, "thrown under," etymologically).

Mr. J. Ramsay Macdonald says :—

> The German Reichstag is not a Parliament. When Bismarck drafted the constitution. . . . he had two leading purposes in his mind. He determined to create a legislature based on the most democratic franchise *but devoid of every particle of real power*, (italics mine) and at the same time to repose the real legislative and executive authority of the confederation in a Bundesrath which was to be so constituted as to be a fortress of the most extreme kind of conservatism. The Reichstag is, therefore, little more than a debating society . . . . . The parties constituting an assembly of debate, which is not an assembly of authority, must be subject to a very different set of influences . . . . . . A Chamber responsible to public opinion for its acts, and free constitutionally to make its will effective . . . . . must make itself responsible for every step in national evolution. The parties in such a Chamber . . . . will be far less able to take purely negative attitudes. (*The Socialist Movement.* p. 108-109).

Mr. Dawson, in his illuminating book, so full of instruction for us, is even stronger in his condemnation of the German constitution and its evil results on the public life of the country. Generalising from that he goes on to remark :—

It is difficult to exaggerate the injurious effect upon public spirit and political thought of the condition of impotence in which the nation is placed by constitutions which are neither absolutish nor democratic, which do, indeed, give to the representative assembly a certain amount of legislative power yet not sufficient to make parliamentary life serious and fruitful...... Legislation owing to its bureaucratic origin......represents too often the limited views and outlook of a narrow class, a class entirely honest and faithful to duty yet not in close touch with practical life and often unable to view the questions from a broad, social and gernerously human standpoint. (*The Evolution of Modern Germany* by W. H. Dawson.)

Two very important factors in the bringing about of a diminution of the academic nature of the work of the non-official members are, (*a*) widely-diffused education of the new kind and (*b*) District Councils. Both these items used to be pressed on the attention of the Government by the late Mr. Gokhale, year in and year out, but to no purpose. The Government would not allow his very milk and water Bill for Free and Compulsory Primary Education to become law, nor does it do a tenth of what it should for spreading secondary education. With regard to the District Councils, the whole force of the Indian Civil Service was thrown against it, as it has been against the separation of the Executive and Judicial powers, now centering in the same individuals, and so this too remains a counsel of perfection. Until the bogey of *prestige* which haunts the dreams of official sleep is exorcised, it will be a very uphill struggle to secure these two indispensable bases, and, so long, the super-structure of the Legislative Councils cannot but continue to be a very ramshackle one.

Coming now to the other criticism, namely, that we are but a congeries of races, infinitely divided up, and that the phrase *Indian Nation* is devoid of all content, the word India being but a geographical expression, I will content myself with one single quotation from a work written by an Indian Civilian nearly seventy years ago. This gentleman was Sir George Campbell, M. P., had a vast and varied experience of the country as a whole, and more specially from Punjab to Bengal, of which latter Province he finally became the Lieutenant-Governor. He recognised our fundamental unity, based as it is on the allegiance to one basic culture. He says:—

It is the peculiarity of the Indian population that it is one in many respects. The same systems, manners, and divisions of the people prevail throughout the country. And yet in every part there is a great variety of different classes dwelling together, but in many points altogether dissimilar. Although there are many classes, almost all the classes are found more or less everywhere, and hence the same general features of society exist alike in every part of India, even when there is a considerable difference in personal appearance and language. In effect it has become one country, and, though many different races have entered it, and have been, by peculiar institutions, kept in many respects separate, each has in its own sphere pervaded the whole country; all have become united in one common civilization; the same system of Hindoo polity has been overlaid by the same system of Mahomedan Government; inhabitants of one part of the country have served, travelled, and done business in all other parts indiscriminately; and so altogether, while the different degrees in which different elements have been mixed produce exterior differences, the essential characteristics of all are the same. Especially in the details of Government we found the same phases throughout, a result principally due to the centralising and uniform system of the Mahomedan Government, and the frequent change of functionaries from one part to another. Most of the supposed differences are of modern origin, and originate in the different views of different Europeans settling at remote points and pursuing different courses. The more one studies the subject, the more identity one finds in the state of things in all the different parts of India.

The different nations of Europe may have been, in some measure, so assimilated in former days, when successive waves of conquest and population broke over the whole continent and left the *debris* to ferment together into nations; when all united in common Crusades, and English yeomen took service at Constantinople. But now widely different national characters have sprung up, and there are bold distinctions which, for the most part exist not in India. That country is common to all its inhabitants, and the most close intercourse exists throughout. Even the Mahomedan is not the fierce, proud foreigner. His character and his blood are in general much more nearly allied to the Hindu than to the Afghan.

There is but one exception to this amalgamation of the people. Throughout the interior hills, the remains of the aboriginal race is everywhere found separate and little mixed. They are small and dark, and generally complete savages, and speak a language altogether different from the Hindoos. In the farther south they seem to have been reduced to slavery; more to the north, in and about the Bombay Presidency, they gave great trouble as robbers and plunderers of the adjacent plains. It is, however, a curious fact, which I have not seen elsewhere noticed, that in the Himalayas adjoining Hindustan proper, though much more abrupt and difficult than any of the interior hills, there exists no such race. The population of this part of the Himalyas is pure Hindoo, till it meets the Mongolian Bhooteas of the other side of the hills; and the fact might be a strong argument in favour of the indigenous or very early origin of the Hindoo civilization. The aborigines have, in their features, no trace of the Negro or Mongol, and would seem to be of Caucasian race.

The chief difference in the population of the North and the South of India seems to consist in the larger intermixture with the Hindoos in the one of the later Northern races, and in the other of the population which existed prior to the Hindoo invasion. (*Modern India.* pp. 36-38.)

Dr. Radha Kumud Mukerji's excellent little book *The Fundamental Unity of India* might be read as a commentary on these very just observations of Sir George Campbell; though some very important considerations have been omitted by the work and remain to be supplied—especially the fact of the unity *of Sanskrit literature* which pervades the whole of geographical India.

After such an accurate statement of the position of affairs, the result of the observations of a keep discerning, and sympathetic official, nothing is left for me to add. Our differences are mostly surface ones and not so deep and wide as the selfish interests of adverse critics would make them out to be. We are what our circumstances have made us. And our prayer to the great British nation is to help us to an environment where we may be better able to fulfil our destiny of achieving a complete national life.

CONCLUSION.

The ever true statement that 'eternal vigilance is the price of liberty' requires to be supplemented to make it a complete truth. If 'well and rightly instructed intelligence' is wanting, no amount of mere vigilance will save the situation. Nor will the vigilance even when *instructed*, if it be of a few only of the nation, be strong enough to ward off evil. The maxim should, therefore, run in some such wise—*eternal vigilance of the well and rightly instructed intelligence of the majority of the individuals of the community is the price of liberty.* This is essential to every scheme of Self-Government, whether it be of the individual as an ethical unit, or of the community as a political unit. The better and wiser nature of the individual as of the community should be strengthened, developed and made more and more pervasive, while the lower and worse nature should be equally studiously curtailed and restrained. The frivolous spirit that unfortunately usually prevails in the so-called "uppermost units" at the 'top' of the community because of too much leisure, of too much wealth, and too little responsibility, has as much to be brought under control and cured as the spiritlessness of dull grind at the 'bottom' of the community, due here to too little leisure, too little wealth, too little instruction. The electorate must not allow itself to become powerless. It should make itself a

> continuously operative instrument of control over the Executive and Legislative elements of the political system, so that the political power of the nation shall only be delegated to the smallest possible extent, and for the shortest possible period that is compatible with its unimpaired and legitimate activity, and so that every citizen shall feel that he is not only called to exercise his electoral power of decision from time to time, but that the community demands of him a continual, intelligent supervision of its affairs, and commits to his hands a means of making his criticism or judgment instantly heard when, in his opinion, there are circumstances which call for its utterance. (*The Essentials of Self-Government* by E. T. Powell, p. 23).

The sub-title of this above-quoted very helpful book "*A comprehensive Survey . . . of the Electoral Mechanism as the Foundation of Political Power, and a Potent Instrument of Intellectual and Social Evolution; . . .*" shows how rightly a very high value is placed by the writer on a proper organisation of the Electorate.

It may be that the over-zeal of the specialist for his own subject is hidden in this extract, and that such an all-absorbing devotion to the political aspect of the national life may starve the other and equally-important aspects, if permitted to persist beyond certain limits. Yet, it has to be said that for a little while in the immediate future, in India, this even excessive attention has to be paid to the aspect of politics, without the rectification of which as the very basis of the *organised* life of the nation, no other aspect could be properly rectified. For (as explained in the Mahabharata, *Shantiparva*, ch. 15 and 122) *Danda Niti*, law and politics, make national and social life possible and *danda* means, not mere 'punishment' in the ordinary sense but 'the political force and authority of the sovereign power of compulsion' which is the very basis of the State, and on which all government rests (see Woodrow Wilson's, *The State*, ch. XIII). The nature and the limits of this *danda* must first be *rectified* before everything else, as is also explained there.

If India is to be rescued from the slough of Despond into which it fell wellnigh ten centuries ago, it must knock off the shackles of a spurious Vedanta and its misbegotten, bastard cosmopolitanism *(Vasudhaiva Kutumbkam)* making us pessimistic and invertebrate; and it must also mercilessly chop off the tentacles of the socio-theological octopus which has so ordered our daily individual life that a full-bodied national life has been all but choked out of the country. The Mussalman too has to so order his life that all conflict with its environment will cease.

The three most potent modern instruments for the consolidation and uplift of a Nation are, universal education, universal suffrage and universal military service. How vital this latter is needs no special dwelling upon, with this hideous war devastating Europe for the last four years before our eyes. Even that *beau ideal* of Anglo-India, the model of what a sober Indian politician ought to be, and whose Presidential speech in the Bombay Congress of 1915, received the high imprimatur of the endorsement of the Government of Lord Chelmsford, uttered a most scathing indictment of the policy which by a total withholding of all military training had so emasculated us that we were scarce fit to fully shoulder the responsibilities of real citizenship. It is the inalienable birthright of every nation that every sane and adult man or woman of it should receive proper education, that every man of it be trained to defend his home and hearth, and that they be all, as a nation, governed by the trusted men of their own choosing. Industrial regeneration will develop of itself hand in hand with this. When that glorious day dawns, may be generations hence, then will come true for India the burning words of Milton—the heroic rebel against Kingcraft and Popecraft—which he wrote for his own magnificent Nation :

> Methinks I see in my mind a noble and puissant nation rousing herself like a strong man after sleep and shaking her invincible locks. Methinks I see her as an eagle, mewing her mighty youth, and kindling her undazzled eyes at the full midday beam, purging and unscaling her long abused sight at the fountain itself of heavenly radiance, while the whole voice of timorous and flocking birds, with those also that love the twilight, flutter about amazed at what she means. *(Areopagitica.)*

SUMMARY.

1. The Imperial Legislative Council should be called the Senate; and the Provincial, the House of Representatives.

2. These should be housed in buildings of their own, and under their own control, and not in the palaces of the Viceroy and the Governors.

3. The Presidents of these should, in the first instance, be appointed for 5 or 7 years by the Speaker of the House of Commons from amongst experienced Parliamentarians; and the Deputy-Presidents by the Councils concerned, subject to the veto of the Governor-General-in-Council or the Governor-in-Council, as the case may be. The salaries of the Presidents should be the same as those of the Ministers; the Deputy-Presidents should be unsalaried; both should be provided with residences in the grounds of the Legislature buildings.

4. The number of the Senators and of the Representatives should be on a population basis, say, one Senator per three millions of population, and one Representative per half a million. This for the Senate would come to roughly 85 elected for British India, about thirty elected for *Indian India*, and about thirty *ex officio*. For the House the numbers would approximate to 50 to 100, elected for the Province; 12 to 25 *ex officio*; and another 12 to 25 from the Indian States,

which are *geogrophically* included within the Provinces; if it be thought desirable to give these last also a representation.

5. The Senators should be given a consolidated salary of Rs. 6,000 (£ 400) and the Representatives, Rs. 3,000 (£ 200) per year.

6. The Senate should meet not less than once every 3 months, the total number of meetings occupying not less than 40 days in the year. The House, not less than once a month, the total number of meetings occupying not less than 60 days in the year.

7. The quorum should be a fairly high one.

8. There should be no creedal register of electors, instead, there should be a creedo-professional register of candidates, according to the original suggestion of Lord Morley. The Congress-League agreement about the number of members of each community considering the circumstances, has to be accepted, even though it gives to Muslims, in some cases, a preponderance of more than twice their actual percentage in population, for instance, in the United Provinces they number only 14 per cent. of the Hindus; though such large over-representation is scarcely justified after the agreement that no resolution or bill or any clause thereof introduced by a non-official member affecting communal interests shall be proceeded with if three-fourths of the members of that community oppose it. The agreement is :—

33	P. C.	Moslems	for	Bombay
15	"	"	"	C. P.
25	"	"	"	B. and O.
40	"	"	"	Bengal.
30	"	"	"	U. P.
15	"	"	"	Madras.
50	"	"	"	Punjab.

provided that no Muslim shall participate in any of the other general elections to the Imperial or Provincial Councils.

With regard to the last Province it would be equitable to allow 20 per cent. to Sikhs, reducing the numbers of both the Hindu and the Muslim candidates by 10 per cent. In those Provinces where there are an appreciable number of Indian Christians arrangement should be made for their representation also.

9. The Senate should have one-third Muslims, also Indian Christians and Sikhs. The non-official European community, whether domiciled or floating, would, of course, be well represented here as well as in the House.

10. The right of asking supplementary questions should belong to any member.

11. Freedom of speech should be guaranteed (though publication might, in special cases of marked extravagance, be restrained by special order of the Legislature in which the speech was made).

12. Resolutions passed by the Senate and the House by substantial majorities twice within thre

years and again repeated in a new House or new Senate should be binding on the Government, their veto being nullified under the circumstances. But in the case of the Senate, if the Governor-General-in-Council so likes, he may refer the resolution to the Judicial Committee of the Privy Council, for their verdict on the matter.

13. The term of office of Representatives should be the same as that of the Governor and his Cabinet, namely, 5 years unless their tenure of office is reduced to 4 years, in that case the tenure of the Representative' should be reduced to 4 years also. Their age should be 30 and over.

The tenure of the Senators should be 5 years also, unless the tenures of the Governor-General and his Cabinet are reduced to 4 years; in that case the term of the Senators should be also reduced by one year. Their age should be 35 and over.

14. If one-eighth of the elected members wish to introduce a Bill or wish to move a Resolution, the veto powers of the Government should be suspended and Government bound to provide every reasonable facility for their introduction and discussion.

15. As the Senate (The Imperial Legislative Council) would be a sort of Upper House for the whole of India, its present power of concurrent legislation in all Provincial matters, with the House of Representatives (the Provincial Councils) which are a sort of Lower House should not be curtailed in any way.

16. Indian conditions are such that no *second* chambers—whether Provincial or Imperial—will be the least good.

17. A strong committee of the Legislature should be appointed to revise the Regulations governing the procedure with regard to the work in the Councils as also the Regulations governing the electors and the candidates.

18. The interest of the adult members of a Hindu joint-family, as electors or candidates, otherwise qualified, should be safe-guarded. As the Regulations stand at present, they are debarred from being either elctors or candidates.

APPENDIX.

Circumstances have forced me to publish at once the first five chapters of the book, and not to wait for writing out of the whole work which would have meant considerable delay. Many of the remaining chapters require special knowledge to which I can lay no claim. It was my intention, therefore, to invite gentlemen possessing this special knowledge to write those chapters. The full scheme contemplates three more volumes each of about the size of the present one. The chapters that have yet to be written are mentioned here in the hope that Mr. G. A. Natesan may be able to arrange for the necessary syndicate of writers and get the work completed at no very distant date.

CHAPTER.	HEADING.
6.	Local Self-Government.
7.	District Administration.
8.	Village Organisation.
9.	Laws and Law Courts.
10.	Police.
11.	Prisons.
12.	Education.
13.	Sanitation.
14.	Forests.
15.	Famines.
16.	Agriculture and Fisheries.
17.	Commerce and Industries.
18.	Shipping and Harbour Administration; Port Trusts.

CHAPTER.	HEADING.
19.	Communications—Post, Telegraph.
20.	Public Works.
21.	Public Careers: Railways; river, canal and coastal vessels.
22.	Foreign Banks.
23.	Finance and Currency.
24.	Imperial Public Services.
25.	Provincial Public Services (Gazetted and Non-gazetted.)
26.	The Defensive Forces.
27.	Newspapers and Journals.
28.	Religious Endowments: management of places of worship; of burial places and cremation grounds; the Ecclesiastical establishment (of the Government of India.)
29.	Economic condition of the People.
30.	Excise (liquor and other intoxicants.)
31.	Frontier Policy.

INDEX.